NATIVE AM

of California and Nevada

by
Jack D. Forbes

REVISED EDITION

Naturegraph Publishers, Inc.
Happy Camp, California

Library of Congress Cataloging-in-Publication Data

Forbes, Jack D.
Native Americans of California and Nevada

Includes bibliographical references and index.
1. Indians of North America—California. 2. Indians
of North America—Nevada. 3. Indians of North
America—
Government relations. I. Title
E78.C15F6   1982   979.4'00497   82-7906
                                        AACR2

ISBN: 978-0-87961-119-4

Copyright © 1982 by Naturegraph Publishers
Cover painting by Douglas Andrews

2013 printing

Naturegraph Publishers has been publishing books on
natural history, Native Americans, and outdoor subjects since
1946. Free catalog available

Books for a better world

Naturegraph Publishers, Inc.
PO Box 1047 ● 3543 Indian Creek Rd.
Happy Camp, CA 96039
(530) 493-5353
www.naturegraph.com

PREFACE & ACKNOWLEDGMENTS

Leaders in Indian education and Indian affairs have frequently asserted the need for an introductory synthesis dealing with the history and sociocultural evolution of native groups living in the Far West. This book is primarily designed to provide an introduction to the evolution of Native American peoples in this region with strong emphasis upon California-Nevada and especially in relation to those historical-cultural experiences likely to have contributed to the present-day conditions of native communities and individuals. Secondarily, it is designed to provide an introduction to the basic concepts relating to Indian studies (for those who wish to delve deeper or to construct curricular units) and to the multicultural, community-responsive approach to Indian education.

Every effort has been made to utilize native groups' names for themselves in order to avoid a kind of "colonialism" in nomenclature. Unfortunately, many groups still have not made their own choices clear. Therefore, the reader should not regard the names utilized herein as the "last word" on the subject, but rather should check with local Indian organizations as to their current preferences.

This handbook, it should be pointed out, does not give complete detailed descriptions of native cultures at the time of initial European contact. Excellent sources, such as A. L. Kroeber's *Handbook of the Indians of California*, R. F. Heizer and M. A. Whipple's *California Indians: A Source Book*, and Lowell Bean's *California Indians: A Retrospective*, are available to fill the need for that kind of information.

It is regrettable but true that many Indians and most non-Indians in the United States have received a "mis-education" regarding the story of the Indian experience in North America. This "mis-education" is largely the result of the ignoring of factual Indian history in the schools, thereby allowing romantic mythology and stereotypical mass media to fill the vacuum so created. The tragic result is that while most non-Indians have a vague idea that Indians were "wronged" at some remote time, they have no accurate notion of what actually took place or of the *continuing* reality of Indian life in this country up to the present date.

The Indian experience in the Far West since 1769 has been an especially ugly one. The author has made no effort in the pages which follow to "tone down" or soften the often harsh realities of native history. Some non-Indians who are unfamiliar with this reality may be offended by this approach, but it is believed that corrective steps to alter the problems apparent in contemporary Indian conditions *must* be based upon an absolutely frank understanding of the real world which has surrounded native life. It would be unfair to the educator or worker in Indian-related projects to do otherwise.

The author does not assign any kind of "collective guilt" to the white population for what has happened in the past. The future, though, is a different matter; we all have a responsibility which cannot be brushed aside. The kind of society which is now being brought into existence is *our* collective challenge.

The viewpoint represented herein is that of the writer and not necessarily that of the various Indian organizations whose members have generously reviewed the manuscript.

Lastly, the author wishes to acknowledge the assistance of many individuals, including especially the research assistance by Tina Bergquist and the typing by Theo Campbell.

Jack D. Forbes

TABLE OF CONTENTS

David Risling, Jr., Hoopa-Karuk-Yurok, founder and president of the California Indian Education Association, and co-founder of D-Q University.

I. INTRODUCTION:
THE SIGNIFICANCE OF THE NATIVE
AMERICANS AND THEIR HERITAGE

The Biological Legacy

It is estimated that there are more than 30,000,000 Americans speaking native Indian languages living in the Americas today, while perhaps as many as 200,000,000 Americans possess some degree of native ancestry. The native genetic heritage is clearly the *dominant* strain in Paraguay, Bolivia, Peru, Ecuador, Mexico, Greenland, and most of Central America, while indigenous ancestry is one of the important elements in the racially-mixed populations of Chile, Colombia, Venezuela, Brazil, and Panama. Elsewhere in the Americas, as in the United States, Canada, the West Indies, Uruguay and Argentina, the Indian racial heritage has been important in certain regions or provinces but has tended to be absorbed within a dominantly African or European population. Nonetheless, "Indians" and tribal groups survive in every mainland American republic (except in Uruguay where a rural *mestizo* or mixed-blood population alone survives) and even on a few Caribbean islands.

It is difficult to estimate the number of persons of native descent currently residing in the United States because the census has never sought to enumerate all such persons and because much mixture took place during the colonial period. There are, however, at least 25,000,000 individuals with a significant degree of Indian ancestry, including some 1,400,000 members of tribal organizations; the bulk of the Mexican-American, Central American, and Puerto Rican populations. Afro-Americans, French Canadians, and other persons often possess varying degrees of native descent. Black Americans, in particular, share in the Indian genetic legacy. One survey indicates that about one-third of the Afro-Americans sampled know of an Indian ancestor. Historical records indicate extensive African-Indian intermingling in the West Indies and in the southern United States during the colonial period. Entire tribal groups were absorbed into the black population in the South and in the West Indies, and that process continues in some areas to the present day.

Therefore, it is quite obvious that the genetic legacy of the Native American is great indeed, especially as one considers the whole of the Americas. It is also apparent from population statistics that the Indian and part-Indian peoples of the Americas are increasing in number at a rapid rate, particularly as compared with predominantly middle-class European-derived groups. In the United States, as well as in Latin America, the Indian and part-Indian populations possess very high birthrates and the proportion of persons of native descent in the total population will doubtless steadily increase in the future (although sterilization programs and abortions are reducing the fertility rate of the native and part-native populations).

It may well be that as many as 30,000,000 (maximum estimate) or 10,000,000 (minimum estimate) United States citizens possess some degree of indigenous American ancestry. For the majority of these people, of course, the amount of Indian "blood" is proportionally slight, but the fact of a firm genetic connection with America's ancient past is a reality nonetheless. For example, a person whose last pure Indian ancestor was born in approximately 1800 could be descended from as many as 2000 Indians who were living when Christopher Columbus first landed in the Bahamas. Interestingly, because Indian "marriage circles" in the United States (the group from which marriage partners were normally obtained) seldom numbered more than 3000 persons, a person of 1/64 Indian descent today, whose last pure Indian ancestor was born in ca. 1800 can statistically possess as many Indian ancestors living in 1400-1440 as a person of "full-blood" Indian ancestry living today. Thus, a person with a small proportion of native ancestry has a significant connection with the history of the given group of Native American people to which he is related, supposing, of course, that he is aware of the connection and its ramifications, and supposing also that he is inclined to identify in any way with distant ancestors or relatives.

Should intermarriage rates between persons of part-Indian and non-Indian descent continue to climb, it is theoretically possible that by the period 2050-2100 the majority of United States citizens could be of part-Indian descent, although the knowledge of any

Indian ancestor will be nonexistent for most individuals. At the same time, however, the population of many tribal groups (such as the Navaho) should be significantly larger than today.

In summary, the biological or genetic legacy of the Native American is of considerable significance, especially from Mexico to Paraguay. In the United States, it would seem clear that the modern North American people have collective roots which extend not only to Europe, Africa and Asia, but also back into the ancient American past.[1]

The Historical and Cultural Legacy

The way of life of the dominant population in the United States is often referred to as "Western European" or simply as "Western" (i.e., a part of "Western Civilization"). In point of fact, however, much that is basic to this way of life originated in the Middle East and North Africa (the wheel, monumental architecture, supra-tribal political organizations, horticulture, Christianity, Judaism, etc.). The culture of the dominant North American population is thus a very mixed or heterogeneous heritage.

This mixed heritage, which has become the common legacy of all North American people, also derives a significant part of its character from contributions made by Native American groups. To a considerable degree, all who reside in the United States have become "Indianized" while at the same time, of course, Indians have become "Europeanized." Unfortunately, this process of borrowing from the Native American population has been largely overlooked by students of so-called "American Civilization" and is, therefore, not well understood by the average citizen.

The various European groups which invaded North America several centuries ago were all proud and ethnocentric peoples. They ordinarily considered themselves to be superior to other, culturally different populations, and even, in some instances, held themselves to be divinely-ordained conquerors or "civilizers." This supremely egotistical viewpoint led the English and the Spanish, in particular, to minimize the native influence upon the styles of living which gradually evolved in the conquered portions of North America. That the English of Virginia and New England were economically dependent upon Native American inventions (such as tobacco, maize, hominy, squash, pumpkins and maple syrup) did not lead to more favorable attitudes towards the Indians, nor did this dependence lead to any early intellectual recognition of the presence of a modified culture.

Tragically, the ethnocentric insularity of English-speaking Anglo-Americans did not diminish with time. Even as the English way of life was being modified by forest warfare tactics, the fur trade, the Indian slave trade, dressed deerskin clothing, the canoe, the toboggan, the political influence of the Iroquois confederation, thousands of native place names, hundreds of Indian words, and numerous other items, the Anglo-American persisted in obscuring the origin of these changes. The way of life and style of dress of Daniel Boone, for example, was highly Indianized, but Boone was not, and is not, considered an Indianized person. Rather, his type of deerskin clothing has been regarded simply as a "pioneer" variant of Anglo-American cultural styles. Each trait borrowed from the native was emotionally "assimilated" and thereby became, in the popular mind, a non-Indian trait. In the same manner, the Anglo-American has taken over Afro-American musical contributions and made them emotionally his own. The significance of this is that while the European has indeed become Americanized (Indianized) and Africanized, this process has not served to diminish an ethnocentric conviction of cultural superiority. This conviction is sustained, in great measure, by sheer ignorance of the origin of much of what the Anglo regards as "his own."

Contributing to this ignorance has been the fact that Anglo-American scholars who write about North American history have tended to be products of their own ethnic past; that is, they have ordinarily seen historical events through the eyes of Anglo-American "pioneers" and "empire-builders." Thus, most general histories of the United States are not histories of North America as a region, nor are they histories of all of the many peoples who have resided in and contributed to the evolution of the United States. On the contrary, most such works are essentially chronicles of the Anglo-European conquest and of the development of the English-speaking white people during the succeeding four centuries. One test of any work which purports to be a general history of America is whether it commences with the 20,000-year story of the Native

Americans or whether it dismisses the "aborigines" as a part of the "environment" and focuses its initial attention upon the "Old World" heritage of the colonists.

As this writer stated some years ago,

> If the history of America is properly only the Anglo-European conquest, then the history of England would be only the Germanic conquest and subsequent events, which would obviously be absurd. English history begins with the earliest period that English historians can discover and then deals with the various Celtic groups, the Roman occupation, the later Celtic states, and finally the Germanic conquest. To leave out the pre-Germanic period would be to leave out an important part of the history of England, and in the same way the leaving out of the story of the Native American has rendered American history incomplete.[2]

It is clear that Anglo-American ethnocentrism, whether displayed by scholars or laymen, has contributed to the obscuring of the actual extent to which modern United States culture is of non-European origin. In addition, this ethnocentrism has often prevented European-Americans from becoming a real part of the region in which they reside. Fostered in great measure by public school curricula, a process has developed wherein Anglo-Americans largely ignore the rich past of the region in which they live in order to focus attention upon increasingly tenuous connections with the Atlantic Seaboard colonial period and even more tenuous connections with "Old England."

California public school pupils, for example, learn a great deal about Plymouth Colony and the *Mayflower* but very little about the native pioneers of the "Golden West." They are, all too often, cut off from meaningful contact with the history of the hills and valleys in which they actually live. This is because educators, following the lead of the historians referred to above, still tend to be engaged in an essentially ethnocentric approach to curricula. This approach is focused upon the Anglo-American past, which is, of course, largely alien to the history of the hills and valleys of a region such as California.

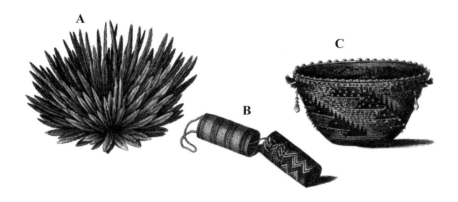

A Indian feather headdress. **B** Decorative basketry tubes. **C** Pomo feather basket. Old drawings by G. Langsdorf. *(Courtesy of Bancroft Library, University of California, Berkeley.)*

The Indian People

The significance of the Native American legacy does not consist solely in the biological or cultural contributions made to society at large. It also consists in a rapidly growing population of modern Indian people who will continue to make a rich contribution to American life, and who, in many areas, will comprise the dominant population. In that region of the Americas sometimes referred to as Indo-America (the region from Mexico to Paraguay), Indian and part-Indian people comprise the majority of the population. It may very well be that the Guarani, Quechua, Maya, and other native-speaking peoples of Indo-America will, in the not too distant future, acquire the political and social dominance in their respective homelands which their numbers warrant.

In the United States and Canada, the 2,000,000 members of tribal organizations or native communities constitute a small minority of the total population, but their significance is all out of proportion to their total numbers. In part, this is because native people tend to be highly concentrated in certain regions, such as the Southwest, Oklahoma, the Dakotas and the Alaskan-Canadian arctic, as well as in certain counties or districts within other areas.

The contemporary significance of the Native American is also derived from their importance as continuous contributors to our sociocultural life. And here one must go beyond such items as ceramics, basketry, painting, sculpture, folklore and music, to the even more significant realm of religion, world view, and interpersonal relations. In religion, for instance, modern theologians (as well as "hippies") are arriving at world views strikingly like those of many ancient Native American religions. It is to be suspected that these modern thinkers and experimenters have a great deal to learn from Indian religion and philosophy, which, after all, arrived at similar viewpoints centuries ago. Many might agree, for example, that the Indian concepts of *Manitou* (the all-pervading "divine" power or spirit) and Wakan-Tanka (the Great Mystery or Great Spirit) represent very appropriate ways of referring to the ultimate spiritual foundation of life.

Of great importance is the fact that American Indian religions, like all great traditions, focus upon the development of moral men possessing a deep awareness of their relationship with the total universe. The Sioux religious leader Black Elk (Hehaka Sapa) has stated,

peace . . . comes within the souls of men when they realize their relationship, their oneness, with the universe and all its powers, and when they realize that at the center of the Universe dwells Wakan-Tanka, and that this center is really everywhere, it is within each of us.[3]

John Epes Brown, who studied under Black Elk, points out that

such knowledge cannot be realized unless there be perfect humility, unless man humbles himself before the entire creation, before each smallest ant, realizing his own nothingness. Only in being nothing may man become everything, and only then does he realize his essential brotherhood with all forms of life. His centre, or his Life, is the same centre or Life of all that is.[4]

The sociopolitical implications of the Native American approach to life could, indeed, be traced in several profound dimensions. This writer has suggested that

In this age of "mass" culture and revolutionary social change, in this era of large-scale alienation and personal anonymity, it is especially important that the small folk society be provided with the means of survival and development.

Modern nations have, with little thought, allowed the development of industrialized mass society to proceed in such a way as to destroy many of the social and cultural relationships which give meaning to human life. The results speak for themselves: crime, juvenile delinquency, high suicide rates, widespread mental illness, escapist activities of all kinds, and an often cheap commercialized way of life which affords no real satisfaction for the average person. Loneliness in the midst of crowds and nothing meaningful to do in the midst of hyper-activity typifies the modern mass culture. ...

Mankind has at least one hope, however, and that is that the numerous tribal and folk societies which still survive in almost every part of the world can be provided with the means for self-protection and self-realization. ... Tribes and folk societies can and do provide their people with a way of life which is usually much more psychologically healthy and meaningful than do mass cultures, and ... we must allow the smaller societies to preserve themselves in order to provide mankind with *a continuing alternative to the super-culture and super-society.*[5]

John Collier, Commissioner of Indian Affairs from 1933 to 1945, felt that the world at large had a great deal to learn from the socioreligious orientation of still-functioning native societies:

They had what the world has lost. They have it now. What the world has lost, the world must have again lest it die. Not many years are left to have or have not, to recapture the lost ingredient. ... What, in our human world, is this power to live? It is the ancient, lost reverence and passion for human personality, joined with the ancient, lost reverence and passion for the earth and its web of life.

This indivisible reverence and passion is what the American Indians almost universally had; and representative groups of them have it still.

If our modern world should be able to recapture this

power, the earth's natural resources and web of life would not be irrevocably wasted within the twentieth century, which is the prospect now. True democracy, founded in neighborhoods and reaching over the world, would become the realized heaven on earth. And living peace—not just an interlude between wars—would be born and would last through ages. . . .[6]

Finally, the Indian people must be regarded as an extremely significant portion of the North American population because in their present condition and in their life-history since the 1580's they serve as perhaps the key witness to the "true" character of the dominant Anglo-American group. As this writer wrote in 1966,

> The Indians are a looking-glass into the souls of North Americans. If we want to dissect the Anglo and analyze his character we must find out what he does when no one else cares, when no one is in a position to thwart his will—when he can do as he pleases. And with the Indian the Anglo has done what he pleased, with no one to care, and with the Indian ultimately too weak to resist, except passively. . . .[7]

The North American native people, then, constitute a unique "test" for the real intentions and most deeply-held values of Anglo-Americans. The history of the North American white population, their present beliefs, and their future behavior cannot be understood without examining very closely the treatment accorded those relatively powerless native groups under their control and subject, ultimately, to their will.

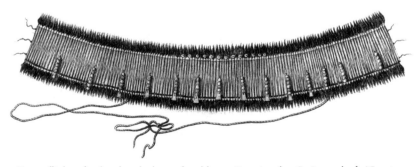

Pomo flicker feather-band, dance headdress. Drawing by G. Langsdorf. (*Courtesy of Bancroft Library, University of California, Berkeley.*)

II. THE EVOLUTION OF NATIVE CALIFORNIA AND NEVADA

The Origin of the First Westerners

The ancient past of the native peoples of the Americas is shrouded in mystery, and it is quite possible that this will always be so. Virtually all native groups in the Americas have regarded themselves as having been created in or at least near their own homelands, and certainly it is true that in an important psychological sense most Indians had become literally a "part" of the locality in which they lived. Native Americans ordinarily exhibited an extreme attachment to their place of birth and to their environment, a degree of attachment hardly to be comprehended by semi-nomadic European-Americans. Thus, no matter where the ultimate geographical "home" of American Indians may have been, their spiritual "home" is located firmly in the Americas.

The European newcomers to the Americas could not believe that their holy book, the Christian Bible, had failed to take note of the history of the Native Americans' ancestors. The Europeans were, of course, in possession of their own origin myth, borrowed from the Hebrews (who in turn had adapted it from earlier Semitic peoples). It was doctrinally necessary that American Indians be linked to this origin tale, and the most common device, first conceived by Spanish writers, was to suggest that the American natives were descended from one of the "lost tribes" of ancient Israel.

"Lost tribes" or not, subsequent European writers almost always look for Indian origins outside of the Americas, although increasingly this search took the form of pseudo-scientific or scientific scholarship. Unfortunately, this endeavor has failed to yield evidence answering any of the basic questions apt to be asked by a layman.

Certain concepts seem to be supported by growing bodies of data, such as the thesis that all present-day humans belong to a single species with a common ultimate origin (perhaps in Africa), and that the ancient Americans possessed occasional contacts with Asia, Polynesia, and Europe. (These documented contacts are, however, too late in time to explain the initial peopling of the Americas, especially in the case of Polynesia and Europe.) If it is correct that all peoples originated in Africa or Eurasia then, of course, it would follow that the Native Americans' ancestors must have migrated to the Americas from elsewhere. A glance at a map would suggest a route from Asia via the Bering Strait to Alaska; but thus far no solid evidence has been found to document this thesis. No archaeological remains found in either Siberia or Alaska are ancient enough to shed light upon such far-off migrations, and it may well be that most of the early sites were along the coast and are now covered with water due to the post-glacial rise of the level of the oceans.

The physical characteristics of Native American peoples were at one time thought to link them with the so-called Mongoloid peoples of Asia, but the problem is now generally seen to be much more complex than was formerly supposed. For one thing, the American Indian peoples did not comprise a physically uniform population. Although the variations in physical type found in the Americas are not as great as those found in Eurasia or Africa, they nonetheless are great enough to suggest that perhaps several different ancestral groups mixed either before or after migration to this hemisphere.

In any event, it would be a mistake to think of Native Americans as part of a "Mongoloid" racial family since several of the more important characteristics of the so-called classic Mongoloid type are virtually absent among American Indians (such as B and AB blood types and the epicanthic eye-fold). This writer would suggest that Native Americans, by and large, comprise a population standing somewhat between the extreme Caucasoid and Mongoloid types and may represent either the end-product of the mixture of several Mongoloid and Caucasoid type groups or the survival of the type from which Mongoloid and Caucasoid are both derived. The reader should, however, be aware that such terms as Caucasoid, Mongoloid, Negroid, etc., are almost completely discredited as referring to "races" (groups of people who are genetically distinct) and are used herein only as simplistic illustrative devices.[1]

In point of fact, one must (initially at least) deal with each Indian people as a separate descent group (usually coupled with its immediate neighbors), with physical characteristics which are unique. We may collectively use such terms as "Americanoid" or American Indian, but we do not know that such different peoples as the heavily bearded natives of San Francisco Bay, the light-skinned delicately featured natives of central Panama, and the sharp-featured Indians of the central-eastern United States do, in fact, have the same genetic history. In all likelihood, they possess both common and divergent ancestries.

In summary, the current stage of knowledge in relation to Native American origins is such that the prudent student should refrain from accepting sweeping theories and should maintain a skeptical attitude. We simply do not possess any certain answers, and it is best to frankly acknowledge this fact.

The Earliest Americans

Throughout the Americas, archaeologists have been studying sites which may indicate that man has been present here for 125,000 to 250,000 years.

Perhaps the oldest sites dated to everyone's satisfaction are to be found in California. Thanks to a newly-developed amino-acid dating method, we now know that numerous settlements existed along the southern California coast in the 40,000-50,000 b.p. (before present) period; and material near Sunnyvale has been dated at near 70,000 b.p. These sites definitely mean that Indian people were here in the Americas during the last "ice age" and possibly earlier.

Many other early sites also exist, geologically dated around 100,000 years ago; however, the "chopper" tools and the organic matter found (which is dateable) in some cases might be of natural origin.

The last ice age endured from roughly 40,000 b.p. to 13,000 b.p. Glaciation is thought to have covered virtually all of Canada and the northern United States, making travel across such a barrier impossible, although parts of Alaska and Siberia may have been clear. The ocean was doubtless much lower than today and many California village sites of that period are probably along bluffs below the present sea level.

Another complication in terms of locating early Indian sites in California arises from the fact that during the period of non-glaciation prior to 40,000 b.p.—and especially around 100,000 to 125,000 b.p.—the ocean level was much higher than today, thus destroying many coastal sites and backing up water into the Great Central Valley. Salt water doubtless reached as far as Sacramento and Stockton, and fresh or brackish water probably filled much of the rest of the valley. Earth movements have also been altering the geography of the state with resulting uplifts—hills or raising elevations—and with some depressions.

Interestingly, some California Indian traditions refer specifically to a time when the Central Valley was filled with water. One makes explicit reference to the Golden Gate being blocked and the water flowing out to the ocean via Pajaro Valley (although the Petaluma area could have offered a second outlet). These traditions may indicate that geologic activity within the past few thousands of years has considerably altered the landscape.

During wet periods associated with glaciation, many sections of Nevada and the Great Basin were also covered with lakes or inland seas, while the Gulf of California extended northwards as far as Indio and Palm Springs. Thus we must think of the ancient Far West as a very different place from today. For example, during the last ice age the Sierra Nevadas, covered with glaciers, probably served as an impassible barrier, and the coolness of climate may well have forced the native people to congregate along the seacoast. Even the water-filled Central Valley and the lake-covered Great Basin may have been cold during the winter months. Certainly, two radically different ways of living would have been developed by the coast and in the high elevations of the wet but cold interior, a contrast perhaps comparable to that between coastal southern New England and Ontario or upper Minnesota in the present day.

These early American ways of living apparently preceded the development of stone projectile points and seem to have featured the use of simple percussion tools and, perhaps, items made of wood or cane. This way of life seems to have changed around 13,000 to 9000 b.p.

From 13,000 to 10,000 b.p. the appearance of a unique spear-point technology may have stimulated a shift from maritime sea-mollusk and vegetable-food gathering emphases to greater dependence upon hunting. On the other hand, many Indians in historic times knew how to kill big game in a variety of ways, such as driving small herds over cliffs.

At this point we can say little about the physical appearance of these earliest Americans, except that they were probably of "modern" type, as evidenced by skulls found in Los Angeles (26,000 b.p.), Laguna Beach (17,000 b.p.), and elsewhere.

Ancient American Cultures

Beginning about 13,000 years ago, ancient Americans began to produce spear points and knives which represent, especially by 11,000 b.p., an impressive command of point-making technology. Little is known about the material culture of these people aside from their "points" and unlined hearths, and almost nothing is known of their non-material culture or physical appearance. It does seem almost certain, however, that they were big game hunters, moving about in pursuit of large mammals such as the now extinct large bison, the mammoth, and the mastodon, and that they may have been largely responsible for killing off, by 9000 b.p., the old Pleistocene herd animals.

Interestingly, projectile points of a basically similar nature have been found in southernmost South America dating as early as 11,000 b.p., thus indicating that the Americas as a whole were going through an ancient "technological revolution" virtually simultaneously. Also quite significant is the fact that the projectile point tradition developed in the Americas was unlike that of interior Asia. It was apparently an independent development, and later spread to northeastern Asia *from America*. It should also be noted that the "Big-Game Hunting" complex described above was apparently not very significantly developed in the California-Nevada region, although points of this early type are found in the Far West on occasion.

Perhaps as early as 12,000 to 10,000 b.p., vegetable-food-grinding tools appear in the southwestern United States at one site. This represents an important event, for between 10,000 and 9000 years ago the Big-Game Hunters were forced to alter their style of life due to the gradual disappearance of the large herd mammals— although the mammoth may have survived to 8000 or 7000 b.p. in southern Arizona. The "economic revolution" which ensued in both Americas is typified by the appearance of food-grinding tools (such as manos, milling stones, and, later, mortars and pestles), new kinds of spear and atlatl (spear-thrower) points, and by the presence of human burials.

This stage of development in most of the Far West and Southwest is called the "Desert Culture" stage, because the area was becoming progressively drier. This tradition, which endured for thousands of years, was typified by the importance of tools useful in vegetable food consumption and by the relative unimportance of tools designed for hunting (except in certain localities). In the Intermountain West, the Desert Culture also featured the use of caves or rock-shelters for housing; bark or grass beds; twined basketry; netting; matting; fur cloth; sandals (moccasins rarely); the atlatl; relatively small projectile points; flat milling stones; scrapers and choppers; digging sticks; fire drills and hearths; wooden clubs; tubular smoking pipes; seashell ornaments; deer-hoof rattles; medicine bags or pouches; birdbone whistles; and other items.

It is quite clear, thanks to the preservation of wooden and fiber materials in dry caves, that the American westerners of 9000 to 8000 years ago possessed a rich inventory of utensils and that they were resourceful and inventive people. (It is likely that many of these traits evolved during the preceding Big-Game Hunting period, but the open camp sites of that era would not have allowed for the preservation of perishable materials.)

Farther west, in the southern California deserts, a series of sites reveal what some writers have termed a "Western Hunting Culture" because food-grinding tools are largely absent. Between 9000 and 7000 years ago, the natives of this area produced heavy projectile points (for the atlatl probably) and a small number of other stone tools, but these assemblages are largely found around the high shorelines of now dry lakes (such as Lake Mohave) or in other unprotected sites, so that wooden or fibre materials could not be expected to survive. A very similar culture, or series of cultures, also existed along the Pacific Coast, modified to some degree by the gathering of shellfish (California coastal seashells were being traded in the Great Basin as early as 9000 years ago).

About 7000 b.p. the Desert and Western Hunting traditions began to experience changes in southern Arizona, where the

Cochise Culture developed, and in California, where the Milling Stone Horizon appeared. The Cochise tradition gradually moved into a pre-horticultural phase which placed great emphasis upon wild vegetable foods, and then, after coming under Mexican influence, into a horticultural period which ultimately evolved into the advanced cultures of Arizona and New Mexico.

In the coastal regions of southern California (and into the San Joaquin Valley) about 7000 b.p., or perhaps later, the Milling Stone Horizon featured a way of life emphasizing vegetable plant gathering, shellfish collecting, and minimal hunting. Projectile-point technology appears to have declined in this period, probably because the hunting of large game was no longer important. Sites are characterized by deep-basined metates, manos, scrapers, choppers, hammerstones, some bone tools, and burials (with the body flexed, extended flat, or subsequently reburied).

Local variations are apparent among the coastal peoples, as along the Santa Barbara coast where shellfish were apparently not being utilized (indicating perhaps an occupation by interior-dwellers who were new to a coastal environment). In the interior desert areas, in the meantime, the Western Hunting Culture apparently endured with little change until about 5000 b.p. when the Pinto spear-point (used on the atlatl) appeared, along with some milling stones. Thus, the southern California desert peoples appear to have been moving in the direction of the Desert Culture stage (with vegetable food utilization) but the hunting of game apparently remained of greater importance than in areas farther east and north. Post holes found near Little Lake, California, seem to be the first evidence of houses found in this portion of the West.

On the whole, the California desert from Owens Valley to the Mexican boundary remained a conservative area, changing but little until about 2000 b.p. Coastal southern California also changed slowly, although in the Santa Barbara region a number of new traits appeared, including the basket-hopper mortar (perhaps indicating the perfection of the important acorn-leaching process), the mortar and pestle, heavy projectile points (with an emphasis upon hunting and shellfish), massive bone- and shell-beads, and flexed burials with the grave materials covered with red ocher coloring.

In northern Nevada, the Desert Culture tradition underwent a series of changes after 4000 b.p. as a part of an adjustment to life along the shores of a number of large lakes which existed at that time. Duck decoys, nets, fishhooks, feather robes, cordage, snares, twined bags, and twined and coiled baskets were made by these early Nevadans, along with many stone, bone, and wood tools. By 2000 b.p. some early traits, such as the use of the atlatl, were dropping away (to be replaced by the bow and arrow), but a large number of characteristics continued into more recent times as a part of the way of life of the Northern Paiute and adjacent peoples. As Jesse D. Jennings has stated, "the facts are that one can argue for a cultural continuum, with increasingly marked regional variation in technological details, in the Great Basin up until historic times."[2]

At about the same time as northern Nevadans were adjusting to a lakeshore environment, in the 4000s b.p., central Californians were entering what is known as the Early Horizon. In this, the first well-known culture for the northern two-thirds of California, the Native Americans exhibited a considerable interest in afterlife and religion by rigidly disposing of the dead in a face-downward, fully-extended manner with extensive grave offerings. The material existence of the people included the use of large, heavy projectile points, shell ornaments, slab metates, mortars, fiber-tempered, baked-clay balls, and twined basketry. The atlatl was the principal weapon, and warfare appears to have been uncommon (due to the absence of skeletons exhibiting signs of violent death).

By 3500 b.p., the central Californian way of life was altered somewhat by the introduction of flexed burials, some cremating, coiled basketry, the wooden mortar, barbed harpoons, and the bow and arrow (used in addition to the atlatl). Village sites were larger, indicating a more extensive population, signs of warfare are common in burials, and grave goods are uncommon except in connection with cremations. Increase of grave offerings may indicate an increasing emphasis upon wealth-display and accumulation by certain individuals, a characteristic typical of north-western California at a much later date.

During the 3000s (at the latest) people began to live in villages along the shores of San Francisco Bay, where their dependence upon shellfish gradually led to the building up of large "shell mounds." Farther south, natives began inhabiting the bulk of the Channel Islands (Santa Rosa Island may have been inhabited earlier), thus indicating the evolution of a strongly maritime way of life.

Cultural Elaboration and Variation in the Far West

Important changes began to take place throughout the Southwest and Far West shortly before the time of Christ, stimulated in great measure by the existence of advanced cultures in Mexico. As early as 5000 to 6000 b.p., a crude variety of maize horticulture had apparently spread from Mexico to southern New Mexico. During the period 3000 to 2000 b.p. new crops (beans, squash, and better varieties of maize) were acquired by border-area Southwesterners, and a new stage, that of Horticultural Desert Culture, ensued. By 2300 b.p. pottery was borrowed from Mexico and a line of cultural evolution commenced (known as Mogollon) which contributes in many ways to the development of the Anasazi (Pueblo Indian) heritage farther north.

At about 2000 b.p. another significant tradition appears in the Gila River area of southern Arizona, a tradition now thought to be ancestral to the later Ootam (Pima-Papago) way of life. This tradition included such traits as horticulture (not very advanced), cremation, pottery, and the carving of fine bowls and utensils from stone. These traits are significant because they appear to spread into California gradually. For example, southern Arizona-type horticulture reached the Colorado River between 1000 and 1200 A.D. and still later spread westward as far as the southern California desert areas and to near the coast in northern Baja California. Southern Arizona-type pottery spread to the Colorado River in the 1000 to 1200 A.D. period also, and later spread towards the coast, reaching the San Luis Rey area only, in about 1500 or 1700 A.D. Carving bowls and utensils of soft stone spread more rapidly (apparently) to the Pacific Coast, perhaps reaching the Channel Islands region by 500 to 1000 A.D., or earlier. Interestingly, this steatite (soapstone) industry came to dominate the Santa Barbara-Los Angeles region to such an extent that the spread of pottery apparently greatly slowed down. Whether cremation spread solely from southern Arizona or originated independently in central California is not clear, but it seems highly likely that the cremation practiced in southern California after 500 to 1000 A.D. was largely or wholly derived from the southeast.

By 2000 b.p. the Horticultural Desert stage appears also in the San Juan River drainage area of Utah and Arizona where it is known, somewhat erroneously, as "Basketmaker." We shall refer to it as Pre-Anasazi, since it leads directly into the later development of Anasazi cultures. Between 2000 and 1600 b.p., the San Juan–area natives developed a way of life which was transitional between the Desert Culture and the Anasazi, and which resembled the Horticultural Desert stage in southeastern Arizona–New Mexico and the much later cultures of such desert groups as the Yavapai, Hualpai, Havasupai, and Southern Paiute. This stage lacked pottery (present in later Horticultural Desert cultures) but possessed a poor variety of maize, squash, slab-lined cists, cave-storage areas—where baskets, bags, sandals, nets, and cords have been found—and, rarely, houses of wood enclosed in mud mortar. The atlatl served as the principal weapon.

It is interesting to note that the crops planted by the Pre-Anasazi (and by the later Anasazi as well) were not derived from the Mogollon or Pre-Ootam cultures, but apparently came from Mexico via the Texas-Plains area.

About 1600 b.p. (400 A. D) the Pre-Anasazi Americans came heavily under the influence of natives to the south and east, acquiring traits such as semi-subterranean houses lined with stone slabs, pottery, beans, and new varieties of maize. The bow and arrow appeared later, perhaps near 600 or 700 A.D., probably coming in from the north. (The bow and arrow appeared in the Desert Culture of northern Nevada before 2000 b.p. and in the Middle Horizon of central California before 300 A.D.)

Anasazi cultures, as such, appear after 700 A.D. in the "Developmental Pueblo" period (also called Pueblo I and Pueblo II). At this time great experimentation occurred in housing, with both semi-subterranean and surface structures and rectangular and round plans. The houses were often constructed with many rooms and were made of either stone slabs, adobe bricks, or wattle and daub. Kivas (underground ceremonial or storage chambers) were also in use; pottery greatly improved in quality, cotton fabrics appeared (doubtless a Mexican influence), and a heavy emphasis upon sedentary horticulture was apparent. This early "Pueblo Indian" way of life proved to be very popular among peoples previously influenced by the Horticultural Desert stages. Between 700 and 1100 A.D. it spread over most of Utah and southeastern Nevada, with Anasazi pottery of this period also appearing in the

Mohave Desert of southern California, probably as a trade item. (It is also possible that Anasazi miners worked turquoise deposits in the Californian desert during this era.)

Between 1100 and 1300 the central Anasazi area entered into a period of great cultural elaboration while the Utah-southeastern Nevada-northwestern Arizona regions continued to preserve the Developmental Pueblo style of life to some degree. At the same time, the boundaries of Anasazi-style occupation became more circumscribed than before 1100 (except in the Flagstaff to Verde Valley area of Arizona where Anasazi influence was strengthened between 1100 and 1300). After 1300 Anasazi cultures retreated to roughly the modern Pueblo Indian areas of Arizona and retreated to New Mexico, but the natives of southern Utah, southern Nevada, and northwestern Arizona preserved, in essence, a lifestyle reminiscent of Horticultural Desert, Pre-Anasazi times (with pottery, some horticulture, where feasible, and other features of the Desert Culture tradition referred to earlier).

Farther to the south, in the Phoenix-Tucson region of south central Arizona, other events took place during this general period which are of significance in understanding later southern California culture. At about 1000 A.D. (according to recent thinking) a culture referred to as the Hohokam spread from Mexico into the Gila-Salt basin. The Hohokam culture featured a number of new traits, including the construction of great irrigation systems, Mexican Mayan-style ballgame courts, pyrite mirrors, curvilinear art, red-on-buff pottery, intensive horticulture, an emphasis upon trade, the development of an intensive pottery manufacturing center at Snaketown, Arizona, and, perhaps, Mexican-style emphases on military activities.

By 1070, a Hohokam "colony" existed near Flagstaff while Hohokam pottery was being utilized on the Colorado River and being traded into the San Fernando Valley of southern California. Between 1250 and 1300, the Hohokam way of life was largely replaced in south-central Arizona by a modified Ootam-like culture and an Anasazi-like, multi-story pueblo-building complex, derived either from northern Mexico or central and eastern Arizona. Similar types of pueblos were also constructed on the Colorado River, probably before 1400.[3]

The Hohokam way of life, with some pre-Ootam elements, did

not disappear completely after 1250, however. By 1150 to 1250 the ancestors of the Hamakhava (Mohave), Halchidhoma, Quechan (Yuma), and other Yuman-speaking Colorado River peoples were developing their European-contact period cultures, utilizing many Hohokam traits (including a style of pottery which remained very similar to Hohokam, as well as cremation, similar houses of a semi-subterranean type, clay figurines reminiscent of Hohokam work, Hohokam-type horticultural crops, and a military orientation which may have derived from Hohokam behavior). Some Hohokam traits also survived in southern Arizona, among the Maricopa and Ootam peoples.

The developments described for the Anasazi, Hohokam, and other southwestern traditions, occurring after 2000 b.p., were paralleled in general by trends towards cultural elaboration and differentiation apparently taking place throughout California and the Great Basin. (It should be borne in mind that the richness and diversity of more recent cultures may sometimes be more apparent than real due to the greater likelihood of complete assemblages of goods being preserved in more recent archaeological sites.) In general, archaeologists are able to distinguish cultures in the 300 to 1000 A.D. period which they believe are directly ancestral to those of Native American cultures contacted by Europeans.

In central California, what is known as the Late Horizon commenced about 300 to 500 A.D. and endured with relatively little change, so far as material traits are concerned, until the period of European invasion. Archaeological traits which characterize this era include cremation, grave offerings, wide-ranging trade, elaboration of ornaments, small obsidian arrow points, large stone mortars, and tubular steatite smoking pipes. In general, the Late Horizon is based upon the Middle Horizon and there is no evidence of sharp cultural discontinuity in central California for a period of at least 4000 years.

During the Late Horizon, Anasazi influence reached central California, not so much in terms of material goods—although Anasazi-influenced Great Basin pottery does spread into the southern Sierra Nevada area—but, rather, in terms of ceremonial-religious behavior. In particular, the Kuksu religious system, found among natives of the Central Valley of California in the nineteenth century, would appear to be closely related to Anasazi ceremonial patterns. Robert F. Heizer has stated, "Based on both archaeological and ethnographical evidence, central California seems to have come under fairly strong influence from the Southwest over the last millennium."[4]

The development of advanced cultures in northwestern California is not well understood, primarily because early archaeological sites are lacking generally in the coastal region from northern California through southern Alaska. Shell-mound sites in northern California reveal that by 500 to 1000 A.D. a way of life had evolved which was essentially the same as that of the eighteenth century in so far as material goods are concerned. On the other hand, the earliest levels at Humboldt Bay featured burials with a lavish burning of goods in a pit, with the corpse placed on top of the still-burning embers, while upper levels revealed the development of the later practice of using extended burials with no burned goods. This change is perhaps quite significant since it would seem to indicate that these Californians shifted their value system from one emphasizing wealth-destruction (so as to facilitate the well-being of a departed person in the afterlife, as well as perhaps to prevent wealth-accumulation by individuals) to one emphasizing wealth-accumulation and display (typical of later Northwest Coast cultures). Gradually, therefore, the stratified society of northwestern California, with certain families dominant because of their possession of wealth, evolved during the past 1000 years.

The development of the Pre-European Culture in northwestern California was closely connected with the general development of maritime-oriented, complex cultures all along the Northwest Coast of North America. In turn, it is now thought by some scholars that this maritime stage was closely related to early Eskimo developments and, in fact, it has been suggested that the cultures of the coast of Canada and southern Alaska developed from an "Eskimoid" base (as early as 2500 to 2400 b.p.). Unfortunately, little time-depth exists in most coastal sites in this general region. (But it should be pointed out that a Columbia River site near The Dalles, with a date of 8000 b.p., shows the beginnings of a riverine-maritime orientation which is earlier than any Eskimo developments.)

The Eskimo-type sea-hunting culture of the Bering Sea region appears to have developed around 3000 b.p. on the Asiatic side of the Bering Strait. It is now generally believed that this maritime culture was largely derived from the coastal and island maritime heritages of East Asia's Pacific rim and certainly not from interior Siberia or the Siberian Arctic coast. On the basis of this approach we might suggest that Asiatic maritime influences gradually spread north to the Bering Sea region by 3000 years ago and then subsequently were diffused to southern Alaska and down the coast as far as northwestern California. Still further, it is possible to suggest that certain traits found along the Northwest Coast were spread in some manner to the Santa Barbara region of southern California, bypassing the central California coast.[5]

One possible mechanism for the diffusion of maritime cultural elements may well have been Asiatic travelers drifting or sailing from East Asia by means of the Japanese Current. This current, which flows from the Philippine Sea to the Californias by way of the Gulf of Alaska, comprises the only easy, natural sea-route to America from Asia. It was utilized continuously between 1565 and 1821 by Spanish galleons and by perhaps as many as sixty drifting Asiatic crafts in the century after 1770. Japanese junks, with living survivors, are known to have reached Santa Barbara and Sitka during the early 1800s, and Asiatic ceramics have been found in Indian sites from the western Canadian coast to the central California coast (although some of these ceramics may have been carried by European vessels). It has also been suggested that there is evidence of much earlier Asiatic contact with the Americas in connection with the appearance of Japanese-like pottery in Ecuador (dated several thousand years ago) and the existence of certain Oriental traits in the Mayan-Mexican region. Significantly, Chinese records mention the voyage of a group of Buddhist monks to what must have been some part of North America, and a return voyage to China, in the fifth century A.D.

It is very unlikely that maritime influences could have been derived from Polynesia, both because of the recency of the occupation of Hawaii and because there are no favorable currents to carry visitors from the South Pacific to the Americas. On the other hand, Polynesian–South American contact, initiated primarily from South America, seems well-established.[6]

Southern California cultural development entered into the Late Pre-European period at about 500 to 1000 A.D. During this era the ways of life first seen by Europeans evolved, with several centers of development. The most distinctive cultural tradition was a rather complex, maritime way of life developed along the coast from Point Conception to, perhaps, Orange County with its center in the Santa Barbara–Goleta area. Another interesting development consisted in the appearance of certain Anasazi-like traits, such as ground-paintings comparable to Anasazi sandpaintings, in the Vitam-speaking (Shoshonean) sections of central southern California.

The exact process whereby different Anasazi-like traits reached separate zones in southern and central California is not known, but several possible avenues can be suggested. First, the Anasazi-influenced people residing in southeastern Nevada, northwestern Arizona, and Utah prior to 1100 to 1300 A.D. might well have maintained direct trade relations with California, as is suggested by the diffusion of pottery, possible turquoise mining in the Mohave Desert, and California seashells found far in the interior. (It is remotely possible that central California Indians, who later followed the Kuksu religion, visited Anasazi communities. This would help to explain how Anasazi practices came to have a counterpart far to the northwest.) Second, middlemen may have helped to diffuse specific items both before and after 1100 to 1300. It is known, for example, that the Hamakhava of the Colorado River visited both the Hopi, in the east, and the San Joaquin Valley, Los Angeles area, and Ventura in the west during the eighteenth century (or earlier). It is also known that the Halchidhoma served as middlemen between the Riverside area and Arizona, and that the Quechan and other Colorado River Yumans traveled to the Pacific Coast in the west and to the Zuni in the east as early as the 1540s.

A third possible source for the diffusion of Anasazi elements into southern California were the pueblos, mentioned earlier, which existed on the lower Colorado before the 1500s. Unfortunately, it is not known whether these people possessed such Anasazi traits as groundpaintings.

Finally, it has been suggested that several Vitam groups (the Tongva, Maringayam, Iviatim, etc.) were newcomers from the northeast, arriving in southern California ca. 1150 A.D. If this theory is correct, then these people might have been living in those Great Basin areas directly involved in Anasazi culture of the

Developmental Pueblo stage, and later might have carried certain aspects of that heritage into southern California. Unfortunately, their failure to maintain the horticultural aspects of the Anasazi tradition argues against such a process.

In summary, it is quite clear that California and the Great Basin were not completely isolated from developments taking place elsewhere. Influences from Mexico and the Southwest and from the Northwest Coast are especially apparent during the period after 500 A.D., but earlier ages also reveal evidence of trade and cultural interchange. On the other hand, the natives of much of the California–Great Basin area tended to be rather conservative in terms of the basic characteristics of their cultures, and archaeology tends to reveal processes of gradual culture change rather than sharp shifts. On the whole, it is difficult to see much evidence for any widespread migrations in the Pre-European contact period. If such migrations did take place they apparently took the form of extremely slow changes which failed to introduce cultural schisms. Where changes in language occurred, as they doubtlessly did, it is very likely that the process was similar to that which took place in the Kupa (Warner's Valley) area after 1769, in which Kamia-speaking villages absorbed Iviatim-speaking newcomers to such an extent that the valley people gradually became Iviatim in language although continuing to trace their ancestry to both groups.[7]

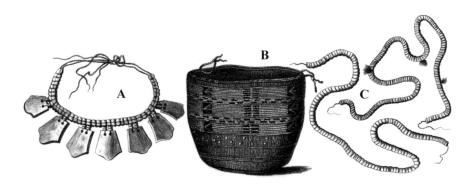

A Indian ground shell necklace. **B** Storage basket. **C** Strings of ground shell money. Drawings by G. Langsdorf. *(Courtesy of Bancroft Library, University of California, Berkeley.)*

Prelude To Invasion

From the 1530s through the 1760s or later, depending upon the region in question, natives of the California–Great Basin region were on the periphery of European expansion, exposed to occasional raids or exploratory forays but not confronted by any permanent attempts at conquest. Points of direct contact with Europeans were limited to 1) Spanish, English, and Dutch vessels along the coast; 2) Spanish land and sea expeditions to the Colorado River; 3) Spanish contacts at the Hopi villages and pueblos of northern New Mexico; and 4) little-known contacts with Spanish traders in the Ute territory of Colorado.

Direct contact with Europeans commenced when Hernando de Alarcón sailed up the Colorado River to the Yuma area in 1540. A few months later Melchior Diaz traveled from Sonora to the Colorado River by land, hoping to meet Alarcón and thus open up a maritime source of supplies for the Vásquez de Coronado expedition, then invading New Mexico. The Diaz party, of some interest because it was the first European group to definitely enter the present state of California, assumed in practice the form of a raid, largely because the Spaniards precipitated hostilities on the Colorado River by seizing and torturing Indians as a "preventive" device. (Early Spanish groups tended to use extremely harsh procedures on occasion, in order to frighten natives into prompt submission.)

Subsequently, the Colorado River area was visited by the Juan de Oñate expedition in 1604-1605 (coming from New Mexico), by several groups led by Father Eusebio Kino during 1699-1702 (coming from Sonora) and by groups led by Father Jacobo Sedelmayr in 1744-1750 (coming from Sonora). In addition, frequent Spanish activity in the Hopi–Verde Valley region and in northern Sonora–Arizona had an impact upon the Yumans of the Colorado.

Various coastal areas of California were visited by Juan Rodriguez de Cabrillo in 1542-1543, Sir Francisco Drake in 1579, Pedro de Unamuno in 1587, Sebastian Rodriguez Cermeño in 1595, Sebastian Vizcaino in 1602-1603, by unrecorded landings of the Spaniards' Manila galleon (sailing each year after 1565), probably by Dutch and English "pirates," and perhaps by occasional Oriental craft. Dutch and English buccaneers frequented the Baja California coast after 1587 and could have visited southern California waters. The evidence for Asian contacts is less convincing. There is a second-hand story of two small strange-looking vessels with golden pelicans as figureheads in the Gulf of California in 1540, whose sailors had both "Negroid" and straight hair and who said that they came from across the Pacific Ocean. Eight strange (non-Spanish) vessels were seen off the coast of Colima, Mexico, in 1573. Indians gave accounts of a ship carrying non-Indians that wrecked near San Luis Obispo ca. 1747. Non-Spanish nautical debris was seen near Monterey Bay in 1774, and metal goods (pieces of swords, a new "machete" and copper rings) were in the possession of Northwest Coast natives in 1775 which the Indians said always came from the North. These instances can, however, be explained in part by possible unrecorded European voyages as well as by Asian visitors.

The natives of the interior Great Basin area were probably not visited directly by Europeans before the 1770s, but they may well have contacted Spaniards among the Hamakhava (1604-1605) or among the Utes of Colorado (1600-1680 and after 1695). It is certain that Southern Paiutes often traded at Hopi during this entire period, but it is not known if any were from north of the Colorado River. In any case, indirect knowledge of the Spaniards' presence in the Southwest is certainly suggested.

Virtually all of the contacts described above were of a friendly or at least non-hostile nature, although it is suspected that occasional vessels visiting the coast created difficulties, perhaps through the actions of sailors seizing native women. This likely explains the native attack upon Unamuno's crewmen near San Luis Obispo in 1587, where one of the Filipinos with the expedition was killed along with some of the attacking natives.[8] In 1595, Cermeño's vessel was wrecked on the Marin County coast at the same bay visited by Drake twenty years previously. At first the natives were friendly, as they had been with Drake, but fighting commenced after a time, perhaps due to the Spaniards' gathering of Indian food supplies.

The brief contacts with Europeans prior to 1769 had little direct effect upon Indian cultural patterns, but certain influences need to be noted. European trade goods, Chinese silk, etc., were acquired, but not enough to alter the native material cultures, except perhaps in northwestern California where a demand for iron led to some metal-reworking. Horses began to be used by Indians in northwestern Sonora as early as the 1690s, but their diffusion towards the Colorado River was quite slow. The Ootam of southern Arizona received a few horses by 1700, the Halchidhoma of the Colorado were trading for them in 1744, and by the early 1770s the Quechans possessed numerous mounts. Horses had perhaps begun to spread into desert southern California by 1774 but they were not very numerous, and the Colorado River was the "frontier" for horses at that date. To the east, horses began to be acquired by the Pueblo Indians, Apaches, and Navahos during the seventeenth century, and to spread northwards to the Utes and Shoshone-Comanches, who were living adjacent to each other in the Wyoming region during the seventeenth and early eighteenth centuries. It is not known when the Great Basin Numic-speaking groups began to acquire horses, but it would seem likely that they were commencing to receive them by the 1770s, at least in the Utah area. (The Lewis and Clark Expedition found the Shoshones of Idaho well mounted.)

Wheat was introduced on the Colorado River in 1702, and by the 1770s the Hamakhava were raising it in addition to their native crops. It later spread to southern Utah and was subsequently introduced into New Mexico as "Paiute Wheat." By 1823 the Cahuillas of Coachella Valley were raising wheat—perhaps derived, along with their other crops, from the Colorado natives.

Another effect of Spanish contact was the spread of disease. It seems quite likely that the coastal population was reduced after 1542 by this means, and it is probable that a similar decline took place along the Colorado River. The Quechans, for example, appear to have dropped from 4000 natives in the 1700 to 1750 period to 3000 by the 1770s, and it is probable that some reductions along the river had occurred before the 1690s. Increased warfare and slave-raiding, stimulated by the Spanish slave trade, also took its toll in Arizona and along the Colorado River during this same general period. It is possible, also, that Southern Paiute captives were being seized by Utes and others for resale in New Mexico, as they were after 1800.

We know little about native cultures during the 1540-1769 period, other than archaeological knowledge pieced together from European accounts or inferred from ethnological research. (It should be stressed here that the detailed descriptions of Western American cultures found in works such as A. L. Kroeber's monumental *Handbook of the Indians of California* are based primarily upon data gathered between 1900 and 1930 from Indian individuals whose personal memories rarely extended back beyond the 1840s.) The archaeological evidence, as already cited, argues for continuity throughout this period in terms of the material aspects of native cultures. The evidence of European visitors does, however, suggest that changes not likely to be seen in archaeological sites were sometimes taking place.

The Colorado River area is the best-recorded portion of the California–Great Basin region prior to the 1770s. In this locale it appears from the documentary evidence that a number of important changes took place. For example, in 1540 the Spaniards found some seven or eight Indian sociopolitical units residing on the river below Yuma, only two of which, the Kohuana and Halyikwamai, can be equated definitely with later groups. Several of these units were bilingual and it seems likely that Ootam-speaking people were residing on the river along with Yumans. By 1604 and 1605, only five groups were residing below Yuma, in the following order: Halchidhomas, Kohuanas, A-ha-yes (perhaps the later Kaveltcadom), Halyikwamais, and Cocopas, all Yuman-speaking. Upriver from Yuma, at the mouth of the Gila, were Ootam-speaking people, Bahacechas (Quechans) and Hamakhavas. By the 1690s, the Quechans had moved south to Yuma, the Halchidhoma had moved north to the Blythe area, the A-ha-yes had disappeared (perhaps going east along the Gila), and the Ootam group had retreated to the east.

Evidence exists, therefore, for considerable movement as well as for the disappearance of several small groups in the delta. It may well be that the Colorado River peoples were in the process of achieving their later stage of political unification, especially between 1540 and 1604, i.e., evolving from small, single-village or band units into multi-village, multi-band "tribes" or republics.

Other changes can be discerned along the Colorado River before 1769, including perhaps a slight decline in trade relations (the trips being made to the Zuni area in 1539 and 1540 were replaced by shorter excursions into northern Sonora), although travel to the Pacific Coast remained common. It also seems that warfare gradually increased in intensity in the Colorado River-southern Arizona area, perhaps largely as a result of the desire to acquire horses and other trade goods through the sale of captives to the Spaniards of Sonora.

The material cultures of the River Yumans, in so far as it is revealed by pre-1769 diaries, is largely the same as that of later years, although some differences can be noted. For example, Alarcón observed in 1540,

> these Indians were adorned in different ways. Some had streaks covering their faces almost entirely. Others had their faces half-covered, all blackened with soot.... Some wore masks of the same color, shaped like their faces. On their heads they wore a deerskin... helmet, and on it a small crest with some feathers.... They have their ears pierced with many holes in which they place beads and shells. All of them, both small and large, wear a multicolored sash about the waist; tied in the middle is a round bundle of feathers which hangs in the back like a tail.[9]

In many respects this description could apply to a River Yuman of the 1880s, but the use of masks, skin helmets, sash around the waist, and feather bundle appear to have dropped out later in favor of complete nudity for males (except for a blanket occasionally thrown over the shoulders). In 1540 the leader of the Halyikwamai "wore a garment closed in front and back and open on the sides, fastened with buttons worked in a chequered black and white. It was made of fiber or rattan."[10] Such distinctive dress for leading men also disappeared in later years. These examples may indicate a decline in the complexity of Colorado River material cultures after 1540.

The European accounts relating to those few California coastal Indians actually visited reveal few differences from later years. The Hukueko people of Marin County apparently changed little between the visits of Drake and Cermeño (1579, 1595) and the 1800s. Likewise, the major characteristics of the advanced maritime cultures of the Santa Barbara–Catalina Island area are in evidence by 1542 and 1602. Many village names recorded by Rodriguez Cabrillo were still in use in the late eighteenth century, such as Misopsno (Carpinteria).

During this two-century period the Indians of California, with the partial exception of the Colorado River natives, failed to prepare politically and militarily for the Spanish invasion, as is rather understandable. They had no previous experience at interacting with aggressive Europeans, a people long at ease in the context of imperialism and Machiavellianism. They had no reason to expect an invasion, nor did they, at first, understand that the democratic, non-unified nature of their societies would inhibit effective resistance.[11]

The Spanish Invasion and Native Response

The Spanish-speaking persons who invaded California in 1769, although of American Indian and African as well as Spanish descent, were participants in a cultural legacy very different from that of the unconquered Native Americans. Basically, these Hispanos (Spanish subjects of whatever race) were citizens of an authoritarian state, members of a mass (i.e., populous, complex, and widespread) society, and participants in a legacy of religious intolerance and conformity, a legacy of centuries of almost constant warfare involving conquest, a legacy of messianic fanaticism (stressing both "Hispanidad"–Spanish culture in general and Catholicism in particular), and a legacy of Machiavellianism, i.e., the willingness to use duplicity on a large scale in order to achieve hidden goals destructive to other people. Hispanic culture also possessed certain morally positive characteristics, such as a relative lack of racial prejudice; however, it is the negative traits which appear to be crucially important in explaining the initial success of Spanish imperialism in the various sections of the Americas.

The Native Americans of much of California possessed almost an exactly opposite way of life, featuring the almost total absence of warfare in the European sense (local feuds, involving few casualties, were the natives' infrequent adventures in warfare), a total absence of the concept of conquering or exploiting other peoples (except in the case of debt slavery in the Northwest and of other rare forms of individual exploitation), a relative absence of the Machiavellian-type of mentality (Indians tended to be direct in their approach to achieving goals, rather than developing complex, devious strategies and deceptive tactics), and a general tolerance of differing approaches to religion and purely individual behavior. Further, most California Indians functioned within very small political units of fifty to five hundred persons whose leaders seldom possessed more than ceremonial authority.

Given these differences, it is not surprising that a few hundred Hispanos, equipped with guns, steel-tipped lances, swords, leather jackets and pants, horses, and, especially, with years of aggressive military experience, were able to initially overcome, and in a short space of time, many thousands of ill-equipped natives. The latter not only fought in small groups on foot, but possessed no body armor and few missiles capable of penetrating the invaders' leather clothing. The Hispanos possessed a significant psychological advantage in knowing the ultimate purpose for their initial intrusion, while the natives, except in the extreme south, could only suppose that the newcomers intended to leave after a time, or that they merely intended to befriend the natives, which was what Spanish propaganda asserted.

In 1769, when Spanish garrisons were established at San Diego and Monterey, a long-term interest in northwesterly expansion by the Spanish Empire was realized. The motives for this advance were varied and included: the ambitions of a senior official in Mexico (José de Gálvez was personally responsible for the move), the desire for the exploitation of the reputed wealth of the region, a desire to control the Colorado River and thereby pacify hostile Indians in Arizona, and anxiety over the possibility that the Russians or British might seize the harbor at Monterey (San Francisco Bay was not known to the Spanish until later in 1769). Missionary motives were also present but should not be overemphasized since thousands of natives farther south had not yet been Christianized.

Between 1769 and 1800, the coastal zone as far north as San Francisco and southern Alameda County was brought under Hispanic control with the establishment of forts (presidios) at San Diego; Santa Barbara; Monterey and San Francisco; smaller garrisons of soldiers at each of some two-score missions; and irregular militia units at three civilian towns (Los Angeles, San Jose, and Santa Cruz). In addition, between 1780 and 1781 two "military colonies" existed on the Colorado River at Yuma, and in the 1790s artillery companies were stationed at the major ports. Although seldom exceeding 500 men, the Spanish military force was highly mobile and was capable of rapidly congregating at points of danger, an important consideration in view of the fact that they had to control or deal with up to 70,000 Indians in the coastal zone.

California during the Spanish era was essentially a military colony with no civilian government except at the lowest levels. However, the military officers in control of the province shared authority with the Franciscan missionaries, who were also salaried employees of the King of Spain, although doctrinally subject to the Pope in Rome. The missions of California were indeed royal, governmental institutions, erected on land belonging ultimately (according to the Spanish viewpoint) to the Crown, although reserved to the natives with the missionaries as trustees. The purposes of the missions were several, but "Indian control" can be identified as the most important initial purpose. Subsequent purposes included the assimilation of the natives into Hispanic society, the development of a means of economic support for the military and clerical establishments, and the conversion of the Indians to Spanish Catholicism.

The kind of mission implemented in California was of the *reducción* or *congregación* (reduction or congregation) type, a variant of missionary activity developed in north central Mexico in the 1570s and utilized throughout Coahuila, Texas, Chihuahua, northwestern Sonora and Baja California. This type of mission was not erected in an already existing pueblo with sufficient population to support a church, but was utilized as a device for gathering together (congregating) natives who were dispersed in small villages, and for "reducing" them from their "free," "undisciplined" way of life to that of a disciplined subject of Spain. It should be clear, then, that the missions of California were not solely religious institutions. They were, on the contrary, instruments designed to bring about a total change in culture in a brief period of time.

The California missions were also authoritarian, coercive institutions ("totalitarian" best describes their nature). One cannot comprehend the effect of the missions upon Native Californians unless one realizes that Indians inducted into a mission were not free to leave (except for brief periods under license) and were constantly subject to the absolute control of the Franciscan missionaries, overseers, and soldiers. Physical force was used to keep the natives from leaving and to maintain discipline, including such punishments as: whipping with a barbed lash (for both men and women), use of the stocks and hobbles, solitary confinement, mutilation, branding, and even execution.

We do not know in every case exactly how Indians were initially recruited into the missions, but it is clear that few came voluntarily for religious reasons. In the early years natives were ordinarily recruited by the offer of "free" meals and gifts (not realizing that they would soon be working harder for their food and clothing than they ever had before). Subsequently, a standard device was to baptize young children in their home villages and then to require them, as "converts," to enter the mission at ages 5 to 7. Normally, the child's mother followed to be with the child and the father followed to be with his wife. By the 1790s, however, the reputation of the missions as places where Indians were "unfree," and as "deathtraps," made it necessary for the missionaries to resort to outright force, beginning especially in the San Francisco Bay area. Spanish military expeditions ordinarily brought back *gentiles* (unconverted Indians) as well as *cimarrones* (runaways). Another common variant was to bribe or frighten a village leader into supplying quotas of converts, as in the following incident:

[In January 1804 a Franciscan from San Miguel Mission] went with a soldier to Cholan [Cholame] rancheria fourteen leagues away and asked Guchapa, chief of all the rancherias in that region, to let him have some of his young men to make Christians of them. Guchapa refused and repulsed the friar and his escort with threats, declaring that he had no fear of the soldiers since he knew perfectly well that they died like other men. It was important to modify this chieftain's views, and [Captain] Guerra despatched a sergeant with thirteen men to arrest Guchapa, which was effected after a brave resistance; and as a captive the chief, being duly rewarded with beads, agreed to bring in all the Christian fugitives in his jurisdiction, and left his son as a hostage for the fulfillment of his contract.[12]

Within the missions, the Franciscans and their soldier escorts exercised complete control over the "neophytes" (as the converts were called); this control even extended to regulation of sexual behavior, splitting off children from parents (e.g., locking up all unmarried girls above the age of seven in a "nunnery" each night and the males in another building), forbidding native marriage and divorce practices, and, of course, attempting to suppress all aspects of Indian religion and curing practices (Indian doctors or curers were flogged whenever apprehended).

From several viewpoints the missions were an immense success. The natives of the coastal zone were indeed congregated in a few places where they could be more easily controlled. Their threatening numbers were reduced by the extremely high deathrate in the missions—from 70,000 to about 15,000 by the 1830s. Tens of thousands were baptized—and buried—as at least nominal Catholics. Perhaps most important of all, an economic base was provided for the Hispano ruling classes. By about 1800, the neophytes were providing much of the support for the Spanish clergy and army, including, especially, food. After 1811 they literally provided the entire support for the province. The *gente de razon* ("people of reason" or Spanish-speaking persons) were entirely dependent upon the products produced by the converts for both food and other supplies (the latter either being manufactured directly by the "neophytes" or obtained through the sale of their goods).

From the native viewpoint, the missions were a catastrophe of indescribable magnitude, since the coastal population was largely eliminated by sickness induced by concentration in unhealthy mission compounds, new foods, new styles of labor, probably an insufficient diet (often with little meat), and, perhaps most important of all, a state of psychological depression. It is indeed disheartening to read diaries of pre-mission travelers commenting upon the vigor and enterprise of the natives and then to read the accounts of later visitors who almost invariably note the apathy, lethargy, and depression exhibited by long-term neophytes. Although the missionaries did attempt to mitigate the "slave-labor camp" character of the missions with Catholic religious pageantry, musical groups, and rarer educational programs, the net effect of the experience was apparently quite devastating for the average Indian. For those few who cooperated openly with the conquerors or who were enthusiastic converts life was perhaps a little better, but for the masses it was apparently tragic indeed.[13]

The mission was not the only instrument of conquest introduced by the Spaniard. Three others need also to be mentioned briefly: the presidio, the pueblo, and the rancho. The presidios or forts not only served as centers for military control but also were places where Indian labor was exploited. The presidios (and almost everything else in Spanish California) were erected by Indian labor, unpaid in the case of converts or prisoners, or poorly paid in the case of *gentiles*. All of the soldier families acquired native servants and thus, as time passed by, each presidio became a town composed of a *gente de razón* ruling class and native laborers. The pueblos (civilian towns), such as Los Angeles and San Jose, developed in a similar manner, with the settlers (most of whom were retired soldiers) utilizing Indian labor on a sharecropping or board-and-room basis. A number of coastal natives preferred to become laborers in the towns rather than converts in the missions (and the Franciscans often protested that natives were become *ladino*, i.e., Hispanicized, without being missionized). The settlers and soldiers, needing cheap labor, were not averse to this process.

The rancho (literally an isolated hut off in the countryside) provided another means whereby Indian labor was integrated into the Hispano economy. Beginning in the 1780s, soldiers and settlers were allowed to graze stock and raise crops in the countryside, using Indian labor entirely. Gradually, these grants of land became more formal; but several things should be noted: title to the land always was retained by the Crown, Indian village rights were never quieted by a rancho grant, and the ranch owner almost always lived most of the year in town, leaving his stock and crops in the hands of Indians working on a sharecropping basis. Gradually, especially after the 1830s, the Indians became serfs, and an economy similar to that of the Deep South of the late nineteenth century developed.

The Spanish Empire was able to expand successfully with a relatively small number of fighting men largely because the Spaniards understood very well the process of conquest and colonialization. Thus, terror was the basis for control (rebellion was usually dealt with severely) but this was supplemented, as in the case of Guchapa, with bribes and privileges. The Spaniards often attempted to recruit the Indian leadership into the imperial system by means of favors which ranged from uniforms, staffs of office, titles and other gifts, to annual salaries and the right to exploit Indian labor (these latter privileges were given primarily in Mexico and farther south). In addition, enthusiastic converts to Catholicism, frightened individuals, and native women who intermarried with Hispanos often served imperial purposes. Thus, when a native rebellion was being planned, the Spaniards ordinarily had informers available who would warn them in advance. Very few Indian revolts (and they were frequent) took the Spaniards by surprise.

Intermarriage between Spanish-speaking persons and California Indians was quite common and was officially encouraged by the Crown as a device for facilitating the control and Hispanicization of the native population, and as a means for meeting the needs of the numerous unmarried soldiers sent to California. Unfortunately, intermarriage failed to improve the position of the Indian masses because both the Indian partner in the marriage and the children were ordinarily absorbed, socially and psychologically, into Hispanic society. That is, every effort was made to maintain a social and cultural wall between Spanish-speaking persons (who were often Indians from Mexico) and California Indian converts or *gentiles*. It might have been militarily disastrous for the empire to have allowed *gente de razón* of Indian blood to have developed a feeling of unity with the native masses.

During the period under discussion, 1769 to 1821, native groups in the interior were very much affected by the Spanish invasion. This was due partly to continued efforts at expansion of the empire, as with the abortive effort along the Colorado River in 1780 and 1781, the successful expansions to San Rafael in 1817 and in the San Bernardino to San Diego backcountry between 1818 and 1823. But in great measure, this Spanish influence was due to other types of activity. The natives of the Marin-Sonoma-Solano and Sacramento-to-Bakersfield areas of California were very much affected by raids for converts. By the 1830s several thousands, from as far away as the Sierra Nevada foothills, had become neophytes along the coast. The Southern Paiutes of Utah and southern Nevada were affected by slave raids conducted by New Mexicans and Utes (and, perhaps, Navahos) designed to supply the servant needs of northern Mexico.

Numerous Spanish expeditions were sent out between 1769 and 1821, reaching north along the coast to as far as Alaska, the interior of California (except east of the Sierra Nevada), virtually all of southern California, and much of Utah. It is possible that irregular parties of Hispanic fur traders and slave raiders also crossed Nevada since the Indians of central California were certain that they had been visited by, or told of, Europeans coming from the east who had crossed or approached the Sierra Nevadas. All of these exploring parties, and especially the raids, had a considerable impact upon native society. Diseases were undoubtedly introduced, the ethnic boundaries were probably altered to some degree, and part-European children were doubtlessly left behind.

In almost every instance the Native Californians responded initially in a friendly, albeit sometimes shy, manner towards the Spanish intruders. The natives tended to believe the Hispano assertions of friendship, and usually aided in the process of erecting temporary buildings as well as supplying the food which made the Spanish intrusion possible. Not many months or even weeks had passed, however, before the raping and seizure of Indian women and the appropriation of native property began to alter the situation. Incidents soon took place, as at San Gabriel, where Indian heads were mounted at the entrance to the mission because an outraged husband had dared try to avenge an assault upon his wife. More serious incidents often occurred as well, as at San Diego, where the Kamia actually destroyed the infant mission in 1775, killing three Hispanos. The coastal Kamias were not pacified until late in 1776.

At San Francisco the Indians fled across the Bay (allegedly due to an attack by the Indians of San Mateo) and then returned in December 1776 to attack the Spaniards, with little success however. Elsewhere the same pattern tended to be followed during the 1770s, with the Indians occasionally becoming irritated enough to fire off a few arrows, but with the Spaniards easily thwarting their efforts.

During the 1780s and 1790s, Indian resistance stiffened somewhat along the coast and reached major proportions along the Colorado River. The river area had long been an important objective of Spanish imperialism because it was seen as a key point on the land route to California and as a means for outflanking the rebel Ootams and hostile Yavapais and Apaches of Arizona. The Quechan people at Yuma were persuaded to allow the Spaniards to establish posts in their territory after their kwoxot (leader) Olleyquotequiebe (Salvador Palma) had been regaled in Mexico City and after they had been promised many gifts, clothing, etc. In 1780, two military colonies composed of soldier-settlers were established across from Yuma and at Xuksil (Algodones), and it was expected that the Quechans would be Christianized and settled in these colonies. Unfortunately, the soldier-settlers, priests, and officers offended the Quechans at every turn, whipping the leading men, damaging native food supplies, and behaving overall in an exploitative manner.

On July 17 and 18, 1781, the Quechans and some allies under the leadership of Salvador Palma, Ygnacio Palma (his brother), Francisco Xavier (a Halyikwamai raised in Sonora) and others, staged a well-planned revolt which totally destroyed the Spanish establishment. Fifty-five to ninety-five Hispanos were killed, seventy-six or more were captured, and the Quechans were free again. During the balance of 1781 and 1782 the Spaniards repeatedly launched large-scale military assaults upon the Quechans, but the latter, with extreme bravery and fortitude, threw back every assault. The Quechan liberation struggle was ultimately successful and the Spaniards were forced to admit defeat in 1783. Thereafter, the Colorado River was completely under Native American control and the provinces of Sonora and California were cut off from each other.[14]

Perhaps as a result of the Quechan example, other Indians became more troublesome to the invaders during the 1780s. In October 1785, led by the Hapchi-vitam and by a female religious leader, Toypurina, the Tongva attempted to destroy San Gabriel Mission. This rebellion was discovered and thwarted by Spanish vigilance (Toypurina was captured and deported to the north where she later married an Hispano), as was another rebellion in July 1786, in which the Hapchi-vitam again planned a revolt in alliance with the Indians of Atongaibit (Victorville) and the Colorado River. In 1794, Indians were arrested at San Luis Obispo and Purisima for planning a revolt.

In the San Francisco Bay area, northern California's first hero known by name appeared on the scene in February 1793. Charquin (Charkeen) fled from San Francisco Mission and began struggling against all those who favored the missionaries' objectives. Serious resistance to the invaders was soon provided by the Saklán of the Contra Costa County region and their allies, the Cuchillones ("Little Knives") of the Karkin Strait area. From 1795 to 1797 these native groups defeated parties of San Francisco neophytes sent to recover runaways from the mission. In July 1797 the Spaniards attacked the Saklán and Cuchillones (who had dug pits to prevent the soldiers from using their horses effectively). The invaders captured nine *gentiles* and eighty-three runaway neophytes. The Saklán put up a brave resistance, wounding two soldiers and losing seven of their own men. The establishment of San Jose Mission at that time on the east shore of the Bay, greatly irritated the Saklán, and several incidents occurred, including a raid by the Spaniards in 1800 killing a chief and capturing twenty runaways. Thereafter, the Saklán disappear from the record, but their neighbors to the north and east continued sporadic fighting through 1810. In one battle at Sespesuya, on the north shore of Karkin Strait (Estrecho de los Carquines), the natives preferred to perish in their burning houses (set aflame by the soldiers) rather than surrender.

Considerable sporadic resistance also occurred at San Juan Bautista where the Ansayanes stubbornly fought, Mission Santa Clara, and elsewhere during the 1790s and early 1800s, but it was generally put down with ease. More serious, because difficult to combat, were neophyte efforts at poisoning or murdering the Franciscans. In 1801, four or five priests became ill from alleged poisoning at San Miguel and San Antonio, and in 1812 the priest at Santa Cruz was killed by some of the neophytes of that mission. Other plots were frequently reported.

Although in 1810 and 1811 the neophytes of San Gabriel, in alliance with Mohave River natives and the Hamakhava and Quechans, planned an abortive rebellion, the coastal natives' will to fight seemed broken between 1800 and 1820, when they offered little resistance, except as runaways. In the interior, however, great changes were taking place during these two decades, changes which were to produce greater resistance in later years. Perhaps most important of all was the continued spread of horses from the Colorado River into southern California during the 1780s and 1790s. Also, by the latter period, natives near the coast were acquiring horses either by serving as cowboys for the Hispanos or by theft. As early as 1783, Indians ran off horses in the San Jose area while in later years horses became so numerous along the coast that it was no problem acquiring them. By 1818 a Spaniard was expressing great fear because of the San Joaquin Valley natives' growing habit of using horses.

At the same time as they were acquiring horses, the Indians of the Central Valley were also becoming more knowledgeable about Spanish fighting tactics and more aware of what Spanish conquest would mean. Hundreds of runaways lived among them and they knew full well what the missions were like. Thus from San Diego to Sacramento and Clear Lake, along the whole frontier, mounted Indians were preparing themselves for increased warfare during the period from the 1820s through the 1840s. This process, perhaps more than anything else, was to prevent Hispano-Mexican expansion into the interior of California.

The Native Californians also offered various other forms of resistance of a more passive nature, the most obvious of which was flight to the interior. Indians ordinarily ran away singly or in small groups, but, on occasion, mass flights took place, as when 200 natives fled from San Francisco in 1795 or when, in 1803, the entire Kamia population of Santo Tomás Mission (in northern Baja California) fled to the Colorado River. The exploits of many of the individual *cimarrones* are rather interesting. In 1812, for example, one Salvador fled from San Juan Capistrano all the way to Sonora but was shipped back in 1819. Much earlier, a Baja California Indian, Sebastian Taraval, forced to serve in California, fled from San Gabriel to the Colorado River, being the first Christian to use the land route between California and Sonora.

Runaways became so numerous in the early 1800s that, on occasion, large sweeps were made through the Central Valley by troops looking for them; and smaller squads of soldiers were constantly out. In 1818 a Franciscan reported that the refugees and *gentiles* had set up "a republic of hell and diabolical union of apostates" in the tulare marshes of the San Joaquin Valley. Other refugees fled to the Colorado River, where some were met by Jedediah Smith in 1826.

This form of resistance was not only effective in keeping the Spaniards busy, but also contributed to the diffusion of horticulture, horseback riding, and other Hispano-Mexican traits, to the interior. By the late 1820s, crops were being grown by refugees in the Kern County area. Horticulture was even more widespread in the Central Valley in the 1830s and 1840s. By 1823 the Cahuillas were also growing crops, but theirs may well have been derived from the Colorado River.[15]

Religious resistance was also offered to the invaders. In general, the natives did their best to secretly preserve their ancient religion in the missions, although it became increasingly difficult to do so. Native revivals are known to have occurred, such as in the Santa Barbara area in 1801. At that time (after a destructive epidemic) the deity Chupu (Ashoop) appeared in a neophyte's vision. Chupu revealed that all who were baptized as Christians would die unless they were washed clean again and made offerings to their old deity. It would appear that virtually all of the region's Indians dedicated themselves to Chupu without the priests being aware of the movement until much later. In 1810 a priest reported that the same Indians were still worshipping Chupu but that he was making progress against the practice.

Clearly the missionized Indians seldom if ever became completely Christianized. This was partly because few lived very long in the missions and partly because new *gentiles* were constantly being brought in. Many pre-Spanish religious beliefs were retained by the coastal Indians, albeit in a garbled form, after the missions had been abolished.

Self-willed death may have also been another form of passive resistance, although it is uncertain whether any Indian *intentionally* induced psychosomatic depression. On the other hand, it does seem clear that large-scale abortion was sometimes practiced to prevent the birth of children in the missions. (However, it should be noted that in many cases what appeared to be abortion might actually have been the result of syphilis, introduced by 1775, or measles.) Apathetic work habits may also be cited as a form of passive resistance.

During this era other Europeans also appeared in the Far West, including Russians, Britons, and Anglo-Americans. The Russians and Anglo-Americans together had the greatest impact, being largely responsible (along with the missionaries) for the depopulation of the islands on the southern California coast between 1800 and the 1820s. Russian and Yankee ships frequently hunted sea otters and seals along the shores of the islands, and the crewmen and Aleut and Kodiak Eskimo hunters reportedly slaughtered many natives. The balance were carried off to the missions on the mainland.

Spanish, Russian, British, and Yankee ships also stopped in northwestern California after the 1770s, usually at Trinidad Bay. Although the Spaniards in 1775 found the Yurok people of Trinidad friendly, contacts with later visitors soon led to hostility. In 1805, a Yankee ship, the *O'Cain*, with 100 Aleut hunters, four Russian overseers, and fifty bidarkas (sealskin boats) hunted in the area, but the Yurok were unfriendly and one native was killed. That this incident occurred is not surprising since the intruders were catching fish and animals belonging, from the native viewpoint, to the Yurok.

Beginning in early 1809, the Russians commenced visiting Bodega Bay, establishing close contacts with the natives of this area north of San Francisco. Aleut hunters actually carried their bidarkas overland from Bodega in order to hunt in San Francisco Bay. Sporadic contacts continued until 1811 when the Russians and Aleuts explored the Bodega and San Franciso bay areas and ventured up the Shabaikai (Russian) River for fifty miles. In 1812, ninety-five Russians and part-Russians, and eighty Aleuts or Kodiak Eskimos, founded Fort Ross at Mad-shui-nui on the coast. Every effort was made there to befriend the Kashia Pomo and Hukueko. In general, the natives north of San Francisco were happy to have allies against the Spaniards (who were frequently recruiting neophytes north of the Bay). However, it is reported that the warlike Sotoyomes (a Pomo-speaking group living near Healdsburg) first tested the Russians mettle in a battle. Later they became allies. Very few Russians remained at Mad-shui-nui, but those that did, along with the Aleuts and Eskimos, appear to have intermarried with the nearby Indians and to have been consistently friendly.

Anglo-Americans, Britons, French Canadians, and New Mexican Hispanos were also entering the interior Far West in this period. With the exception of the Hispanos, however, none are known to have definitely reached as far as the Great Basin. Certainly by 1800 to 1820, New Mexicans were traveling to the Utah Lake–Great Salt Lake area to trade for furs and slaves, and rumors reached the coast which can be taken to indicate that some penetrated as far as the Nevada and Colorado River areas. Anglo-Americans and French Canadians traveled along the Snake River after 1810, and it is possible that Nevada Indians made contact with certain of these parties.

Quite obviously the years from 1769 to 1821 were of vast significance for the Native Americans of the Far West. By the latter year, virtually all of the coastal natives were living in the missions or on nearby ranchos, and the ancient villages were depopulated. In 1818, Governor Vicente de Sola could report that 64,000 Indians had been baptized and that of these, 41,000 were dead. In fifty years the coastal population had been reduced from perhaps 70,000 to slightly more than 20,000. (It should be noted that the Spaniards were well aware that mission Indian deathrates were high prior to the invasion of California.)

The interior population had also been vitally affected, with losses in numbers undoubtedly taking place through raids for "neophytes," slave raids in Utah, and the spread of disease. On the other hand, the interior natives were becoming more warlike, were mounted, and were better prepared to resist future aggression.

It also seems likely that certain movements of people were taking place due to European intrusion. It is possible, for example, that there was a general southerly and southwesterly migration of Shoshones and Northern Paiutes caused by the Crow, Blackfoot, and Cheyenne occupation of former Shoshone lands in Montana and Wyoming. Likewise, the Southern Paiutes may have commenced a westward-southwestward movement to escape from New Mexican, Ute, and Navaho slave raids. These movements may, in turn, have partially displaced groups such as the Washo, although the Southern Paiute were able to occupy territory in the Mohave Desert vacant due to Spanish missionization. Nearer to the coast it seems possible to suggest that certain areas depopulated by the missionaries were occupied by new groups, but this is less clear for the period before 1821.

The Europeans had arrived, this time to stay, and the Far West was never to be placid again.

The Mexican-Indian Period

An independent Mexican state came into effective existence, in so far as California was concerned, in 1822, after a dozen years of warfare in central Mexico. Unfortunately, the Mexican Indian masses who had shed their lives struggling for independence since 1810 were not at first to benefit materially from independence, for power fell into the hands of wealthy persons of largely European descent.

The new Mexican republic (or empire, as it was briefly called) began its existence in the midst of numerous serious contradictions, contradictions derived from the antagonistic desires of wealthy European landowners, ambitious semi-Europeanized mixed-bloods, and the predominantly Indian peasant masses.

Fundamentally, the Mexican republic before 1910 served the interests of the landowners and the ambitious, although the constitution of 1824 guaranteed equality of citizenship to all persons, including, theoretically, the conquered natives of coastal California, southern Arizona, and central New Mexico.

Between 1822 and 1825, California remained a military colony, a colony of Mexico rather than a colony of Spain, but the rulers were essentially the same as before. After 1825 the pace of change began to accelerate, but, by and large, the Indian masses were not to benefit. Republican ideals and political structures were introduced, but, in essence, these served merely to allow ambitious mixed-bloods to acquire power and property, often at the expense of Indians. By the 1840s a feudal society had developed wherein a new class of large rancho owners with military followings vied for political power and wealth, with the Indian as only a peripheral participant. The native witnessed many changes, but much remained the same in practice.

The Mexican government was weaker militarily than that of Spain and likewise lacked the religious and cultural fanaticism which had led the Spaniards to seek new conquests. For these reasons, as well as because of increased resistance, the Mexicans were unable to expand the territory under their control appreciably, except in the Sonoma region north of San Francisco Bay. In point of fact, the areas under Mexican control often tended to be smaller than the areas under Spanish control, as in the San Diego–San Bernardino backcountry after 1834-1840, in northern Baja California, and elsewhere in northern Mexico and the Southwest.

The missions in California and elsewhere were, in theory, to be abolished and the Indians were to be granted equality of citizenship. This did not happen immediately in California, however, because the Spanish-speaking population continued to be economically dependent upon the forced labor of the "neophytes" and because the Hispano-Mexicans were afraid that liberated Indians would either refuse to work, would rebel, or would flee to the interior. During the early 1820s, therefore, the missions continued to exist exactly as before 1822, except that the Franciscans had to go farther afield to recruit new converts. All of the coastal natives were missionized (or living in the towns) and it was necessary to reach out into the areas north of San Francisco Bay, to the Central Valley, and to the mountain and desert areas for converts, the bulk of whom would appear to have been recruited by force.

In 1823, San Francisco Solano Mission was founded at Sonoma after a bitter struggle between the priests in charge of the old Bay Area missions. The three existing missions were entirely dependent upon far-off regions, principally north of the Bay, for converts, and their priest-managers were afraid that a mission at Sonoma would cut off their supply. It was charged (by a San Francisco priest) that the missionaries of San Jose Mission were in the habit of raiding the Suisun region for converts, forcibly seizing *gentiles* and killing those who resisted.

In 1825, Lt. Col. José Maria Echeandia was appointed in Mexico to be Governor of California, and when he came north he brought with him new ideas of Mexican republicanism, equalitarianism, and *mestizo* upward-mobility not previously apparent in California. Echeandia possessed a democratic style of behavior, typified by his shaking hands with the African-Indian-Spanish mayor of Santa Barbara (an act which made a great impression upon the mayor, Rafael Gonzalez). He also wished to abolish the missions, not merely to liberate the Indians but, also, in all probability, to break the economic power of the Franciscans and provide wealth for the ambitious Mexicans who were his supporters.

Several actions initiated by Echeandia changed the missions forever. In July 1826 and January 1831 he issued decrees to begin the process of "secularizing" the missions, that is, to turn each mission into an Indian town. These decrees did not lead to any immediate formal change, because their intent was thwarted by the Franciscans and by a new Governor, Lt. Col. Manuel Victoria, but they did stir up the Indians' hopes and led to a decline in mission discipline. More significantly, in 1832 Echeandia recruited hundreds of Indians to fight with him in one of California's many armed political struggles, and this act, an unprecedented one for California, set the stage for growing native unrest.

From 1834 to 1836, Governor José Figueroa, a *mestizo* of Aztec background, was finally forced by the Mexican government to commence the formal secularization of the missions. The plan put into effect by Figueroa and his successors was not, however, emancipation in any real sense. The absolute rule of the priest was simply replaced by that of Mexican civilian officials (administrators and *mayordomos*), and virtually all of the elements of physical coercion were retained. The situation may actually have deteriorated, for what ensued was a "sacking" of the missions by some of the more powerful Mexican families of California.

Typically, a secularized mission was to be an Indian pueblo (or, if the mission had branches, several pueblos) with one half of the property belonging to the natives and the other half being used for support of the priests and secular officials. In fact, however, many missions were plundered of their resources (livestock, tools, and even portions of buildings) during the first few months, and, therefore, the Indians in pueblos began life at a considerable disadvantage.

During the era of Juan Bautista de Alvarado (1836-1842) and thereafter, the Indian pueblos were largely destroyed, not through any laziness or incapacity on the part of the Indians, but rather because the secular administrators managed to appropriate most of the mission wealth for themselves, while they and other Mexicans (usually their relatives) were granted the best lands formerly under mission control. At the same time as this official looting was occurring, the Indians were still subject to forced labor for the support of church and state, and physical punishment was used to control their actions as during the pre-1836 mission regime.

Understandably, the ex-neophytes tended to abandon the mission-pueblos in favor of more favorable surroundings. Many fled en masse to Mexican towns, where they could at least work for themselves with a greater degree of freedom. Others returned to the interior or to the sites of their former villages.

In the towns the Indians tended to fall under the influence of the worst aspects of Hispano-Mexican secular culture, including alcoholism, excessive gambling, and sexual promiscuity. Syphilis and other diseases took their toll, so that the Indian population tended to decline steadily, while a portion of the people were lost in the process of Mexicanization and intermarriage.

A somewhat similar process occurred in the rural areas of the coastal zone where the natives came to be dominated by the Mexican rancho owners. The typical Mexican rancho was based, economically and socially, upon the exploitation of Indian labor, a labor which was virtually unpaid except in the sense of possessing a certain share in crops raised and in meat slaughtered. Native villages or settlements were able to survive within rancho boundaries only because the rancho owners needed Indian house servants and agricultural laborers. Fortunately, Indians living in rural communities were able to preserve or revive something of their pre-mission cultures, with the rancho owners apparently having little interest in suppressing such traits.

The Mexican-Indian period saw a marked increase in armed native resistance to outside aggression and in somewhat improved fighting ability. In general, the entire frontier from Sonoma to San Diego was a "war zone" which the Mexicans were often unable to control in spite of an increased Spanish-speaking population along the coast. Perhaps the greatest Mexican successes occurred north of San Francisco Bay after the establishment of San Francisco Solano in 1823 and the civilian settlement of Sonoma in 1835; but these successes occurred only after a great deal of warfare.

During the 1821 to 1824 period, the Hukueko of Marin County put up their last resistance, under leaders such as Pomponio, Marin, and Quintin. Pomponio was a San Rafael-area native who had been missionized at San Francisco. He later escaped and for several years raided his enemies from San Rafael to Santa Cruz. One of his associates, or perhaps Pomponio himself, once escaped from imprisonment by cutting off the heels of his feet so as to slip off the iron rings or stocks which confined him.

In 1824 Pomponio was captured at Novato and executed, but in the meantime the activities of Marin and Quintin made extended campaigns by the Mexicans necessary. Marin was forced to take refuge on an island, where he at first successfully defended himself; but he and Quintin (after whom San Quentin point and prison are named) were both ultimately captured.

A period of relative quiet ensued, perhaps encouraged by the fact that hired *gentiles* were used as laborers at Solano during the late 1820s, in place, apparently, of the zealous recruitment of neophytes. An epidemic which swept through much of northern California in the early 1830s may also have effected the north Bay area.

In 1834, Mariano Vallejo, an ambitious and energetic Mexican, became Administrator of Solano Mission and Commander of the new civilian settlement at Sonoma. Thus commenced a process whereby the Vallejo family and its relations secured control over much of the Napa Valley, Sonoma, and Petaluma–Santa Rosa regions and of the wealth of Solano Mission, all at the expense of the Native Californians. As a part of this process, the Vallejos constantly were in need of cheap Indian labor (which was sometimes not voluntary) and of the use of force to sustain what amounted to a vast private empire. To accomplish this the Vallejos secured an alliance with Samyetoy, a Suisun leader who came to be known as Solano, and waged warfare against the independence-loving Sotoyomes (Pomo-speaking people from Healdsburg and perhaps elsewhere), "Guapos" (Miyakama), Yolos, and others.

The details need not concern us here, but from 1834 through 1843 warfare between the Sotoyomes and Mexicans was almost constant, with the "Guapos" and Yolos also joining in, especially before 1840. The Sotoyomes were aided by the Russians in some degree, who furnished arms in exchange for furs and skins, while the Vallejos were aided by Solano and his Suisun warriors who were armed and trained by Salvador Vallejo (and on occasion by other groups, such as the Kainama). On several occasions the Mexicans reached as far north as Clear Lake; for example, in 1837, when they captured Zampay, a Yolo leader, and forced Succara, a Sotoyome leader, to agree to a temporary peace treaty.

The Vallejo policy of using Indian auxiliaries is an excellent example of colonialist strategy, taking advantage of native divisions and rewarding leaders (such as Solano) who were willing to become instruments of the invaders' policy. Unfortunately for the Suisuns and others who aided the Mexicans, disenchantment usually set in, but often after native strength had declined. In April 1840 Vallejo's Indian infantry attempted to rebel, but they were crushed, with many killed and nine leaders executed. In spite of this, many Indians continued to fight for the Vallejos, a service which was crucial in insuring Mexican control over the Sonoma region.

In March 1843, the Vallejos, with 270 men, raided the Clear Lake region for servants, forcing the Sotoyomes, Tuleyomes and others to take refuge on an island. In his usually bloody style, Salvador Vallejo slaughtered 170 Indians and a Negro fugitive from the United States who had taken refuge with the natives. This cruel campaign appears to have ended major resistance in the north Bay area, although other factors were also at work: the abandonment of

Fort Ross by the Russians, the increasing Mexican population in the area south of Santa Rosa, and the decimation of the native population by disease. Several epidemics are reported for the 1830s. A smallpox epidemic spread from Ross to Sonoma in 1838 and raged throughout the north, killing 70,000 Indians according to Mariano Vallejo.

What fighting remained north of San Francisco Bay was primarily the result of Mexican raiding. For example, in 1845 a group of Mexicans from Sonoma raided the peaceful Kashia Pomo in the Ross area to secure captives. Some Indian men were killed, two women were raped, and 150 servants were obtained. Anglo-Americans took up this practice of capturing Indian laborers in the late 1840s and 1850s, as will be discussed below.

Northern California generally was very much affected by European intrusion during this period, although data is often scanty. From the south the natives of the Sacramento Valley were subject to raids for converts and laborers by the Mexicans and later by the intrusion of John Sutter and Anglo settlers. From the north the Indians were subject to visits and raids by Oregon Indians and those who were trading with natives and Europeans along the Columbia River. It is not known when Oregon Country natives began to visit California, but such visits probably commenced with the 1800-1810 period when they acquired horses. A Spokane woman is reported to have been in California before 1814, a Walla Walla band as early as the 1800-1810 period. In 1814, trappers in the Willamette Valley met traveling Shasta, Walla Walla, and Cayuse who invited traders to come live among them, and it appears that some did visit the Shasta and upper Sacramento later that year. The John Work expedition of the summer of 1832 found the natives of the Cow Creek–Upper Sacramento River area very much afraid of horses and subject to slave raids by the Shasta. The Shasta not only held slaves themselves but actively traded them north to the Columbia River, as did the Walla Walla and other groups. At The Dalles an annual fair was held where "the southern tribes brought Modoc, Pitt River, Chasty and California Indians—prisoners—to sell as slaves." A similar fair was held at Yainax, east of Klamath Lake, where came

> Klamaths, Modocs, Summer Lake Snakes from the east; Warm Springs people from the north; Shastas and Pitt

Rivers from Northern California; all those fraternized, and each October, when the earth had yielded it fruits . . . they met here in grand conclave, with Nez Perces and Cayuses, and others from the Cascades to the Rockies; from California to the Columbia River. . . . Here also was the great slave mart of the mid-mountain region.[16]

In 1841, some Walla Wallas and Nez Perces were reportedly planning to journey south to the Shasta groups to trade for furs and horses, while in 1844, 1846, and 1847, other Walla Walla groups went as far south as Sutter's Fort to trade for cattle and other items.

Fur trappers and other non-Indians generally found the northern California Indians friendly in the 1820s and 1830s, but by 1837 the Sacramento River and Shasta groups were often hostile towards trespassers. Through the late 1830s and 1840s battles between travelers and natives were frequently reported. (From 1830 to 1833 as many as half or more of the Sacramento Valley Indians were wiped out by malaria introduced from the north.)

The Central Valley frontier presented the Mexicans with great problems, although the native villages to the west of the delta and San Joaquin River were all depopulated by the 1820s.

In 1827 or 1828, a neophyte known as Estanislao (Stanislaus) escaped from San Jose Mission, and, with another native, called Cipriano, established a band of refugees and *gentiles* in the northern San Joaquin Valley. Estanislao vigorously attacked the missions and attempted to stir up a revolt at San Jose and Santa Clara, with considerable success. Several campaigns were launched against Estanislao in 1828 but they were failures. In May 1829, an expedition of forty soldiers with a swivel gun, accompanied by militia, set out for the River of the Laquisimes (perhaps the Stanislaus River). The natives were entrenched in a wooded area near the river and the entire day of May 7 was devoted to a fruitless effort to force them out. May 8 was also entirely devoted to fighting, with two soldiers killed and eight wounded. Thereafter, the siege was abandoned and the Indian "freedom fighters" were left victorious while the Mexicans retreated to San Jose. This represents, therefore, a great day in northern California history, being the first substantial victory gained by Native Californians over the invaders.

The Mexicans could not accept permanent defeat, and late in May a very large expedition was organized, composed of perhaps 100 men including auxiliaries. On May 30, the army confronted the Indians at the scene of the former battle. Unable to penetrate the native defenses, the Mexicans set fire to the wooded area, but they were still unable to dislodge the defenders. On the next day the Mexicans advanced into the woods, finding pits, ditches, and barricades, but no enemies. The troops immediately followed the Indians up the River of the Laquisimes and on the following day surrounded a portion of the "freedom fighters" in a thicket. The Indians declared that they would rather die than surrender and they fought doggedly behind ditches and earthworks in spite of the brush being set on fire again. That night many of the Indians escaped; others were killed. The next morning at least three women were captured, and perhaps one man, and all were apparently murdered by the soldiers.

During this same period the Central Valley natives were being visited by Anglo-American, British, and French Canadian fur trappers, accompanied by eastern Indians, Negroes, and even an occasional Hawaiian. These fur trappers, coming from Utah, New Mexico, and Oregon, were generally friendly and traded with the natives, especially for horses. The Mexican priests at missions such as San Jose were disturbed by the presence of these newcomers, being afraid that the Indians would be encouraged to be even more hostile towards the Mexican regime. Such a process may well have taken place, although the Joseph R. Walker party of 1833-1834 actually aided the Mexicans in slaughtering a group of San Joaquin Valley Indians. On the other hand, Canadians, Anglos, and Shawnees combined with California Indians to raid the coast from 1837 until the 1840s.

During the early 1830s the natives of the Central Valley were struck by a serious epidemic of malaria, or perhaps by a series of epidemics, which greatly reduced the San Joaquin Valley population, which dropped from 83,000 to 19,000 between 1800 and 1851, as estimated by one scholar.[17] Understandably, this reduction in population made offensive warfare against the Mexicans more difficult, and it may well have staved off a major effort at driving the Mexicans from central California.

In 1833, several Mexican expeditions went into the Central

Valley, one in November resulting in the death of twenty-two Moquelumnes.[18] Many of these expeditions were now becoming slave raids, as was charged in relation to the frequent fighting of 1835. The need for neophytes no longer existed, but Indian laborers were beginning to be needed on the ranchos and many expeditions were apparently designed in part to meet that need.

Sometime during the early 1830s one Yoscolo staged a rebellion at Mission Santa Clara, liberating 200 Indian girls from confinement, carrying off herds of cattle, and fleeing to Estanislao in the Mariposa region. The Mexicans were unable to defeat Yoscolo until he retired to the Santa Cruz Mountains, after a successful raid on the missions in 1839. In the Santa Cruz area he was finally defeated after a hard battle, and his severed head was subsequently displayed on top of a pole at Santa Clara.

Little is known of the later career of Estanislao, but it appears that he and his men were still fighting the Mexicans as late as 1838-1839. During 1838 the Moquelumnes, under Sinato, Nilo, and Crispo, were very active, while another leader, Ambrosio, was captured and shot. Vallejo's Suisun allies, under Solano, raided the Moquelumnes in March of that year, but in August, fifty of the latter, under Cumuchi, sought to steal horses from Sonoma. Cumuchi was captured and executed, but before he died he confessed that his people had large numbers of Mexican horses near the lower Sacramento River.

During 1839 the Mexicans staged a large campaign as far as the Kings River country of the Sierras, capturing seventy-seven Indians (chiefly women and children; men over ten years old were to be killed according to an 1839 decree). Later in the year, however, other Mexicans were surprised on the Rio de Estanislao, losing most of their weapons and suffering ten casualties. In general, warfare continued along the frontier from the San Luis Obispo region to Contra Costa between 1840 and 1847 with much cruelty but with neither side gaining the upperhand militarily.

In 1848, Governor Pio Pico contracted with Dr. John Marsh and John Gantt to rid central California of its Indian problem by private enterprise. They and their men were to receive one half of all of the livestock obtained and 500 beeves, while the government was to get the women and children captives. Indian men would be killed if they resisted.

The establishment of a fort at Sacramento in 1839 by John Sutter, three other Europeans, ten Hawaiians, and an Oregon Indian had a great impact upon the natives of the Central Valley. Sutter shrewdly emulated Vallejo's Indian policy by allying himself with Narciso, a former "neophyte" who headed the Ochecames of Sacramento, as well as with other nearby natives. These Indians, many of whom were ex-mission converts and knowledgeable about agriculture and various crafts, were hired to construct the fort, raise crops, catch fish, hunt for furs, and serve as soldiers. Sutter also utilized them and his non-Indian employees for raiding distant villages for captives who were usually sold to rancho owners near the coast, thus supplying Sutter with perhaps his most reliable "crop." The Indian made Sutter's success possible, and in turn the local Sacramento natives benefited somewhat from Sutter's protection, but ultimately at great cost.

Sutter's Fort during the 1840s became a center for arriving Anglo-Americans who were encouraged by the Mexican government to take up land in the lower Sacramento Valley. By 1847 a number of such ranchos existed, almost all utilizing local Indian labor. After 1848, however, this Mexican-style system rapidly gave way to an "Indian removal" process more typically Anglo-American. Although all of the Mexican grants, including Sutter's, stipulated that Indian property rights had to be respected, Anglo-Americans almost always ignored this fact.

The Tulareños, natives and former converts in the southern San Joaquin Valley, constantly raided the coast from the 1830s through the 1840s, often in association with Shawnee, New Mexican, and non-Indian adventurers. In 1844, John C. Frémont passed through the southern San Joaquin Valley, meeting several "dark-skinned, but handsome and intelligent Indians." He learned that

> the Indians of the Sierra make frequent decents [descents] upon the settlements, which they keep constantly swept of horses; among them are many who are called Christian Indians, being refugees from Spanish missions. Several of these incursions occurred while we were at [Sacramento].[19]

At Tehachapi Pass Frémont met an Indian from San Fernando who rode into camp well dressed, with long spurs, and a sombrero, and speaking Spanish fluently... an Indian face, Spanish costume, jingling spurs, and horse equipped after the Spanish manner... he had obtained from the priests leave to spend a few days with his relatives in the Sierra.[20]

This Sierra native pointed out a place, on the east slope of Tehachapi Pass, "where a refugee Christian Indian had been killed by a party of soldiers which had unexpectedly penetrated into the mountains." Frémont was able to purchase a Spanish saddle, spurs, and a horse from four other Indians, friends of the San Fernando cowboy.

Thus it is clear that the natives of the southern San Joaquin Valley and Sierras were in both hostile and friendly communication with the coast, and that they were becoming partially Mexicanized through this process.

The coastal region in the Santa Barbara area is of some interest because it was here that the only large-scale revolt against Mexican rule occurred among long-missionized Indians, and this revolt had considerable impact upon the natives of the interior. The Tsamalá-Kagimuswas of Purisima and Santa Inés and the Tsmuwich of Santa Barbara had apparently become disturbed at their continued exploitation by the soldiers and other Mexicans of the Santa Barbara district. In fact they were being forced to virtually support the entire military establishment. It would appear that the chief architect of the revolt, Pacomio (along with Bernabé, Benito, and Mariano), had long been planning some action, although the immediate cause was the flogging of a Purisima neophyte. In any event, simultaneous revolts occurred at Santa Inés and Purisima, with the latter being captured and fortified by the natives. Messages were sent to the Yokuts-speaking villages of the San Joaquin Valley, and the Santa Barbara neophytes under Andrés seized their mission, defeated a Mexican attack and fled with their belongings to the Buenavista Lake area of the southern San Joaquin Valley. Many Tsamála rebels soon joined them, along with neophytes from San Fernando and elsewhere.

On March 16, 1833, a large Mexican force succeeded in capturing Purisima, imprisoning Pacomio and the other leaders. In April another large army attacked the refugees in the valley but failed to accomplish anything. The offer of pardons and the presence of a still larger army in June did, however, persuade many of the Santa Barbara Indians to return to their mission in June and July. Large numbers remained at liberty, though, and took up permanent settlement along the Sierra foothills north of Kern River. In the spring of 1834, they were visited by a party of Anglo-Americans:

> After we halted here we found that these people could talk the Spanish language . . . and on inquiry ascertained that they were a tribe called the Cancoas, which tribe some eight or ten years since resided in . . . the missionary station near St. Barbara, on the coast, where they rebelled . . ., robbed the church of all its golden images and candlesticks, and one of the priests of several thousand dollars in gold and silver, when they retreated to the spot where we found them. . . . This tribe is well acquainted with the rules of bartering for goods or anything they wish to buy—much more so than any other tribe we met with. They make regular visits to such [Mexican] posts where they are unknown, and also make appointments with ship-traders to meet at some designated time and place. . . . These people are 7 or 800 strong, their houses are constructed of poles and covered with grass, and are tolerably well supplied with house-hold furniture which they brought with them. . . . They follow agricultural pursuits to some extent, raising very good crops of corn, pumpkins, melons, etc. . . . They are also in the habit of making regular visits to the settlements for the purpose of stealing horses, which they kill and eat.[21]

Very little resistance continued along the coast itself after 1825, although a native known as Valerio carried on a quasi-guerrilla style of raiding near Santa Barbara for a few years until being killed by the Mexicans.

The Indians of the Los Angeles region, although significant as virtually the only workers during the Mexican period, failed to organize any significant armed resistance, although a few former converts raided from their villages on the Mohave River (two campaigns of 1845 literally wiped out these refugees, including their brave leader, Joaquin, who had been mutilated earlier by a *majordomo* at Rancho Chino). More serious were the frequent raids of Utes and New Mexicans, the former coming from Colorado under Walkara. Throughout the 1840s and 1850s the Utes, sometimes in combination with New Mexican traders, camped in remote areas in order to steal livestock in the Los Angeles Basin. They also contributed to raiding by Southern Paiutes, since the latter were being forced by Ute pressure to move westward into the Mohave Desert. By 1842, at latest, minor Paiute raiding in southern California had commenced.

The Hamakhava of the Colorado River also came into the southern California coastal plain as they had in earlier years. Prior to the period of 1800 to 1820, their visits had been friendly trading enterprises, but the Spaniards had forcibly interfered and thereafter the Hamakhavas aided rebel neophytes in various hostile actions. By the 1830s and 1840s, the Hamakhavas were stealing horses in the Los Angeles Basin, usually in alliance with Mohave River rebels or in connection with general periods of native unrest.

After 1826 the mission Indians of the San Juan Capistrano–San Diego region gradually became more restless, in great measure due to Echeandia's attempted reforms. A few battles with Kamias and Cahuillas occurred along the frontier in 1826 and the Mexicans also attempted, unsuccessfully, to establish a post on the Colorado River. From 1827 to 1832, the frontier was quiet in the south, but by 1833 a new era of Indian warfare commenced, largely brought about by the collapse of Echeandia's reforms and by increased Mexican aggressiveness in the matter of land acquisition.

In February, 1833, it was reported that the San Diego natives, together with others as far north as San Gabriel, were demanding that the missions be turned over to them. This did not occur, and in the spring Tomás Jayochi, a Kamia, organized a rebellion in alliance with the Quechans. The Mexicans learned of the plot and stopped it, but the following year brought even more serious events. Santa Catalina Mission was attacked in northern Baja California by Kamias, Paipais and Cocopas; Kamias and Cahuillas were raiding farther north; and the mission Indians rebelled at San Bernardino, destroying that place with attacks in 1834 and 1835. During the latter year, mission Indians largely abandoned San Juan Capistrano, and the Cahuillas were hostile, planning to converge upon San Jacinto (Hemet) for a general uprising. Between 1836 and 1842, warfare was almost continuous from San Diego to San Bernardino, with Quechans, Kamias, Cahuillas, and Hamakhavas becoming even more aggressive. San Diego was virtually captured by the natives at one point and several missions in northern Baja California were permanently destroyed. The Mexican population steadily declined in the San Diego region and numerous ranchos were either abandoned or never occupied.

Gradually, however, a state of equilibrium began to be achieved in the San Bernardino–San Diego region between Mexicans and natives. In 1839, the two leaders of the Kamias of Jacumba, Cartucho and Pedro Pablo, had been planning to recover California which they claimed belonged to them. They claimed that they were not alone in their plans, but in actual fact, most southern California native groups, once having thrown off the yoke of the missions, were quite willing to live peacefully with the Mexicans if the latter would respect their local autonomy and village land rights. By the 1840s the Mexicans south and east of Los Angeles were simply forced to agree, informally, to such a live-and-let-live relationship; and when they did, warfare largely ceased.

Mexican rancho owners and officials also learned to emulate the Vallejo-Sutter style of utilizing Indian allies as soldiers or auxiliaries. In 1839 a group of Cahuillas had moved westward to settle near Jurupa (Riverside), and after 1842 a band of mountain Cahuillas under Juan Antonio served as an auxiliary force for the Lugo family in the Colton–San Bernardino region. In a similar manner, Cabezon, a Cahuilla leader in the Coachella Valley, became a Mexican ally, and Jatiñil, a Kamia leader in northern Baja California, aided the Mexicans until becoming disillusioned after 1837. These auxiliaries proved useful in helping to capture or kill runaways and in at least diminishing thefts of livestock. No really serious warfare occurred in the San Bernardino–San Diego region between 1842 and 1851, however—with the minor exception of an attempt in 1846 by the Kupanga-kitom and their neighbors in the Warner's Valley area to obtain revenge on the Mexicans during the U. S.–Mexican War. The natives' aid was not appreciated by the invading Anglo-American army, and a force of Mexicans and Cahuillas under Juan Antonio put down the rebels.

Mexican travelers and Anglo-American fur trappers were able to visit the Colorado River frequently during the 1830s and 1840s, but always at the sufferance of the still vigorously independent

Yuman peoples. The latter were, in turn, engaged in rather constant intertribal warfare, greatly increased over earlier periods. The Quechans and their allies, the Hamakhavas, Yavapais, Kamias and others were continually at war with the Halchidhomas, Maricopas, Cocopas, and their allies, doubtlessly stimulated in part by the fact that the Halchidhomas and Maricopas had aided the Spaniards against the Quechans in 1781 and 1782. This warfare gradually led to the decimation of the Kohuanas and Halyikwamais, who were forced to abandon their rich delta lands and flee to the Halchidhoma near Blythe. By the 1820s and 1830s the Halchidhoma were forced to gradually retreat eastward to the Maricopas on the Gila River, while the Kohuana and Halyikwamai remnants returned to the delta. During the 1830s and 1840s the Halyikwamai were further reduced in number and were forced to disperse, some joining the Cocopa, others fleeing to the eastward-retreating Maricopa, and some being absorbed by the victorious Quechans, Kamias, and Hamakhavas.

In 1848, therefore, the lower Colorado River was controlled by three groups only, the Hamakhavas, the Quechans, and the Cocopas; with some Southern Paiutes (called Chemehuevis), Kamias, Paipais, and Halyikwamai-Kohuana remnants living nearby but at the sufferance of the more powerful groups. This process is interesting if only because it illustrates two important tendencies: 1) the continued emphasis placed by native groups upon traditional inter-Indian rivalries as opposed to unification in the face of European and Mexican aggression; 2) the many changes in traditional boundaries occurring as a result of the indirect and direct consequences of European and Mexican influences. It is very likely that similar changes took place throughout much of the Far West, although detailed documentary evidence is lacking.

Reference should also be made to the extreme conservatism of the Colorado River Yumans who, in spite of 300 years of contact with Europeans and Mexicans, chose not to significantly alter their societies or cultures. Again, this is fairly typical of native populations in the Far West.

The Great Basin region was also affected by alien influences during the period from the 1820s through the 1840s, although to a lesser degree than was California. Most affected were the Southern Paiute groups of Utah and Nevada, which were continually being raided by New Mexicans, Utes, and, to a lesser extent, Anglo-Americans and Navahos. Illustrating this process is an account in the diary of an Anglo-American who joined a New Mexican caravan in 1839, traveling from Los Angeles to Taos—

> hurrying on, I discovered that our New Mexicans had surrounded a rancheria of Piutes. I saw one little Indian boy, about 12 years old with his arm nearly shot off.... I began to scold the New Mexicans and called them a pack of damned brutes and cowards—and they were so.
>
> There was one old Indian standing with his bow and arrow—they wanted to take and kill him, but were afraid to approach near enough to come within reach of his arrow—I went up to the Indian and asked him for his bow and arrows—they had solemnly promised me not to hurt him if I succeeded in disarming him—the Indian handed them to me—and I shall never forgive myself for having taken the word of those villians, for villians they were ... as soon as they saw the Indian without arms they came near and riddled him with bullets....
>
> I found another rancheria ... an Indian came out and by signs asked me if I had come to fight. I said *no*; then he asked me if I was hungry, and ... he invited me to alight and partake of what he had, which was *atole* made of the seed of hogweed, and barbecued trout.... Whilst I was eating up came the confounded New Mexicans [under Tomás Salazar], and the Indians ran to conceal themselves in the brush—all but two succeeded in escaping—those two unfortunate Piutes were taken by the Mexicans, tied, and shot in cold blood.... [The Mexicans stated that] "it is not wrong to kill these pagan Indians."[22]

Farther north, the lives of Shoshones, Northern Paiutes, and Washos were affected by numerous parties of trappers, traders and, after 1841, overland emigrants who seriously depleted the natural food resources of the Humboldt River watershed and often precipitated minor incidents. Nonetheless, little organized warfare occurred, in part because a Northern Paiute leader, Truckee, counseled friendship with the white strangers during the 1840s. Northern Paiutes and Washos occasionally served as guides across Sierra passes, and a group of the Northern Paiutes joined Frémont in

1846 and 1847 in his campaigns against the Mexicans of coastal California.

It is to be suspected also that the great expansion of warfare and slave raiding which occurred in the Oregon Country and northern Rockies during this period very much affected Nevada-Utah native groups. Columbia River–Oregon tribes capable of raiding northern California for slaves were also capable of raiding northern Nevada, while Plains Indian war parties could easily have attacked the Shoshones of northeastern Nevada and northern Utah. It is highly likely, therefore, that few groups in the Great Basin were immune to influences—including slave raiding and disease—likely to lead to significant internal changes and boundary dislocations. (For example, James C. Adams in 1854 joined a group of Mewuk in their annual excursion from the Toulumne River over the Sierras to Walker Lake, where they were accustomed to spend the summer. Such movements could easily have spread the epidemics of the 1830s into Nevada.)

In summary, the Mexican-Indian Period, while not witnessing any great expansion in the extent of non-Indian territorial control, was an era of significant change for native peoples. Although many positive elements can be cited, such as greater unity, increased sophistication in dealing with aggressors, more adequate military ability, and the adoption of certain useful activities (such as agriculture in the Central Valley), the general trend of the period is negative. Aside from the fact that thousands of Indians were enslaved, forced to labor as neophytes or serfs, killed, flogged, separated from loved ones, and pushed into apathy and alcoholism, is the clear evidence that the still-free groups were greatly weakened by disease and warfare. Thus, although the area of free Indian territory remained much the same as in 1821, the numbers of Indians living there were greatly reduced, and those that remained were being more frequently abused by alien incursions.

By 1848 the native population of California had been reduced to about 100,000, with perhaps as many as 100,000 Indians dying of sickness and warfare in one generation after 1821. Thus, the Mexican era was apparently more destructive to the native population than the Spanish period had been (although the loss of at least 50,000 persons between 1769 and 1820 may not be accurate since it does not reflect the possible effects of epidemics in the interior). Nonetheless, the Native American population might well have ultimately recovered (as immunity to disease developed) and remained dominant in the Far West, were it not for the Anglo-American invasion. At the time that invasion commenced, from 1845 to 1847, some 6000 ex-mission Indians were still residing along the coast, along with 7000 predominantly-Indian Mexicans and 700 Europeans and more than 100,000 natives in the interior of California, Nevada, and Utah. The Far West was still overwhelmingly Native American, but a drastic change, for which neither Mexicans nor natives were ready, was in the offing.

The Anglo-American Invasion

The United States–Mexican War had little immediate effect upon the Native Americans of the Far West, since the United States' armed forces concentrated upon subduing Mexican settlements and not upon controlling the vast areas belonging to Indians. The U. S.–Mexican War did not, therefore, result in the conquest of the entire so-called "Mexican Cession" area. On the contrary, this war merely marked the beginning of an era of military conquest which did not cease until a small group of Utes and Southern Paiutes in the area of southeastern Utah were subdued in 1915, although the bulk of the region was conquered by the 1870s.

Nor did the United States acquire, as so many school maps assert, the "Mexican Cession" area as a result of the Treaty of Guadalupe Hidalgo of 1848. The Mexican Government could only cede to the United States that which she possessed, and quite clearly Mexico possessed no sovereignty except in coastal California, southern Arizona, and central New Mexico. Many decades of warfare, and the expenditure of many thousands of lives and dollars, were necessary before the United States could assert meaningfully that its laws were operative throughout the Far West. It is simply another example of anti-Indian prejudice, and of ignorance, that school maps award the Far West to the United States in 1846 (Oregon) and 1848, ignoring the existence and continued independence of numerous native groups.

The conquest of the bulk of California and Nevada was not accomplished primarily by regular soldiers, although they played an important role, especially in remote areas and in later phases of fighting. The conquest was rather the direct result of the westward movement of a vast horde of armed civilians, single men and family units, very much resembling the ancient "hordes" of Central Asia in their mobility, warlike nature, and indifference to the boundary claims and property rights of already established, alien peoples. Unfortunately for Native Americans, these invaders often possessed a hatred of Indians which went beyond the mere desire for acquiring Indian property to the wish for the complete extermination of native peoples. Unfortunately also, these invaders possessed a form of society which provided no real means for Indian absorption (as had the Spanish and Mexican) and forms of government which tended to be immediately responsive to the vilest wishes of the westward-moving masses.

It is not surprising that a historian such as H. H. Bancroft could, in the 1880s, assert that

> the California valley cannot grace her annuals with a single Indian war bordering on respectability. It can boast, however, a hundred or two of as brutal butchering, on the part of our honest miners and brave pioneers, as any area of equal extent in our republic. The poor natives of California had neither the strength nor the intelligence to unite in any formidable numbers; hence, when now· and then one of them plucked up courage to defend his wife and little ones, or to retaliate on one of the many outrages that were constantly being perpetrated upon them by white persons, sufficient excuse was offered for the miners and settlers to band and shoot down any Indians they met, old or young, innocent or guilty, friendly or hostile, until their appetite for blood was appeased.[23]

The United States possesses many sordid chapters in its history, but perhaps none is more sordid than that relating to the conquest of California, typified as it is by great brutality and callousness and what closely approaches genocide. This process cannot be examined in detail, since the bulk of California Indians were conquered, and died, in innumerable little episodes rather than in large campaigns. This fact, of course, makes the sequence of events all the more distressing since it serves to indict not a group of cruel leaders, or a few squads of rough soldiers, but, in effect, an entire people; for the conquest of the Native Californian was above all else a popular, mass enterprise.

A few Indians seem to have naively expected that the United States' armed forces would sympathize with the native viewpoint in the Southwest, since both groups had been fighting against the Mexicans. But, of course, the Anglo-Americans, as soon as the U. S.- Mexican War was terminated, adopted the Mexican side of whatever controversies were in progress, since the Mexican leadership was "white" or "nearly white," and since the property interests of the two former enemies coincided. (It should be noted that throughout the Americas the United States has almost always supported white or near-white elites against the brown or black masses, betraying thereby a deep-seated racial and cultural bias.)

Quite understandably then, United States forces became involved in warfare against California Indians even before the war with Mexico officially ended. Thus, the long struggle of the Central Valley natives against the Mexican ranchers became, by 1846, a struggle also against Anglo-Americans, with U. S. troops campaigning to protect their new subjects in the San Jose area. Similar skirmishes occurred in the south.

The Anglo-American invasion of California and adjacent areas really commenced with the Gold Rush of 1848, although the initial phase, May 1848 to the spring of 1849, did not involve extensive warfare. The incoming miners, many of whom were Mexicans from California and Sonora, South Americans, and Europeans, were intent upon finding gold rather than acquiring land. They likewise were greatly influenced by the Mexican attitude, which favored the hiring or commissioning of Indians to do as much of the prospecting and rough work as possible. Many ex-neophytes were brought from the coast and large numbers of interior natives, both ranch-hands and free Indians, were encouraged to prospect. Such settlers as John Sutter, P. B. Reading, and Charles Weber were especially prominent in using Indian miners. Weber made an advantageous agreement with José Jesus, a former neophyte alcalde of San Jose Mission who had returned to the Rio de Estanislao to fight against the Mexicans and who had succeeded Estanislao upon the latter's death. José Jesus supplied Weber with Indian miners who were so successful in locating coarse gold that they were responsible for a rush of other miners to the Stanislaus River watershed. Other old settlers in California, such as Isaac Williams, used Indian miners in the southern California mountains as early as

1849. Many other natives searched for gold on their own, using the metal as a means for obtaining food in an environment fast becoming difficult to survive in by means of their traditional economy.

Generally speaking, the early phase (1848-1849) of the Gold Rush was localized in the central Sierra foothills, the numbers of miners were not as numerous as in later years, and ethnic hostility was diminished by the relative ease with which gold was located. Nonetheless, hostilities did occur in the most crowded districts, the Colomas and Consumnes both suffering briefly from warfare. Elsewhere, Trinity River natives (probably Hupas) forcibly drove away miners, and minor friction was common along the various emigrant routes from Oregon, across Nevada, and along the Colorado River.

During 1849 the Gold Rush changed in character as tens of thousands of Anglo-Americans, thousands of Mexicans, and others poured into California. During the next few years the miners expanded rapidly northwards to the tributaries of the Feather and Yuba rivers and southwards to the Kern River. They stormed by sea and land into the Trinity-Klamath region, and even prospected extensively in such areas as Sonoma-Mendocino and southern California. The Anglo-Americans also became increasingly hostile towards any class of non-white miners and even against non-Anglo Europeans.

Everywhere the miners went, hostilities soon developed, and understandably so, since the invaders refused to respect any native rights. Villages were uprooted, women were raped or carried into concubinage, men were casually murdered, and, everywhere, the native food supply was ruthlessly destroyed. The Indians responded with retaliatory attacks which almost always led to the organization of campaigns by irregular militia or vigilante units. These campaigns often resulted in the near extermination of whatever Indians might be in the vicinity, including women and children.

A few incidents can be cited here to illustrate the predominant character of warfare in California in 1849 and the 1850s. At Big Oak Flat in 1850, for example, one writer witnessed the following:

> We had been there only a few days when one night a band
> of Mt. Indians made a raid on some of the Miners on the
> Flat and robbed them of a Horse and other valuables,

killing one Miner and wounding another with their arrows. The Miners followed the Indians for 25 miles up into the Mountains, then they found their settlement, and killed old Men, Squaws, and Children, the Bucks having fled. I am thankful that I did not join them as their acts were more foul than the Indians'.[24]

A few years later a group of Wintus living in the McCloud River area were invited by the whites to come to a feast for the purpose of making peace.

About three hundred Indians came.... They had been there several days, feasting and dancing, when some Numsoos from Trinity Center came and warned them of danger, telling of a similar trick played on their people at a place called Kal-le-ke-le where many were slaughtered.... Then Dol-le-ken-til-le-ma [a leader] warned his people to be on their guard. The Indians began to slip away quietly.... The chief then noticed that whenever an Indian left the table, a soldier followed. This alarmed him, so he watched his chance and slipped down to the river. A soldier followed. The chief dived and when he came up the soldier fired at him, but he dived again and escaped. The forty-five Wintoon warriors remaining at the table were all massacred by the soldiers and volunteers.[25]

The natives of the Clear Lake region experienced from 1848 to 1850 a sequence of events : ot by any means untypical. Two white men, Stone and Kelsey, had settled in the Clear Lake area where they established a Mexican-style ranch operation using Indian labor (which, however, they abused more than the average Mexican ranchero would have, with frequent floggings, torture, seizing the women, and even murder). In 1849, Kelsey led a futile expedition to the gold regions, taking a number of Clear Lake Indians along as virtual slaves, few of whom survived. Finally, in the fall of 1849, the exasperated and starving Pomos, led by two Indian cowboys, Shuk and Xasis, executed Stone and Kelsey.

The killing of two white men, even though guilty of great wrongs, naturally led to a military campaign against the Clear Lake natives. The first expedition, in 1849, failed to reach the Indians, who were hiding on an island; but in May 1850, Capt. Nathaniel Lyon led a large force, equipped with boats, to the lake. According to army report, 60 out of 400 Indians were killed on the island while at least another 75 were eliminated near the Russian River in Mendocino County. That this was a "massacre" is revealed, first, by the fact that the soldiers suffered only two non-fatal casualties while more than 135 natives were killed, and, second, by the Indian version of the event:

> The next morning the white warriors went across in their long dugouts. The Indians said they would meet them in peace so when the whites landed the indians went to wellcom them but the white man was determined to kill them. Ge-Wi-lih said he threw up his hand ... but the white man fired and shot him in the arm ... many women and children were killed on around this island. One old lady ... said she saw two white man coming with their guns up in the air and on their guns being a little girl. They brought it to the creek and threw it in the water. And a little while later, two more men came.... This time they had a little boy on the end of their guns and also threw it in the water. A little ways away ... layed a woman shoot through the shoulder. She held her little baby in her arms. Two white men torge the woman and baby, they stabed the woman and the baby.... She said when they gathered the dead, they found all the little ones were killed by being stabed, and many of the women were also killed stabing.... This old lady also told about the whites hang a man on Emerson island.... The Indian was hung and a large fire built under [him]. And another Indian was caught.... This one was tied to a tree and burnt to death.[26]

The Indians of California and the southeastern Great Basin were continually subject to slave raids in this period to supply servants for the towns and ranchos of California and New Mexico. In 1853, E. F. Beale visited San Pablo Rancho in Contra Costa County where he found ninety sick and starving Indians who were "survivors of a band who were worked all last summer and fall and as the winter set in, when broken down by hunger and labor and without food or clothes they were turned adrift to shift for themselves."[27] These natives had been brought from the same Clear Lake area mentioned above by Mexican-Californians who made a business of capturing and selling Indians. (Sad to state, as late as

1857 northern Indians such as the Klamath were still raiding southward to the Pit River country for slaves to sell in Oregon.)

Extreme cruelty in warfare was not limited to the first few years of fighting. As late as 1858 and 1863, horrible massacres were perpetuated in northwestern California, as when the citizens of Eureka slaughtered some 60 unsuspecting natives of all ages and sexes at Humboldt Bay, or when almost all of the males of the Wailaki and Lassik groups were killed during a "round-up" of Indians along the Eel River. One should also not forget the planned extermination of almost 2000 Yanas (most of whom were working on white ranches) by Indian-hating white vigilantes in the area east of Redding and Red Bluff during the single year of 1864.[28]

It must not be thought that all Indians were more or less passive victims of miners and slave raiders. Many native groups, from the Klamath River to the Colorado River, offered notable resistance during the early 1850s; resistance which sometimes won the admiration of their violence-admiring foes. In southern California, for example, the Quechans and Hamakhavas, although generally tolerant of inoffensive travelers, defended themselves well when offended. In 1850, a group of outlaws led by John Glanton, who had been scalping Apaches (and Mexicans) for money in Chihuahua, took over a ferry being operated on the Colorado at Yuma. The Anglo gang not only robbed travelers but destroyed a rival ferry operated by the Quechans. Finally on April 21, 1850, the Quechans rose up and wiped out the outlaws, only thereby to gain the animosity of Indian-haters who held that no Indian should ever be allowed to kill any whiteman, no matter how bad. In the fall of 1850, 125 white militia attacked the Quechans, but the Indians were soon able to force the invaders to retreat back to the coast.

United States troops established a post at the site of Fort Yuma in late 1850 and peace prevailed until 1851 when many southern California natives, exasperated by white encroachment and by attempts to collect taxes on Indian property, planned a general revolt. Antonio Garrá, a Kupanga-kitom, was the chief architect of the revolution. He was soon joined by Quechans, southern Cahuillas, Kamias, Luiseños, Chemehuevi Paiutes, and Hamakhavas, and messages were sent to the San Joaquin Valley tribes. During 1851 and 1852, warfare raged along the Colorado River and in San Diego County, with the river and desert areas being for a time completely under Indian control. Garrá was eventually tricked into being captured by a group of pro-white Cahuillas, and strong U. S. forces subsequently defeated the Quechans, but only after a bitter and protracted campaign featuring the destruction of the natives' food supply.

By the mid-1850s the greater part of central and southern California was conquered, although a little fighting occurred in the San Joaquin Valley in 1857-1858. Much of extreme northern California, all of eastern California, almost all of Nevada, and most of western Utah were still under Indian control, however, and a new phase in warfare tended to develop. The still-free Indian groups generally lived in isolated, rough or desert regions and many had profited from the experiences of their less-fortunate brothers by becoming more knowledgeable about fighting whitemen. Therefore, it was generally necessary for large bodies of regular troops or organized militia to proceed against them.

The most notable areas of resistance centered among several groups: the Hamakhava (1850s and early 1860s), Southern Paiutes (to at least 1869), Owens Valley Paiutes and Shoshones (1850s to 1865), Northern Paiutes (1860s and, for a few, into the 1870s), Western Shoshones (early 1860s), Modocs (to 1873), Pit River groups (to 1867), and Hupas, Whilkuts, and Karoks (to 1864). In all of these wars the Indian people exhibited great bravery in the defense of their homes, or in their efforts to insure a food supply for survival, but they also tended to exhibit the disunity so destructive of native efforts at liberation. There was no simultaneous *general* uprising against the invaders occurring over a wide area. Instead, each group tended to rebel or fight only when pressed to the wall itself and not in alliance with other people in *anticipation* of what might be their own fate at some future date.

The Native Americans of the Far West won a number of notable victories, as when the Northern Paiutes defeated a large militia force sent against them at Pyramid Lake in May 1860; when many Hupas, Karoks, and Whilkuts successfully fought a war of attrition for five long years between 1858 and 1864; when a small body of Modocs under Kentipoos (Captain Jack) courageously held off an overwhelming force of regular U. S. troops in the Modoc lava beds for over three months in 1872 and 1873; and when the ever-diminishing Yahi fought stubbornly for their freedom from 1850 until 1870 and then chose to live a life of complete concealment rather than surrender.

Unfortunately, the many heroic instances of resistance by Indian people ordinarily failed in the long run simply because of the overwhelming numerical superiority of the invaders. It is worth noting, however, that the native groups which fought the hardest often received the best and largest reservations, while those who were defeated early or who were relatively passive received small reservations or none at all. Perhaps deservedly, those Indians who served as auxiliaries or scouts of the whites usually received nothing for their efforts. (It should be noted that the United States during this period often followed a policy of not providing lands or services, except sporadically, for completely pacified or unwarlike groups.)

By 1873, the California–Great Basin region was militarily under the control of the Anglo-American invaders, but at what human and moral cost! The California census of 1870 reveals only 31,000 Indians surviving, a decline of perhaps 70,000 in two decades. But the conquest itself did not end with the military phases—in fact, it was only beginning.

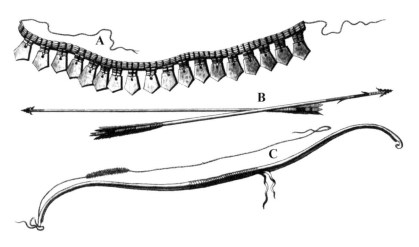

A Ground shell necklace, probably also used as money. B Hunting arrows. C Reflexed bow. Drawings by G. Langsdorf. (*Courtesy of Bancroft Library, Berkeley, California.*)

III. THE CONQUEST: POWERLESSNESS AND POVERTY

The First Thirty Years: Stealing From the Dying

The first thirty years of the conquest were the hardest to bear, especially in California. That this is true is starkly evident in the fact that the native population fell to a mere 16,000 in 1880, indicating a loss of 15,000 in the decade of the 1870s (an almost 50% drop) and a loss of some 80,000 during the entire thirty-year period (an 80% decline).

To be conquered at all is a very sad fate, but to be conquered by those who hate and despise you is the worst of all possible situations. The Native Californians were unfortunate in that they were overcome by a people whose view of them was so filled with hostility that it easily supported genocide.

> We will let those rascally redskins know that they have no longer to deal with the Spaniard or the Mexican, but with the invincible race of American backwoodsmen, which has driven the savage from Plymouth Rock to the Rocky Mountains, and has headed him off here on the western shore . . . and will drive him back to meet his kindred fleeing westward, all to be drowned in the Great Salt Lake.[1]

Along with hostility came contempt and prejudice, as exemplified by numerous viciously-racist statements included in works about California written during the period after 1849. Even a more balanced writer such as H. H. Bancroft could write in the 1880s that "we do not know why the Digger Indians of California were so shabbily treated by nature; why with such fair surroundings they were made so much lower in the scale of intelligence than their neighbors. . . ."[2]

The Anglo-Americans as a whole felt little sympathy towards peoples considered to be both hostile foes and inferior creatures. Bancroft typified white-Indian relations in California during this era as "one of the last human hunts of civilization, and the basest and most brutal of them all." Quite naturally, this brutality extended far beyond the realm of actual warfare and affected every facet of the natives' life, especially wherever whites were numerous.

What were the conditions faced by Native Americans in the first decades of conquest? In practical terms, the Indian existed with neither legal rights nor protection since the constitution of the State of California, adopted in 1849, deprived him illegally of citizenship, since the legislature soon prohibited Indian testimony in the courts, and since white attitudes made the killing, raping, or enslavement of an Indian no crime at all. (Under the Treaty of Guadalupe Hidalgo, the United States was bound to recognize Indian citizenship in former Mexican areas, but the U. S. ignored this requirement.) A similar situation existed in Nevada, and to a lesser extent in Utah where Mormon attitudes were more sympathetic to the Indian as a person. This point must be emphasized: *the Indian, after conquest, existed completely and absolutely at the mercy of whatever sympathy or barbarity existed in the white population.* And there was precious little sympathy!

The white settlers and their governments adopted the unconstitutional attitude that the Indians possessed no property rights whatsoever and that they were "trespassers on the public domain."[3] Thus, although native villages might be allowed to exist for years in an out-of-the-way or undesirable location, the villagers generally gained no "squatter's rights" through longevity of residence and could be removed at will by anyone. For many years, then, most Indians possessed no land or security of residence since reservations served only a small proportion of the population.

Conquered natives were constantly faced with the prospect not merely of being driven from their homes, but of being seized and forced into servitude or concubinage. The Los Angeles Basin was a major center of Indian labor exploitation, with natives either retained as *peones* (unable to move because of debts or having nowhere else to go) or literally worked to death as captive-labor, purchased at auction in Los Angeles (as late as 1869) or simply seized in the countryside. Northwestern California was also a center for Indian slavery. An 1861 report asserted that

> In the frontier portions of Humboldt and Mendocino counties a band of desperate men have carried on a system of kidnapping for two years past; Indian children were seized and carried into the lower counties and sold into

virtual slavery.... The kidnappers follow at the heels of the soldiers to seize the children when their parents are murdered and sell them to best advantage.[4]

The California legislature adopted legislation in 1850 which made it possible for any Indian to be declared a vagabond and sold to the highest bidder for laboring purposes. Throughout the state, Indian women were commonly seized and forced to serve as servants or concubines, in some cases being cast adrift after a time, in other cases becoming a common-law wife. (Legal marriage between whites and Indians was long prohibited in both California and Nevada.)

Another widespread form of servitude developed in both California and Nevada due to the nonpossession of land on the part of the Indians. As whites seized all of the desirable fertile lands, the natives who survived the military conquest found that they had to reside on either nonproductive ground or on a white farm or ranch. In either case, survival depended largely upon being able to acquire food in the white economy since hunting and gathering had become exceedingly difficult. Thus, most natives were forced by economic circumstances to become agricultural laborers or house servants for white people. Our histories of labor ordinarily ignore this fact, but prior to the Chinese, the Indians served as the great exploited agricultural laborers of the Far West.

The vast majority of Indians, therefore, were dispersed as squatters in the rough places or as tenants on white farms and ranches, in either case largely dependent upon white employment and whatever wages, if any, were offered. In many areas, in fact, the natives labored only for room and board and protection, since to be expelled from the farm might mean death either at the hands of white terrorists or by starvation.

Indian labor was especially important in northern California, in the fertile valleys of Nevada, and in southern California. In 1852 it was said that "they [the Luiseños and Kamias] are a large majority of the laborers, mechanics, and servants of San Diego and Los Angeles counties.... The Indian laborers ... are almost the only house or farm servants we have."[5] Unfortunately, the Indian laboring class was not well cared for, and by 1880 there were not enough Indians left to comprise an important part of the labor force, except in a few rural localities.

The fact that the whites of California and the Great Basin desired cheap labor was certainly a major factor in preventing the establishment of adequate reservations. Other factors were, of course, the usual white greed for land and the failure of most Indians to pose a serious enough military threat to justify a "generous" policy.

In 1848, when the United States asserted its claim to the Far West, the coastal zone of California included numerous villages or settlements of former mission Indians. These villages possessed property rights under Mexican law, which rights the United States was required to respect by the Treaty of Guadalupe Hidalgo. The United States, in spite of suggestions to the contrary made by a few experts of Mexican law, chose not to recognize any such titles and, as a result, virtually every village was destroyed from the 1860s to the 1880s by aggressive Anglo entrepreneurs and ranchers. Theoretically, of course, the Indians might have appealed to the courts, but in practice they could not during these years because their citizenship rights and their right to testify against whites were both denied. The viciousness of the white population in regards to the ex-mission Indians is illustrated by the fact that when, in 1870, an effort was made to set aside the valleys of Pala and San Pascual as reservations, the surrounding whites rushed in to seize the land and the Indians were effectively intimidated. The Federal government opened the land to whites again in 1871.

Elsewhere in California and the Great Basin were Indian groups who had never been conquered by Spain or Mexico but whose property rights were theoretically protected by the Treaty of Guadalupe Hidalgo (since the United States chose to base its title upon this treaty), by the Fifth Amendment of the U. S. Constitution (which prohibits the seizure of private property by the Federal government without "due process" and "just compensation"), and by the customary practice of the United States (which recognized "Indian title" as valid until quieted by treaty). Unfortunately, however, the Federal government was extremely negligent in the Far West, allowing local white desires to become sanctioned as fiats in defiance of constitutionality.

In 1851, after vast hordes of whites had already inundated California, the President chose to empower three commissioner-agents to regulate Indian affairs in California. These agents, in conformity with standard procedure elsewhere, toured the State, negotiating eighteen treaties with a large part of the native population. The agents found the natives generally anxious for peace and willing, apparently, to cede most of their lands to the United States in return for eighteen reservations totaling some 7,500,000 acres where they would be congregated, temporarily supplied with food, and aided in becoming agricultural. The text of a typical 1851-1852 treaty included the following:

> A treaty of peace and friendship made and concluded at Camp Barbour, on the San Joaquin River . . . between . . . the United States, and the undersigned chiefs, captains, and headmen of the . . . How-ech-ees, Chook-cha-nees, Chow-chil-lies, Po-bo-nee-chees, and Nook-chees . . . [The Indians acknowledge the jurisdiction of the United States and relinquish all claims to ceded territory.] To promote the settlement and improvement of said tribes or bands, it is hereby stipulated and agreed that the following district . . . shall be, and is hereby, set apart forever for the sole use and occupancy of the aforesaid tribes of Indians. . . . To have and to hold the said district of country for the sole use and occupancy of said Indian tribes forever. [Certain rights, such as for roads, are reserved to the U. S.] *And provided further,* the said tribes of Indians . . . shall at all times have the privilege of the country east of the aforesaid district . . . to the foot of the Sierra Nevada mountains, to hunt and to gather fruit, acorns, etc. . . .[6]

The treaties negotiated in California were implemented in the following three ways: 1) many Indians were actually persuaded to leave their other lands and to congregate upon the reserves in 1851 and 1852; 2) the agents purchased large quantities of supplies for the Indians (although much was diverted for the profit of the agents and other whites); 3) the Indians throughout the state were gradually required to give up their old lands as if they possessed no title. One can argue that the treaties in question were transformed from mere tentative agreements into actual contracts binding upon the Executive Branch of the United States, since, in effect, the treaties were made binding upon the natives.

In any event, Congress, under pressure from California whites, rejected the treaties and caused them to be hidden in the archives. One might well agree that the reservations set aside in 1851-1852 were still bonafide Indian property, both because of the implementation of the treaties by the U. S. and because the "Indian title" had not yet been surrendered to the Federal government; but such an argument matters little since the "White Power" of the day decreed otherwise.

The natives of eastern California, the Colorado River, and Nevada were not even visited by treaty-makers, except for the Western Shoshones, Goshute Shoshones, and Yahuskin (Northern Paiute). During 1863 and 1864, treaties were negotiated with the above groups, but no formal cessions of land took place nor were any lands guaranteed to the Indians (except in the case of the Yahuskin who agreed to give up all of their territory in order to settle at Klamath Lake Reservation). It can be said, therefore, that the United States seized the Indian lands of California and the Great Basin and allowed these lands to pass into the hands of whites (or to become a part of the so-called "public domain") without benefit of even the remotest shred of legality. Can the Federal government possess title to properties forbidden to it by the Constitution? This interesting question has not yet been settled for Indians, although, of course, the answer is "no" if the seized property belongs to whites.[7]

Some efforts were made on the Indians' behalf by the Federal government during these years but they were usually either confined to simple peacekeeping maneuvers or to small-scale, insufficient programs which chiefly benefited white agents and speculators. In 1847 three persons were appointed as Indian agents for California. They had no money to spend, which may have been just as well since the commissioner-agents appointed in 1850 spent nearly $800,000 during 1851 and 1852, very little of which benefited Indians. Cattle, blankets, and flour destined for the natives were either never delivered (with "kickbacks" for the agents) or were sold to Indians and whites. Blankets were cut in half when being distributed to Indians so as to supply a larger number with half-blankets and thereby create a surplus of whole blankets which were then sold to whites. In brief, these agents of 1851 and 1852 set the pattern for later Federal appointees who, almost without exception, used "the Indian business" as a lucrative step towards personal wealth.

In 1852 E. F. Beale was appointed as superintendent of Indian affairs for California, with an appropriation of $100,000 for "presents" to keep the natives quiet. Beale, influenced by the plans for the eighteen reservations rejected by Congress and by a proposal of Benjamin D. Wilson to establish eight reserves ("pueblos") for 9000 Indians in the southern half of the State, advocated the establishment of mission-style reservations. Here the Indians would be gathered and instructed, under the watchful eye of an agent and nearby soldiers. The only difference between this plan and what was being done farther east was the use of Federal employees as supervisor-instructors rather than Federally-subsidized missionaries. Beale is often given credit for initiating a new approach to reservations. However, similar ideas were advocated by Utah agent John Wilson in 1849 and by Oregon agent Joel Palmer in 1853. Farmer-instructors were actually working with Indians in Utah as early as 1851 and formal "farms" were laid out in 1855.

Beale asked for $500,000, received $250,000, and immediately began to lavish his entire effort on one site, the Tejon Reservation at the extreme southeast end of the San Joaquin Valley. The site was a poor choice because it had white claimants (who were never bought out) and because it probably never could have supported a large population. Beale acquired supplies for 2500 Indians, paying very high prices for beeves and other items, but an employee later stated that there were never more than 800 Indians there, including 600 local Tejon-area natives who had already been growing crops before Beale had arrived. Beale himself reported in 1854 that he had gathered 2500 Indians at Tejon, but a friendly visitor found only 1200 three months later. In any event, Beale neglected tens of thousands of Indians, including many who were in desperate condition, in order to provide supplies for a few hundred, most of whom were not directly threatened by white encroachment. Furthermore, the improvements made by Beale were eventually lost because they were made on what became private property.[8]

Beale was succeeded in 1854 by an agent who established Nome Lacke Reservation in Colusa County, Mendocino Reservation at Fort Bragg, and Klamath Reservation along the lower Klamath River. In 1856, Nome Cult or Round Valley reserve was established along with "farms" at Fresno, Kings River, and Tule River. Perhaps as many as 6000 Indians were thus provided for, but at tremendous cost due to the fact that the whole operation was really designed to enrich the superintendent and his accomplices. (In 1856 they claimed that 10,000 of 61,600 California Indians were residing on the reservations.) One aspect of these years was that the reservation Indians were often forced to look for food on their own (in spite of rations, which were resold by the agents to whites) and their labor was also sold to whites by the government employees. The superintendent also allowed white squatters to gain footholds on many of the reserves.

Various investigations were made, including one by J. Ross Browne who summarized the policy of the 1850s as follows:

> The results of the policy pursued were precisely such as might have been expected. A very large amount of money was annually expended in feeding white men and starving Indians. . . . At all events, it invariably happened, when a visitor appeared on the reservations, that the Indians were "out in the mountains gathering nuts and berries. . . . Very few of them, indeed, have yet come back. . . . In the brief period of six years they have been nearly destroyed by the . . . government. What neglect, starvation, and disease have not done, has been achieved by the co-operation of the white settlers in the great work of extermination.[9]

In 1859, the Federal government virtually abandoned the reservations, leaving the Indians more or less on their own and allowing white squatters to seize most of the improvements. Between 1860 and 1866, all of the reserves and farms, with the exception of Round Valley and Tule River, were extinguished or sold. Thus the Indians lost again, including the loss of many miles of ocean-front property along the Mendocino coast. Was it legal for the Federal government to sell or abandon these "Indian" reservations? Obviously, reservations established by "Executive Order" of the President, were insecure places at best.

To take care of some of the northwest California Indians, expensive land was rented from white owners on Smith River in Del Norte County (1861 to 1866), while in 1864 the Hoopa Valley Reservation was established to appease natives who had been at war for five years. The Colorado River Reservation was set aside for the river tribes in 1865. Meanwhile, in the Great Basin, the Utah Superintendency established a number of "farms" (small reserves) in Utah during 1855, and in 1859 briefly set aside two for the

Shoshones (one at Deep Creek and one at Ruby Valley, the latter being six miles square in size). In 1859 also, the Pyramid Lake and Walker River reserves were set aside for the Northern Paiutes. (In 1865 two Washo reserves of 360 acres each were authorized in Washington, but the local agent failed to take action because there were "no suitable lands.") These latter were the only reserves set aside in Nevada until 1873 when the Southern Paiutes received a tiny reserve at Moapa, and both were administered in a typical inefficient and corrupt style. In 1877 the Duck Valley Reservation was established and at the same time some "farms" were rented from whites for the Western Shoshones.

During the 1870s some effort was made to establish schools for California and Nevada Indians (most could not attend public schools), but the early facilities provided were crude and frequently operated by the local agent's wife whether she knew how to teach or not. In California a new experiment was also attempted wherein the Quakers were to administer the northern reservations and the army the rest, but it was the Methodists who actually took over in 1870. The Baptists were assigned to work in Nevada but did nothing, and, all in all, very little happened in California either. In many instances, the church appointees behaved no differently from their predecessors, as for example, when from 1873 to 1876 Tule River Farm was abandoned in favor of a mountainous tract which could support only one-quarter of the agency population. In 1875 Malheur Reservation was established in eastern Oregon, serving Northern Paiutes of Nevada and Oregon, but it was mismanaged, coveted by whites, and soon abandoned. In 1874, a reservation was set aside for Chemehuevi Paiutes on the Colorado River, and two years later eight small tracts were reserved for southern California Indians. Almost all of the latter were surveyed in such a way that the native villages were left out and worthless lands included, or the areas set aside included lands already patented to whites.

It should be noted that although philanthropical endeavors did occur in California in relation to "white causes" during this period (such as helping the Sanitary Commission during the Civil War), no movement developed whose purpose it was to come to the aid of the Indians, even though the circumstances of slavery, starvation, etc., were well-known. These thirty years, and what they reveal of Anglo-American character, cannot be forgotten. Nor can the fact be ignored that the modern Indian people of the Far West possess a burden of conquest from these and subsequent years, a burden which many still carry.

Native Survival

That American Indians survived at all during those thirty years is in itself rather remarkable and is testimony to the fortitude of the Indian people. Those Indians who resided in heavily white-controlled regions had to make revolutionary adjustments in order to survive, although for those in coastal southern California the adjustments were similar to those of the late Mexican period. Everywhere in the heavily occupied regions the native people had to alter their economy, as has been pointed out, in the direction of becoming a rural proletariat or, to a lesser extent, an urban laboring class. Changes in styles of dress, housing patterns, and food habits followed rapidly as traditional items became hard to acquire. Many Indians became dependent for a time upon cast-off white material goods with which they clothed themselves, developed utensils, and built their houses. Gradually, many developed a positive desire to emulate white styles of dress and living because to do so was an indication of being a "civilized" person and was rewarded by white favor.

It should be pointed out, however, that during the transitional period in their changing material culture, Indians were generally the butt of jokes because of the odd combinations of Indian and non-Indian practices which were often followed. White people generally had little understanding of the difficult processes of acculturation taking place.

Many Indians resisted the Anglo-American conquest in passive ways, such as preserving native religious and ceremonial practices, maintaining such crafts as basketry, holding traditional dances, keeping their native language, and holding to their sense of identity as a people. Others, however, succumbed to the alien pressures and became more and more non-Indian, especially in the coastal zones of central and southern California. In these areas many surviving Indians intermarried with Mexicans; by 1889 one observer could report that the Indians north of San Luis Obispo were becoming lost in the Mexican population. In the Los Angeles–San Diego region a similar process occurred, with the younger people often preferring the Spanish language and Mexican dances to their native traditions. In the rural areas many of these Mexicanized Indian groups survived as distinct communities, but in the towns they became simply Mexican-Americans.

Along the Colorado River, in the desert areas, throughout great sections of Nevada, and in isolated pockets in northern California, other Indian groups attempted to maintain their native cultures virtually intact for long periods of time. The Hamakhavas, Quechans, and Cocopas, for example, maintained traditional inter-tribal warfare until the 1860s, and in one case to 1880, along with their religions, ceremonies, and basic orientation towards life (in spite of a somewhat altered material base). In isolated regions a few small native groups simply stayed away from whites, while farther north, Winnemucca, a Northern Paiute leader, and a large number of followers retreated into the rugged areas of northern Nevada and southeastern Oregon in order to live as in the pre-conquest period. In northern California, a small group of Yahi survivors chose to conceal themselves in their beloved Mill Creek canyon and to cut off all contacts with the outside world.

Still another form of resistance was in the development of religious movements based upon traditional dreaming and curing behavior but modified in the context of conquest. One of the better-known of these movements, the Adventist or so-called Ghost Dance religion, apparently developed in Nevada in 1869 when a Northern Paiute religious leader, Wodziwob, dreamed of the return of the Indian dead, and that dancing would aid in their reappearance. Other preachers, such as Numataivo (father of Wovoka), Winawitu, Weneyuga, and Winnemucca spread this doctrine in the 1871-1872 period in Idaho, northeastern California, and elsewhere. In 1871, a Northern Paiute missionary visited Indians on the North Fork of the San Joaquin River and converted Joijoi, a North Fork leader. The latter subsequently made several trips to Nevada, learning songs and dances from a Paiute known as Moman. Joijoi staged dances in the San Joaquin Valley and other converts soon spread the Adventist movement southwards to Tejon and northwards among various Yokuts-speaking groups.

Other missionaries apparently carried the songs and dances to the Mewuk, where, in 1871 and 1872, "Old Sam" was reported to be a great orator and prophet who said that mourning death was not necessary since the dead were to return. About 1872 also, Indians at Pleasanton revived the central California Kuksu religion in connection with Adventist doctrines. This revived Kuksu movement was then spread by native missionaries to the Mewuk, Maidu, Pomo and Wintun peoples where it survived for some time, although the Adventist songs and dances were abandoned farther south and in Nevada after 1875.

The Indians of the Far West were unaware of the possibility of engaging in political or quasi-political action during this period and, with one exception, they confined their movements to "mystical resistance" or to warfare. The exception was Sarah Winnemucca, a brilliant daughter of Winnemucca who had managed to acquire a little schooling. During the 1870s, Sarah wrote letters on behalf of her people and then in the late 1870s commenced an active campaign on behalf of Indian rights as a public lecturer and lobbyist, which activity culminated in two books, *Life Among The Piutes* (1883) and *Sarah Winnemucca's Solution To The Indian Problem* (1885).

The potential for Indian political-civic activity was vastly improved when it became possible for natives to testify against white men in California in 1873. It also seemed as if the Fourteenth Amendment (1869) had given many or all Indians citizenship rights since the amendment asserted that "all persons born or naturalized in the United States and subject to the jurisdiction thereof" were citizens of both the United States and of the state in which they lived. Many whites in California and elsewhere believed that Indians were included, but during the 1880s the United States Supreme Court held otherwise in two blatantly unconstitutional and racist court decisions. Legally, therefore, Indians were held to be aliens, but unlike other aliens they were also held to be "non-persons" and beyond the protections of the Bill of Rights.

The Next Forty Years: 1880–1920s

After the period of open violence had ceased, the Indian people settled down to a still-traumatic life as conquered aliens ultimately without legal privileges and subject to the ever-present threat of terror. But as warfare became confined to Arizona, northern Mexico and the Four Corners region, and as it ceased altogether in the United States after 1915, a changed attitude began to appear among many white individuals. Gradually, that "moral conscience" in which Anglo-Americans have always taken such an inordinate amount of pride began to assert itself, especially in those sections of the country where there were few Indians. Of course it appeared after the majority of California Indians were dead, but at least it did finally appear.

In the late 1870s, as already mentioned, Sarah Winnemucca began lecturing and writing on behalf of her Northern Paiute people. She was soon joined by others, such as Standing Bear of the Poncas who lectured in Boston in 1879. Listening to Standing Bear was Helen Hunt Jackson, a wealthy New England author who soon decided to devote the remaining years of her life to the Indian cause. Jackson's A Century of Dishonor (1881) and Ramona (1884) drew the literate white population's attention to the plight of the Indian in general and of the former mission Indians of southern California in particular. Although vicious attacks upon the Indian people were more typical of the writing of the 1880s (as for example Theodore Roosevelt's Winning of the West, 1889), such works as Jackson's and Sarah Winnemucca's served to awaken a strong tide of pro-Indian sentiment, especially in New England. In 1882, the powerful Indian Rights Association was organized. Religious denominations also became more concerned and a number of "Indian associations" appeared which were essentially devices for supporting various Christian missions. Unfortunately, as shall be pointed out, many of these "friends of the Indians" proved to be enemies in disguise, but others did bring about improvements in Indian affairs.

In spite of their greatly reduced numbers, most Far West Indians still possessed no land recognized as their own. During the 1880s and 1890s, several new reserves were created, such as Fort Yuma (1883), Hoopa Extension (1891), and the Washo allotments (1895). Aided by the Indian Rights Association, the southern California Indians won a court fight to obtain title to the village of Soboba, while the Sequoya League (a "friends of the Indians" group active between 1901 and 1911) helped the Warner's Ranch natives obtain new lands when they were ousted from their ancient villages in 1900 and 1901. Thereafter, exceedingly small parcels were occasionally purchased or set aside for "homeless" Indians, especially between 1910 and 1929. (Most of these "rancherias" in

California or "colonies" in Nevada were designed to provide residential sites only.) The Owens Valley Indians *were* to receive a large reservation (66,000 acres) suitable for grazing purposes in 1912, but for some reason the Indian Bureau never actually made it available to them.

The setting aside of these additional lands must be viewed in perspective. First, they provided homes for only about one-half of California-Nevada Indians; second, most provided no opportunity for future economic development; and, third, these "postage stamp" reserves, as they were called, were set aside during a period when much larger quantities of land were being transferred to white ownership or being set aside as national parks and national forests. (The new national forests often posed a threat to Indian villages. Indians continued to be ousted from their homes as late as 1910.) Millions of acres of timberland, grazing land, and some agricultural regions were still available during this period, and much of it could have been made useful for Indians but was not. The reader should realize that 87% of Nevada still remains today as so-called public domain, thus clearly indicating that the whites of the period in question were not over-generous in meeting native land needs. (Congress often attached riders to appropriation bills forbidding the acquisition, by Indian tribes, of additional lands even with their own funds.) Millions of acres also remained under Federal control in California during this era.

Although we should applaud the efforts of the "friends of the Indians" in spurring the government to acquire some additional land for natives, it is quite obvious that setting aside land for parks and timber reserves was far more popular and successful in this period. The Indian people actually lost a great deal more land than they obtained, as will be noted.

Raw corruption gradually declined in the Bureau of Indian Affairs during the period in question, but Indian people were still the victims of great abuses. Perhaps the greatest of these was the Dawes Allotment Act, pushed through Congress in 1887 by a strange combination of western anti-Indian interests and New England reformers. Unfortunately, the humanitarianism of the followers of Helen Hunt Jackson (who had died in 1885) was often warped by their white superiority complexes; this is, the reformers felt that they knew what was good for Indians without asking

Indian people. And what was good for Indians was, of course, to force them to become Anglo-Americans through a process of destroying tribal organizations and dividing up economic assets among individual families. It should be pointed out that this process of giving individual plots to families had been tried many times before and had almost always failed, due primarily to white chicanery but also to native traditions of collective ownership.

Additionally, the Dawes Act provided that after each family had recieved its 40 to 160 acres the balance of the land was to be declared "surplus" and opened to whites. (The money obtained, held in trust for the Indians, was spent for government operations.) This was a key part of the act from the western viewpoint.

It might be asked how it came about that Congress could by legislation both alter the form of corporate assets and also confiscate a portion of them, but it must be remembered that Indians were not thought of as possessing any constitutional protection. (It is especially ironic, of course, that the individual allotment act was put into effect during a period when whites were moving more and more in the direction of corporate, i.e., collective enterprise rather than individual enterprise. This was nowhere more true than in California.)

In any event, many Indians were pressured into accepting allotments, in part as the only means for gaining security of title or citizenship (the latter was made available to allottees). Such Far West reserves as Walker River, Klamath River, and Hoopa were allotted or partially allotted, although most California-Nevada reserves were totally unsuited for such a process, being too small, too rough, or too sterile. The result was not surprising. Klamath River Reserve was abolished entirely by 1892 while whites were able to gain control of key sections at Walker River and Hoopa reserves. Elsewhere the allotments did not work out well, even where retained by Indians, because of Federal red tape, marginal quality, and lack of capital for development. Federal regulations (and the assumption that the Indian population would remain static) produced complicated heirship problems which even today make many allotments virtually useless.

In brief, the Dawes allotment plan proved to be a disservice to Indians and a net gain for white land-grabbers, not because Indian families did not desire to have their own farms and ranches but because it was an inflexible bureaucratic plan conceived and executed by outsiders. Indian people were not given a chance to work out their own solutions to the land problem.

During this period, Indians also continued to lose land in various other ways. For example, in Nevada the Pyramid Lake Paiutes lost a 20,500-acre timber reserve (set aside in 1864, then abandoned "informally" after having never been developed, but still being shown on maps as late as 1910), and the entire southern part of the reservation around the town of Wadsworth. Both areas were lost due to the influence of the Central Pacific Railroad and in neither case were any legal formalities followed by the government. Additionally, during the 1890s, Senator William Stewart of Nevada sought to abolish the Walker River Reservation entirely and to further diminish the Pyramid Lake Reserve, but fortunately his efforts were blocked by the Board of Indian Commissioners, a body which contributed to improvements in the Indian Bureau during this period. (Senator Stewart did not succeed in taking away much Indian land but, ironically, he did get an Indian school, Stewart Institute, named after him.) In the early 1900s white squatters succeeded in occupying the southern portion of the Walker River Reservation and by 1906 the Indians were forced to give up that area and Walker Lake in exchange for arid desert lands.

Other examples of land lost to the Indians included the Klamath River Reservation of forty square miles, of which, in 1893, the Indians received only 9000 acres, and the Paiute Reservation of 66,000 acres located north of Bishop. The latter was lost by the natives in a rather mysterious way through the machinations of the City of Los Angeles, which during the 1920s was seeking to gain control of as much land as possible in the Owens Valley area. As late as 1954, when hearings were held in Bishop, the head of the Indian Bureau in California could not explain what had happened to the 66,000-acre reserve (but the reserve's value was being subtracted from the award to be made to Indians for lands seized by the Federal government on the grounds that the reserve still existed).

Another manner in which Indians effectively lost the use of their land was through leases (managed by the Indian Bureau) with white ranchers and farmers. In 1925, some 57,000 acres were leased in California, 19,000 were "farmed by Indians," and the balance, more than 400,000 acres, apparently were not being utilized for any agricultural purpose (most being useless).

In 1919, Malcolm McDowell conducted an investigation into California Indian affairs on behalf of the Board of Indian Commissioners. McDowell's excellent report is sprinkled with recommendations for reform, including the following:

> The adoption of a California Indian policy, with appropriate legislation to make it effective, predicated upon the aknowledgement of a legal debt due the Indians because they were dispossessed of their lands without due process of law and without compensation, and based upon the principle of exact justice and not upon sentiments of pity or charity.[10]

Mr. McDowell commented at length upon the "strange" fact that the procedure followed in other parts of the United States in quieting Indian titles had not been followed in California. Unfortunately, McDowell was naive since "exact justice" as regards land rights has *never* been extended to California or Nevada Indians in the fifty years since his report was written.

The period from the 1880s through the 1920s was an era during which the conquered native population was constantly brought under more and more bureaucratic control. Although without constitutional basis, the Indians were reduced legally to the status of "wards" and were regarded as possessing virtually no rights over their "own" reservations. The government actually made it very clear that the reservations belonged to the government and not to the Indian people.

Indian agents in this period often possessed as much power as they wished to award themselves, including authority to suppress Indian ceremonies, cut off adults' long hair, expel "difficult" persons from reservations, imprison offenders, make assignments of land to "cooperative" persons, offer agency employment, recommend certificates of competency, and otherwise control and manipulate the native population. The degree of totalitarian control actually exercised varied naturally from region to region and was generally in direct relation to the proximity of a given reservation to an agent's headquarters. Those Indians not residing on reservations and those at a distance from the agency were comparatively free from supervision.

Most Indian children were, in one way or another, affected by the schools operated by the Indian Bureau. By 1910, 51.3% of California's Indian youth from ages 5 to 20 were attending school, compared with 61.6% for all rural children. By 1920, 60.4% of the Indian youth were in school compared to 68.5% of all California's rural children. The vast bulk of these pupils were enrolled in the elementary grades.

The Indian schools (along with a few public schools) had succeeded very slowly in reducing English illiteracy. In 1910, 63.4% of California Indians over age 21 were still illiterate, while 16.6% of those between ages 10 and 20 were nonreaders. By 1920, these figures had declined to 46.2% and 9.1%, respectively, as compared with 6.4% and 1.9% for all classes of the rural population. Nevada, unfortunately, was even farther behind with 82.6% of the adult Indian population and 43% of those ages 10 to 20 still illiterate in 1910. By 1920, these figures had become 66.9% and 33%, compared with 7.9% and 3% for all classes of the rural population of that State. Quite obviously something was lacking in a program that after some forty years still saw one-third of its older school-age youth illiterate in Nevada, and one-tenth illiterate in California— not to mention rates of two-thirds (Nevada) and one-half (California) of the adults still illiterate.

In 1882 Helen Hunt Jackson found that the southern California Indians were

> all keenly alive to the value of education. In every village that we visited we were urged to ask the government to give them a school. In one they insisted upon ranging the children all in rows, that we might see for ourselves that there were children enough to justify the establishing of a school.[11]

The slow progress actually made by Indian pupils was, apparently, in sharp contrast to the initial enthusiasm of the parents and the young people. In part this situation can be blamed upon the poor quality of instruction received in Indian schools (in spite of evidence that there were some individual teachers with great skill and dedication), but in large measure it must have been due to the overall orientation of the schools. Education, during this era, was conceived of as a means for destroying the native heritage and "liberating" the individual Indian so that he could take his place in society as a "brown-white man." The Indian schools were totally divorced from the culture of the native people and were essentially anti-Indian in almost every respect. It would be quite understandable if most Indian children left that kind of classroom as quickly as possible. On the other hand, some pupils were able to attend vocational boarding schools which sometimes gave them a "trade" even if it alienated them from their Indian heritage.

In 1915 only 316 Indian pupils were attending public school in California, but by 1919 this number had increased to 2199. In general, this was the result of a campaign carried out by Indians, by the Indian Board of Cooperation, and a new government policy of integrating Indians in public schools in areas such as California and Nevada where the native population was intermixed with white communities. Resistance to integration on the part of whites was widespread in California and Nevada at first, but gradually prejudice was overcome, due in great part to the fact that the Federal government paid the local school districts on a per-pupil basis.

By 1919, 11,000 California Indians were residing on Federal "trust" land (reservations or rancherias) with another 5200 to 14,000 scattered elsewhere. Of the 12,725 Indians served by the Indian Bureau in 1920-1921, some 5029 were of mixed racial ancestry with 2308 of these of one-half or less Indian descent. Since it is highly likely that a greater proportion of non-reservation Indians were of mixed ancestry, it would appear that approximately one-half of the California native population was of mixed background by 1920.

In 1882 and 1883, probably less than 1000 Nevada Indians (out of 5000) were residing on "trust" land, but by 1927 about 2500 were on the larger reservations with 2000 at the various colonies and about 500 on their own.

General conditions in the Far West were far from good in 1919 and 1920, after more than a half-century of conquest. McDowell wrote in 1919 of the majority of California Indians that

> more than all else, they have for generations been treated by their white neighbors as an inferior people and have been accepting that appraisement quite as a matter of course. . . . They get their own living with the work of their own hands. . . . With apparently few exceptions the California Indians are seasonal, or casual, work people. The

earning time for the great majority is the growing
seasons.... [Others] of them find employment in saw-
mills, on the surface of mines, in logging camps, and on
railroads and public roads. During sheep shearing these
Indians are in demand.... They herd cattle, milk cows,
and do general farm labor. The women who live near cities
and towns go out by day as domestics and laundresses.[12]

This description was also applicable to most Indians in Nevada,
including perhaps a majority of reservation natives, since the latter
very often had to become seasonal workers in order to earn a living.

During this era the ways of living of the Indian people were
further transformed and, on the whole, their material existence
came to approximate that of poor whites, except in so far as a few
native arts and crafts survived. In clothing styles, house construction, methods of transportation, and personal ornamentation,
"white ways" became the rule, with native clothing disappearing
except for on ceremonial occasions and with most Indian-type
structures, such as community "round houses" and men's sweat
lodges, being allowed to deteriorate and disappear. Generally, Indian
people were under enormous and continued pressure to imitate
white behavior and with the exception of a few arts and crafts, such
as basketry, there was no significant tendency in the non-Indian
community to encourage any retention of the ancient heritage.
Most younger Indians were, of course, deeply influenced by the
anti-Indian heritage bias of their educational experiences and, even
when "turned off" by the schools, were under great psychological
pressure to conform to the dominant society.

Indian people were often rather passive during these forty years
from the 1880s to the 1920s. This is, of course, not at all surprising
in view of the enormity of the shock of the preceding period of
warfare and disorganization and of the immense power and prestige
available to those whites who intervened in Indian affairs. Indian
people operated at a great disadvantage, and to resist at all required
great tenacity of spirit or brilliance of perception. The easy course
was to bend with the hurricane, accepting white views on all
matters from dress to religion.

Spiritual resistance was most in evidence during the early years
of this period, with the revival of the Adventist (so-called "Ghost
Dance") movement by Wovoka, the continued functioning of the

Essie Parrish actively preserves the basketmaking heritage of the Kashia Pomo people at Tsununu-Shinal in Sonoma County. *(Photo courtesy Mrs. Essie Parrish.)*

Sarah Winnemucca, outstanding Nevada Indian writer and lecturer, and daughter of Neh-meh leader Winnemucca (about 1880). *(Courtesy of Southwest Museum, Los Angeles.)*

A Western Shoshone young warrior, known to the whites as "Charlie" (about 1880). *(Courtesy of Southwest Museum, Los Angeles.)*

Wessie (or Wazzie) George, a Neh-meh (Northern Paiute) living at Stillwater, Nevada, splitting willow stems for basket. *(Courtesy of Southwest Museum, Los Angeles.)*

A young Pomo man navigating a tule boat in Clear Lake (about 1880). *(Photo courtesy of Southwest Museum, Los Angeles.)*

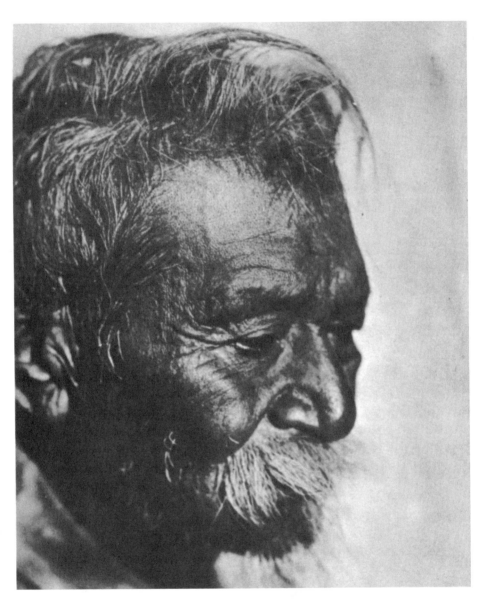

A Koshónomo Pomo man (about 1880-1900). *(Photo courtesy of Southwest Museum, Los Angeles.)*

A California Indian basketmaker in Yosemite Valley (before 1900). *(Photo courtesy of Southwest Museum, Los Angeles.)*

A Mewuk settlement in the Sierra foothills during the period when Indians were driven off all the best sites (about 1880). (Courtesy of the Bancroft Library, University of California, Berkeley.)

San Francisco Bay Area to central California Indians with dance headdresses (early 1800's). *(Reproduced through the courtesy of the Bancroft Library, University of California, Berkeley.)*

Tachahagáchile, a Kato (Nungahl) man (pre-1900). *(Photo courtesy of Southwest Museum, Los Angeles.)*

A Hamakhava (Colorado River) girl. *(Photo courtesy Southwest Museum, Los Angeles.)*

A Nim (Mono) or Neuma (Owens Valley Paiute) girl with winnowing basket (about 1880). *(Photo courtesy Southwest Museum, Los Angeles.)*

A Maidu woman (probably before 1910). *(Photo by E. S. Curtis, courtesy Southwest Museum. Los Angeles.)*

Noverto León, a 105-year-old Soboba (Atahum) man (about 1900-1910). *(Reproduced through the courtesy of Bancroft Library, University of California, Berkeley.)*

A Pomo village near Clear Lake (about 1890). *(Reproduced through the courtesy of the Bancroft Library, University of California, Berkeley.)*

William Robert Cooke, Yurok Indian and an early member of the California Indian Education Association. *(Photograph by Dennis Galloway.)*

Marilyn Stephens (Mewuk) and Frank Canizales (Mewuk), at an Indian education meeting. *(Photograph by Dennis Galloway.)*

The author, Jack Forbes, and David Risling, Jr., (founder-president of the California Indian Education Association) talking with Long Beach State College Indian students at a CIEA meeting (1969). *(Photograph by Dennis Galloway.)*

revived Kuksu religion of central California, and the survival of various curing procedures among a number of groups. Wovoka, a Northern Paiute, became nationally famous when, from 1887 to 1890, his songs and dances spread rapidly from the Walker River of Nevada to the Plains Indians. Wovoka's teachings, emphasizing rededication to a life of virtue and the consequent return of the Indian dead, were opposed vigorously by Indian Bureau officials and the movement collapsed in Nevada, never appreciably spreading into California. Nonetheless, Wovoka was greatly respected by many Indians, and along with numerous other Indian doctors, maintained a tradition of ancient native practices which has endured, to a certain extent, to the present day.

In the Pomo region the Maru religion, an outgrowth of the Adventist-Kuksu revival of the 1870s, continued to function. In that area and elsewhere in California individual native doctors periodically experienced revelations (usually in dreams) which caused them to develop variations in either the Maru religion or the practice of spiritual doctoring. Bureau officials attempted to discourage the native religious movements but often with only very gradual success. In 1919 it was reported, for example, that at Hoopa "some of the old tribal customs and superstitions remain; the medicine man is still somewhat in evidence; some of the old-time dances bring the Indians together once in a while...."[13]

On the Walker River Reservation the agent attempted to interfere with native dances and doctoring but met with resistance. In 1912 the Indians, with the help of a sympathetic white attorney, drew up a petition asking for the removal of the agent, but the effort was largely a failure since the Indian Bureau approved of the suppression of native religion, dancing, and other "excesses."[14]

Many other kinds of resistance were offered by individual Indians, as with pupils frequently running off from boarding school, or with occasional violence, as when in 1910 and 1911 a group of Indians under "Shoshone Mike" briefly raided in northern Nevada. Quite different was the response in 1904 of the Yokayo Pomo people to the efforts of the white man to acquire part of the property which they had purchased for their Indian community some twenty years before. The Yokayo took their case to court and won, thereby protecting their unique Indian-controlled community.

As early as 1882 the people of the Round Valley Reservation

began struggling against Federal bureaucrats, utilizing varied forms of resistance. In that year the agent wrote

> from the time I struck the first blow to prepare the buildings at Camp Wright for a boarding school, I have met with opposition from nearly all parties... and even the Missionary, who was here at the time said, "The Indians will not let their children come, and they will burn the buildings before they will let you take their children into them."[15]

As predicted, the boarding school buildings were burned on the nights of July 20 and July 23, 1883. The agent wrote,

> this is but the out crop of the spirit of hostility to the school that has been more or less expressed since I began to prepare the buildings for that purpose. Added to this the spirit of insubordination... has shown itself lately....[16]

Five of the "largest boys" of the school later confessed to the burnings.

From 1911 to 1914 a new wave of opposition to policies being followed at Round Valley Reservation and the boarding school developed. In 1911 the girls burned their dormitory down; in 1912 the girls set fire to their temporary dormitory on two occasions; and in 1914 the boys twice attempted to burn their dormitory and actually succeeded in burning down the main school building. The superintendent wrote,

> I have every reason to believe that the action of the pupils... is the result of the feeling manifested by the parents of the children and discussed in their presence while at home.... There has always been among these Indians a very strong feeling against the government school.[17]

The Round Valley Indians were aided by the Rev. F. G. Collett, a Methodist preacher who had organized the Indian Board of Cooperation in 1913. Collett helped the reservation residents circulate a petition seeking the removal of their Indian Bureau supervisors, and an investigation followed.

> The Indians were not allowed to tell their stories [except] in the presence of Superintendent Wilson.... We cannot fully appreciate how hard this made it for the Indians to

relate their grievances, only as we take into consideration that the Indians are desperately shy and incomprehensively afraid of ridicule and are cowed under a system that makes them dependent creatures and that the children had been most cruelly flogged on their bare backs until they had suffered for weeks from the outrages perpetrated by these government officials.[18]

Indians also expressed their resentment of Federal policies by seeking to obtain public schools. Captain Odock of an Indian group near Colusa appealed for a school in 1910, with the result that ultimately an all-Indian public school district was established. Rev. Collett's Indian Board devoted much of its energy between 1913 and 1915 to helping Indians in Lake and Mendocino counties establish new public school districts or gain admittance to already existing non-Federal schools.

With the aid of Rev. Collett, the Indians of Lake County discovered another means of advancing their position by means of a court case. Ethan Anderson attempted to register to vote with the Lake County Clerk but was refused, and a test case was set up which eventually reached the State Supreme Court. Ethan Anderson won his right to vote in 1917 and thereby won citizenship rights for all California Indians who did not reside on the larger reservations (Anderson v. Mathews, 174 Cal. 537, 163 Pac. 902). During 1915 and 1916, Lake County area Indians held many meetings to raise money for the case and also to plan challenges to Lake County welfare practices.

Quite obviously, the Native Americans of California were beginning to learn how to engage in political-legal resistance. By 1919, it was reported,

> the rancheria Indians ... living in Mendocino, Lake, and Sonoma Counties ... have organized themselves into an association under the name of the Society of Northern California Indians. This organization was effected under the guidance of Rev. Father Raymond, O.M. Cap. of St. Marys Church, Ukiah ... the coming together of these rancheria Indians, with the set purpose of forming an organization of any kind, is significant and interesting. A few years ago it would have been impossible to unite these rancherias into an organization....[19]

McDowell sat in on a conference of the SNCI at Ukiah where fourteen rancherias were represented.

> The purpose of the society is to promote the advancement of and to secure a peaceful and prosperous existence for the Indians; to obtain and publish a history of their people; to establish a legal department to advise the Indians, and to suggest and obtain remedies for unsatisfactory conditions; to work together for more and better schools for their children and to arrange for lectures on agriculture, stock raising, domestic science, etc.... These are non reservation Indians—Pomos, Concows, Noyos, Sansels, Ukies, Wylackies, and Nomelackies—who, with some exceptions, live on tracts of land owned by the Government.... They want to be more like white men: they want water piped to their little cabins ... they want better living conditions; they want their children to have more and better school facilities....[20]

Somewhat comparable developments took place in southern California where the natives organized the Federation of Mission Indians to improve conditions and promote concerted action. But

> at the federation meetings expressions of ill will or hostility to the Government were occasionally heard. Grievances were aired and complaints, both legitimate and trivial, were uttered. As a result, and under orders of the Department of Justice, some 57 Indians were placed under arrest on the charge of conspiracy against the Government.[21]

The Indian Bureau was able to attempt to deny free speech and assembly rights to Indians because of its doctrine that Native Americans were not protected by the Constitution. Fortunately, friendly whites organized the Indian Welfare League to help the Indians and in March 1922 the Board of Indian Commissioners intervened, finding that the Indian Bureau's policy was both "ill advised and utterly futile." Conditions among the ex-mission Indians were in a bad state; they were "suspicious and their resentment seemed to be justifiable."[22]

Thus, by 1920, the Indians of the Far West were beginning to experiment with new forms of concerted action, ranging from petitions, to law suits, to organizing in order to make their desires known. A new era had not yet dawned, but its birth could be anticipated.

IV. THE NATIVE AWAKENING

The Struggle for Equality of Citizenship

In 1924, the United States Congress, fifty-five years after the passage of the Fourteenth Amendment, finally extended citizenship to all Indians. But Indian people did not thereby acquire citizenship rights equivalent to those of whites. A long period of struggle against the Bureau of Indian Affairs and the various state governments, and local white prejudice was still to be.

For complex reasons, all of which were extra-constitutional, the U. S. Supreme Court had come to hold that Indians were "wards" of the Federal government. Still later, the court came to assert that "wardship" did not end when citizenship was granted. In 1923 the Court held, for example, that

> this duty of protection and power [of the Federal government] extends to individual Indians, even though they may have become citizens.... "The civil and political status of the Indians does not condition the power of the government to protect their property or to instruct them. Their admission to citizenship does not deprive the United States of its power or relieve it of its duty."[1]

The Bureau of Indian Affairs interpreted the granting of citizenship in 1924 as not affecting its authority.

> The act of June 2, 1924 ... did not in any way alter the control of the Office of Indian Affairs over the tribal or individual property of Indians. Nor did it change the laws that apply to the person of the Indian. The unallotted Indian living on a reservation is still not subject to state laws, and he is subject to United States law for only certain specified offenses.[2]

It should be borne in mind that the only special constitutional power over Indian Affairs possessed by the Federal government relates to the regulation of "commerce" with the "Indian tribes," the same power which the Federal government possessed in relation to interstate commerce. The Constitution does not provide the Federal government with any special authority over individual Indians, whether aliens or citizens, nor does it provide that government with any explicit powers over Indian property or territory.

During the 1920s, and ever since, American Indian people have existed in a legal "no man's land" as a result of conflicting congressional statutes, state laws, bureaucratic rulings, and non-constitutional court decisions. First, Indian property or territory had gradually changed from being regions ("domestic dependent nations") not a part of any state and simply under Federal "protection" to areas held "in trust" by the Federal government for Indians—a vast and significant change. Further, Indian areas in California and Nevada were held, again by extra-constitutional processes, to be actually owned by the Federal government and simply made available for Indian occupancy as a kind of "gratuity." All of this is quite significant because it relates closely to the question of "termination," a concept developed quite early but not widely implemented until the 1950s. If Indian lands were beyond state jurisdiction because of their former sovereign political character and "protectorate" status, then the withdrawal, or "termination," of Federal supervision did not per se alter the local tax-free status of those lands; but if Indian lands were the trust property of the United States, then the lands were threatened with state jurisdiction and local taxation at any time when the Federal government chose unilaterally to alter that trust status. The whole question of the legal status of Indian reservations has also been greatly affected by a hodge-podge of conflicting Federal statutes adopted without any prior resolution of the question outlined above.

Second, the legal "no man's land" has persisted because individual Indians were often unable to be either citizens or "wards" since the two concepts, in spite of the Supreme Court, are quite obviously in conflict. Many states, regarding Indians as Federal "wards," refused to make state and local services and voting rights available to individual natives, while the Federal government, regarding them for certain purposes as citizens, sometimes discontinued its welfare programs. This was especially a problem for non-reservation Indians in the Far West, but it was also a problem for groups residing on rancherias and colonies, since these small tracts were often not regarded as being true reservations. The full range of Federal services tended to be available only for persons residing on large reservations.

One might suppose that at long last Indians as citizens acquired the protection of the Bill of Rights, but such was not usually the case. As has been seen, as late as 1922 the Indian Bureau sought to arrest southern California Indians (some or all of whom were citizens) for merely criticizing the Bureau. In a similar manner, the Indian Bureau sought forcibly during the 1920s to suppress the native religion at Taos Pueblo in New Mexico, in clear violation of the First Amendment, while everywhere the Bureau cooperated closely with Christian missionaries.

The Federal government was actively engaged in efforts to forcibly change native cultures, as in seeking state laws to suppress the peyote-using Native American Church (in addition to the police-state tactics utilized on reservations). The Indian Bureau also sought to interfere with traditional marriage practices on reservations, advocating repressive state laws:

> I think it not untimely to suggest the need for legislation subjecting all Indians to the laws of civilization respecting their marital relations . . . there is still too much disregard of the sacred principle upon which conjugal happiness . . . depends. . . . The vicious practice of Indian custom marriage and separation is deplorable. . . . The tribal courts [run by the Bureau] . . . are not sufficient to deal successfully with the loose marital relations of barbaric origin and there should be some means provided for involving State law more effectively . . . before we can have the right beginning of progress toward civilization.[3]

During this period a renewed effort was made to suppress native dances of religious significance. The Commissioner wrote in 1923,

> A long-time tendency of the Indians has been to give too much time to dances, powwows, celebrations, and general festive occasions. . . . To correct this practice a letter was widely circulated among the Indians last year . . . [with] an earnest appeal . . . that they shorten somewhat the length of these gatherings and omit from them use of harmful drugs [peyote], intoxicants, gambling, and degrading ceremonials.[4]

This does not fully convey an idea of the actions that were actually taken to suppress "degrading ceremonials," such as the arrest of many leading men at Taos.

The awarding of citizenship did not at first diminish the enormous power exercised by Indian Bureau officials, including especially local superintendents of "agencies." To understand this situation, one must picture each reservation as a colony administered by civil servants who, formally at least, answered only to their bureaucratic superiors in Washington, D. C., rather than to the people being "served." Indian reservations were communities where the ruling bureaucrats possessed the power to disburse appropriations from Washington, the power to award jobs and land-use privileges, the power to control the local police and courts (in which the Constitution did not operate as a limitation upon procedure), the power to control who received piped water, who obtained a road nearby, who obtained sewage services (when available), the power to influence the securing of jobs from white employers, the power to control movement to and from the reservation, the power to award rights to attend Bureau vocational institutes, and, later, the power to award scholarships to colleges and universities, among other powers. Struggling with these all-powerful, non-elected officers of the Federal government were largely unorganized people who were also exceedingly poor, undereducated, and without powerful allies (since very often the local Bureau officials had tie-ins with local businessmen, farmers, and ranchers due to the awarding of contracts and lease-rights). Very often also, the Indian people were very much afraid to challenge the local Bureau officers, not merely because any such action would endanger them in very concrete ways, but also because of a deep general fear of "white power" imposed by the experience of being conquered.

The terrible power of the Indian Bureau over the lives of individual Indians (and still greater power over the lives of communities) meant that many Native Americans could always be found who would serve as "front-men" and "tools" of Bureau officials. Acting out of fear or self-interest, many Indians made themselves accomplices of the colonial system and served to make it virtually impossible for Indian people to speak with a firm, united voice.

Unfortunately, the power of the Bureau of Indian Affairs still remains almost as great today as it was in the 1920s, especially in relation to smaller and less well-organized Indian communities. The reforms of the 1930s, the Indian awakening, the rise of competing state and Federal agencies (such as the Office of Economic Opportunity), and the decline in Bureau services in areas such as California have all conspired to reduce somewhat the more blatant and obvious violations of Indian peoples' rights to local self-determination, but Bureau officials still possess powerful tools for controlling individual Indians (principally in the awarding or withholding of such items as jobs, scholarships, road projects, public works, and economic development programs, but also in terms of influencing who gets what lands and under what conditions, etc.).

Courageous individuals and small groups resisted the Bureau's totalitarianism during the 1920s and 1930s, but with varying success at the local level. In part this was because the Indian Bureau has always displayed a remarkable ability to project an appearance of making changes while actually resisting change. For example, in 1932 the superintendent of the Sacramento Agency, Oscar H. Lipps, wrote a pamphlet which ostensibly placed the Bureau on the side of reform in California Indian affairs. But Mr. Lipps's program included such items as, 1) recommending a California Advisory Committee on Indian Affairs to be composed entirely of non-Indians, and 2) the expenditure of $12,000,000 of the Indians' own money (an expected award from a land claims case) in "a carefully prepared program . . . worked out in advance by the State and Federal agencies cooperating . . . to rehabilitate the needy and neglected Indians of the State. . . ."[5]

Mr. Lipps, the man "speaking on behalf" of California Indians and exercising great power over the lives of, in his words, "these primitive people," stated,

> The California Indians are not by nature the low, degraded, intellectually inferior people they are generally believed to be. They are a retarded race and their seeming intellectual inferiority is due more to their treatment, poverty and lack of opportunity than to any inherent incapacity. While not the upstanding, proud and noble bearing type of the quaintly picturesque and brilliantly arrayed Plains

Indians, still they possess average native intelligence, and, given a chance, the majority of them can be developed into useful citizens and as such contribute something of value. . . .[6]

During the 1930s reforms were made in Federal policy towards Indians, the principal one being that local native groups were to be allowed to incorporate, possess constitutions, and elect a "tribal" or business council. This small measure of local self-government was rapidly taken advantage of by many Far West groups, including in the first year (1935) the Pyramid Lake Paiute Tribe, the Reno-Sparks Indian Colony, and the Washoe Tribe of Nevada and California. National reforms in Bureau policy were also attempted but, unfortunately, these reforms were entirely dependent upon the continued goodwill of Congress and the appointment of pro-Indian officials. No power at the national or regional levels was actually transferred to democratically-chosen Indian boards and therefore it was possible for many of the reforms to be reversed or sabotaged during the late 1940s and early 1950s, whenever a new President chose an unsympathetic Commissioner of Indian Affairs or Secretary of the Interior.

The reforms were often also meaningless at the local level since the same Bureau officials as before possessed the same power either to control tribal council elections or to manipulate the council members. Gradually many Indian groups were indeed able to acquire some independence and authority, but others remain to this day under practical Bureau domination (or else the council members and local Bureau officials comprise a "partnership" oligarchy which controls local affairs).

Nonetheless, a new spirit came to pervade the Indian Bureau during the 1930s which could not entirely be reversed even during the reactionary years of the 1950s. For example, the outright opposition to Indian traditions largely disappeared except in the schools (and it was diminished even there), the "image" of respecting Indian opinions came to be valued, the loss of Indian land was largely halted, and many persons of Indian and part-Indian descent were allowed to rise in the Bureau hierarchy. (The latter, of course, has a negative aspect since it serves as one of the means for preventing many educated Indians from criticizing the government.)

As the relative power of the Bureau of Indian Affairs declined, only a portion of the authority lost was acquired by Indian communities. A significant part of the Bureau's power passed instead into the hands of white-controlled state and local agencies and this process has tended to accelerate in recent years. For example, during the period after 1912 and through the 1930s numerous small public school districts were established in both California and Nevada to serve Indian populations. The bulk of these districts were potentially controlled by Indians, although many were, in fact, controlled behind the scenes by the Bureau, by white missionaries, or by white superintendents. During recent decades, however, virtually all of these districts have been abolished and consolidated with larger districts, thus ensuring white control.

Increasingly, therefore, and without solving the problems created by continuing Indian Bureau power, Indian people have been forced to turn their attention to state-level politics. At the state level, Indians faced the hard fact that, due to small numbers, they could generally possess no direct representation in the legislature and were dependent upon difficult-to-tap "goodwill" rather than any reliable source of influence. Unfortunately also, both the governments of California and Nevada have tended to adopt a paternalistic approach to Indian affairs, typified by the establishment in 1961 in California of a State Advisory Commission on Indian Affairs, composed entirely of non-Indians.

In the 1950s, as will be discussed below, the Bureau of Indian Affairs commenced the termination of its services to California Indians. Indian people were concerned and so were State officials who were not anxious to accept responsibility for communities which normally were still lacking in such fundamentals as paved roads, clean water, sewage facilities, and defined property lines. The legislature therefore established a Senate Interim Committee on Indian Affairs which held hearings beginning in 1954. The Committee did signal service in calling attention to the gross insufficiency of the Bureau (conditions were not dissimilar from those described in the special investigations of 1882 and 1919) and an opportunity was provided for the, by then, numerous Indian organizations to testify. Unfortunately, the legislators chose to rely entirely upon white Federal and State officials to "do something," and the result was virtually nil.

Since 1961 the California State Advisory Commission on Indian Affairs, composed of whites and almost always employing white staff, has not served to provide Indians with a voice in California Indian affairs (a few appointed Indians have merely served on an advisory committee to the advisory commission). More significantly, the one concrete accomplishment of the commission, the *Progress Report to the Governor and the Legislature* was researched, prepared, and edited by non-Indians. Their recommendations, while often praiseworthy for their concern for material progress on reservations, are much weakened by being written by non-Indians unable to comprehend the fundamental problems of Indian people. Not surprisingly these non-Indians could not, without repudiating their own commission and staff, come to grips with the issue of powerlessness, nor could they face up to land problems whose discussion might irritate powerful white interests.

In 1968 an effort was made by the California Advisory Commission to transform itself into a more powerful agency, but with an all-white membership. Indian people, through intensive lobbying, succeeded in amending the bill to establish an all-Indian commission. This latter amended bill then passed the Senate but was ultimately killed by the chairman of the existing all-white Advisory Commission, Senator William Coombs (who, as author of the original bill, possessed the traditional legislator's right to withdraw a piece of legislation bearing his name).

In Nevada, one Northern Paiute, Mr. Dewey Sampson, briefly served in the legislature, but otherwise the Indian people were not represented at the State level until 1965. In that year the newly-formed Inter-Tribal Council of Nevada and allied tribal councils succeeded in persuading the legislature to establish a State Commission on Indian Affairs to be composed of at least three Indians (out of seven members). John Dressler, the Washo chairman of the Inter-Tribal Council became Commission Chairman and Alvin James, a Northern Paiute, became the first Executive Secretary.

An important step forward has been the continuing development of Indian-controlled organizations, such as the National Congress of American Indians (1944) and numerous local groups in California and Nevada. Unfortunately, the NCAI has never been strong in the Far West, and most California-Nevada groups became embroiled in the land claims cases in such an extent that their effectiveness on other fronts was seriously handicapped.

Of recent significance has been the development of state-wide inter-tribal councils, particularly in connection with the handling of grants from the Office of Economic Opportunity and other Federal agencies. In the early 1960s efforts were made to organize such a council in Nevada but Bureau opposition led to failure. During 1963, however, the BIA changed its position and a number of Indian leaders were ready to move in any case. The result was the establishment of the Inter-Tribal Council of Nevada, Inc., which initially represented only a few reservations and colonies but has since come to include virtually all such communities, and has successfully encouraged the funding of numerous development-action projects in Nevada. *The Native Nevadan*, published by the council, has become an excellent means of communication for most Nevada Indians.

Unfortunately, the fact that the initial meetings of the Inter-Tribal Council of Nevada took place at the BIA office and that a U. S. Public Health Service officer played a major advisory role led many Indians to adopt a hostile position. Furthermore, factionalism already existed among Nevada Indians and, in general, those who were militantly opposed to the government position in the claims cases tended to stay away from the Inter-Tribal Council. Those who supported the Council tended, generally, to be persons who were more willing to cooperate with white officialdom, while those in opposition tended to be extremely suspicious of all white-controlled agencies.

The Inter-Tribal Council of Nevada might well have failed except for the fact that it has become virtually the sole vehicle for the disbursal of Federal grant money to Indians in Nevada. Again we see the power of the Federal government, in that its selection of particular Indian agencies for the receipt of funds powerfully affects internal native politics.

In California a movement to establish an inter-tribal council also developed, but under slightly different circumstances. The Office of Economic Opportunity made the decision during 1964 and 1965 not to fund local tribal groups directly, but rather to use coordinating groups such as inter-tribal councils. During 1965,

OEO stimulated, more or less artificially, an effort to create an Inter-Tribal Council of California. Unfortunately, the Federal representatives became involved with only one of the many factions in the State, with the result that the persons controlling the Inter-Tribal Council have not been nearly as representative as in Nevada. Repeated efforts to secure funding and to achieve a broader base were unsuccessful, but finally, in 1968, the OEO "Indian Desk" decided to make a grant to the Council.

The Inter-Tribal Council of California soon became an important political force in the State, using Federal monies to hire staff throughout the State. Many Indians charged that it was devoted only to building a "political machine," while others were concerned about alleged corruption. Eventually, however, the membership revolted and new leadership was installed. After that the ITC (as it is known) became a more positive force, using Federal grants to help with unemployment, tribal development, and economic enterprises.

Initially, those Indians who supported the Inter-Tribal Council of California were individuals who, in the past, had been "cooperative" with the Indian Bureau and who were willing, for one reason or another, to work with white officialdom. The State Office of Economic Opportunity, under Governor Ronald Reagan's appointees, also exercised a strong influence on the Inter-Tribal Council, pushing it in a conservative direction and supporting "cooperative" Indian leaders. The opposition, as in Nevada, included many natives who had become completely disillusioned with the Federal government and who generally opposed accepting money from the California land claims case. These Indians in California and Nevada, whom this writer denominates as "militant traditionalists," were informally allied with such groups as the Survival of the American Indians, Inc. of the Pacific Northwest (who staged the "fish-ins"), the traditionalist Hopis, and the Iroquois who fought against Kinzua Dam in New York State. Since 1968, "traditional unity" conferences have been frequently held in various states, including California and Nevada, and a widespread, albeit informal, movement has developed.

On the other hand, the several inter-tribal councils have also tended to grow in strength, due, in great measure, to having good access to Federal funding. Still further, moderate elements have been able to oust the more personalistic and factional elements from the California Council since the early 1970s and it has enjoyed greater trust and respect because of that. The ousted group established a "rump" California Tribal Chairmen's Association but it failed to rival the Inter-Tribal Council in spite of BIA sympathy.

A few California and Nevada Indians were active in the National Indian Youth Council and its offshoot for the 1968 Poor People's Campaign, the American Indian Citizen's Coalition. A small number of individuals, mostly young, participated in the summer demonstrations in Washington, D.C. By and large, though, this development had little impact upon the large majority of Indian people in California and Nevada, many of whom, although critical of the government, were not inclined to stage demonstrations or to develop alliances with other minorities.

A change began to develop in 1968 and 1969 when Indian students joined with other ethnic groups to campaign vigorously for Native American Studies programs on college campuses. This trend of collaboration has continued to some degree, but mostly at the campus level or among traditionalists.

In 1968 also, three very significant events occurred: United Native Americans was organized in the San Francisco area by Lehman Brightman (a Sioux), Dr. Jack D. Forbes, Lanada Boyer, and others; the American Indian Movement was formed in Minneapolis; and *Akwesasne Notes,* an influential Native American newspaper, appeared on the international scene. UNA was an avowedly pan-Indian organization which published *Warpath,* probably the first Indian periodical to apply the colonial analogy systematically to Indian affairs.

UNA declined after 1969, as an organization, but its ideas spread rapidly throughout the West. The occupation of Alcatraz, the establishment of Deganawidah-Quetzalcoatl University, the Pit River land struggle, and many other developments all grew out of a coming together of the old-time traditionalist-nationalist movement with UNA ideas about colonialism, decolonialization, and self-determination.

Eventually, by the end of 1972, with the Caravan of Broken Treaties and the occupation of the BIA headquarters in Washington, D.C., the American Indian Movement appeared in California and absorbed many of the UNA-Alcatraz-traditionalist elements.

Note should be taken also of the many outstanding individual traditionalist leaders, such Raymond Lego who exercised a profound influence, on the land struggle especially. A self-educated constitutional law expert, Raymond Lego provided the inspiration for the long Pit River struggle. He died in 1980, as uncompromising as ever.

Tremendous changes have taken place since 1968. The Indian people now have D-Q University, many urban Indian centers and health programs, numerous local projects, and a growing "middle class" (largely dependent upon Federal dollars). On the other hand, drop-out rates for Indian students remain as high at many rural high schools as they were in the 1950s and the bulk of the people are still quite poor.

The future of the struggle for native rights largely depends upon Indian people's achieving a greater degree of unity. Progress has been made in that regard, but much personalism and factionalism still remains; family loyalties are still often more important than Indian (or tribal) loyalties, and there may be a growing schism developing between the middle class and the poor. Partial "success" has perhaps contributed to the loss of a strong sense of direction, and many Indian organizations seem to be drifting or resting only on past laurels.

The Struggle for Land and Compensation

Since 1920 Native Americans have had to continue their efforts to achieve a better economic position in the face of continued white attacks upon the Indian land base, continued existence of a large number of landless Indians, and the opposition of the Federal government to a willing recognition of its debt for land illegally seized in earlier years.

Many Indians still did not possess adequate reservations during the 1920s, as in Inyo County, California, where 759 of 1418 natives were reportedly still "homeless" in 1925. Small plots were being acquired by the Indian Bureau, but on a very protracted and unsatisfactory basis. The setting aside of so-called public lands for national forests, national parks, etc., continued to take precedence over meeting Indians' land needs, both during the openly anti-Indian (and corrupt) administration of Warren G. Harding, and under the later, somewhat improved, administrations which followed. Similarly, the leasing of "public" lands to white ranchers, miners, and farmers possessed a higher priority with the Department of the Interior.

By 1920 many Indian people in California had become somewhat familiar with the idea of using the courts as a means for achieving justice. The Indians of northern California, aided by Rev. F. G. Collett decided at that time to seek compensation for the lands seized illegally during the 1850s. In 1920, Congressman John E. Raker introduced a bill which proposed that any California tribe or band could sue the United States for lands taken away, utilizing private attorneys of their own choosing. Raker's bill and similar ones which were introduced each year through 1927 were all defeated, in great measure because of the opposition of the Indian Bureau. The BIA, the supposed "guardian" of the Indians, was actually disposing of Indian lands during this period (Secretary of the Interior Albert B. Fall was himself seeking lands belonging to the Mescalero Apaches) and, not surprisingly, was hostile to such court cases.

In April 1922 a number of delegates representing California Indians journeyed to Washington, D.C., to attend an Interior Department hearing where they hoped to get a reversal of the Department's stand in opposition. The Commissioner of Indian Affairs reported,

> At this hearing it was made clear that the previous adverse report would not be modified, as the department was unwilling to approve any bill that had for its purpose compensating Indians for the value of lands ($10,000,000) involved in the eighteen treaties which were rejected by the Senate in 1852. . . .[7]

The Department did agree that landless Indians should be provided with homes and that the poor should get further aid, all administered by the Bureau. (It is rather ironic that the Executive Branch during the 1920s, ostensibly dedicated as it was to "rugged individualism" and economic conservatism should favor the "dole" for Indians and oppose what was essentially a self-help measure. The basis for this opposition would seem to have stemmed from a fear of allowing Indians access to the courts, and a basic hostility towards Native Americans achieving any measure of independence from the Federal bureaucracy.) During the late 1920s, various white organizations began to respond to Indian interest in the matter of land claims. In 1926, for example, the influential Commonwealth Club of San Francisco issued a report on native affairs including a recommendation for Federal legislation allowing for a fair determination of California Indian claims. In 1927 the State legislature authorized the State attorney general to bring suit against the United States on behalf of the Indians, provided that Congress approved authorizing legislation; and in the following year Congress did approve such a measure.

The bill finally approved, originally introduced by Representative Clarence Lea of Lake County, empowered the California attorney general to submit the claims of California Indians to the U. S. Court of Claims "for determination of the equitable amount due said Indians" and recognized the failure to secure the lands and goods guaranteed in the eighteen treaties as "sufficient ground" for the suit. California Indians were defined as those resident in the State on June 1, 1852, and their descendents.

Unfortunately, the bill was weak in several respects. First, the Indians were unable to retain their own counsel and while the use of the California attorney generals saved money, they also were elected partisan officeholders subject to replacement every four years (actually three different men, U. S. Webb, Earl Warren, and Robert Kenney, served while the suit was in court). Second, the bill was amended to preclude any award exceeding $1.25 per acre, awards were to be limited to the value of what was promised in the 1851-1852 treaties, all Federal expenses for California Indians over the years were to be deducted from the award as "off-sets," and the award (if any) was to go to the U. S. Treasury "to the credit of the Indians of California," earning therein 4% annual interest. The award was to be "subject to appropriation by Congress for educational, health, industrial, and other purposes for the benefit of said Indians ... and no part ... shall be paid out in per capita payments. ..."[8]

Thus Congress, in effect, recognized the validity of the cessions of lands made by the California Indians in 1851 and 1852 (about 75 million acres) but did not recognize the validity of the United States' treaty obligations to the natives (about 8 million acres) except in terms of possibly awarding a belated $1.25 per acre with no interest (as it turned out). Quite obviously, if the Indians' cession was valid, the United States' establishment of eighteen reservations was equally valid and the Indians were entitled to recovery of the land, or if not that, at least to its actual value plus damages. Many other inconsistencies were also involved, such as: deducting Federal expenses which often never benefited Indians or which were used for coercive purposes; including in the suit many California Indian groups not a party to the treaties; proposing to use the award monies for future Federal expenses. Clearly, the Congress of 1928 was not in either a generous or a fair mood, but at least some kind of action could commence.

The land claims case was initiated in 1929, but disappointment soon set in as the California Attorney General U. S. Webb awakened to the realization that the Hoover Administration was going to bitterly fight the suit. "To the Department of the Interior [the case] was an uninvited intruder in their domain, inspired by ignorant do-gooders." To the Department of Justice it was "a raid on the treasury."[9] As a result, Webb, in 1932, filed an amended petition which made a stronger case for Indian title, asserting that in 1851 and 1852 the Indians "were the owners and entitled to the use, occupancy, and possession of certain lands ... amounting in all to more than seventy-five million acres. ..." Repeated efforts were also made between 1930 and 1943 to obtain amendments to the 1928 authorization act to make it possible for the Indians to obtain a more generous settlement, but Congress was hostile on each occasion except in 1935 and in that year President Franklin D. Roosevelt vetoed the legislation.

The Interior Department and Executive Branch continued their efforts to see to it that the Indians received next to nothing, first by procrastinating on the matter of computing the "off-sets" and then, finally, in 1934, coming up with a total of $12,500,000 allegedly spent on California Indians in almost one hundred years. This total wiped out more than two-thirds of the value of the properties promised in 1851 and 1852 (figuring the land at $1.25 per acre) and exceeded congressional appropriations for the period (the figure for appropriations was finally reduced to $12,029,099 after the Court of Claims refused to allow deductions for corruption, diversion of funds, etc.).

Webb then adopted delaying tactics in the hope of getting Federal legislation allowing the Indians to receive interest, but this effort was a failure. In 1939 Earl Warren became Attorney General (of California) and the case was reactivated; and finally in 1942 the question of liability was settled.

> The plaintiffs [California Indians] are entitled to recover the value of the land set out and described in the ... treaties ... [and goods promised]. As this claim does not involve a taking of land by the Government for which just compensation shall be made, but only compensation for an equitable claim, no allowance of interest is permitted or allowable.[10]

This was a strange decision indeed, denying "just compensation" and holding that "equitable" did not include interest, but the result should not be too surprising as Indians have not done well in the Federal courts as a general rule. Warren tried to obtain a new trial but was turned down, and in 1943 his successor, Robert Kenney, appealed to the Supreme Court without success.

During 1943 and 1944, Kenney attempted to reach a settlement on the basis of the unsatisfactory rulings of the Court of Claims. In essence, an agreement with the government attorneys secured a settlement of $5,024,842 for the Indians after the "offsets" of $12,029,099 were subtracted from the value of the treaty promises (land, goods, and services) set at $17,053,941. Many Indians were extremely unhappy but Kenney went ahead and made the settlement in December 1944, almost two decades after the case had begun. In 1950, Congress finally adopted legislation providing $150 for each California Indian (leaving a portion of the award still in the U. S. Treasury).

The settlement of the 1928 case was, in effect, a shrewd bargain for the Federal government and another fleecing for Indians. The Indian people had been made to pay for almost a century of Indian Bureau expenses relating to California, including funds spent on forcibly removing natives from their homes and on lining the pockets of crooked officials. Or, from another perspective, the government had obtained about 8 million acres of prime land for a 1950 cash expenditure of about 60¢ per acre coupled with $12 million in previously already paid for "services." But this is not the whole story, because the government had already realized more than enough income from the lands in question to pay for the full settlement given the Indians. Therefore, it can be said that the government quieted the Indians' claim at no expense to itself whatsoever; it may well be that the government actually made a profit (if the 8 million acres were sold to whites for more than $2 per acre or if proceeds from timber sales, leases, etc., are considered).

The settlement of the 1928 thru 1944 case was certainly not "equitable," nor was it legally sound. As to the latter, it should be pointed out that *all* California Indians had subtracted from their award money the value (at $1.25 per acre) of reservations (600,000 acres) set aside for only a part of the California Indian population; that *all* California Indians were to participate in the award money regardless of whether they had any real legal interest in the eighteen treaties of 1851 and 1852; and that each person of California Indian descent was treated as having an equal interest in the award regardless of whether he possessed sixteen Indian ancestors living in 1851-1852, or only one.

One interesting effect of the procedure followed in the case was the apparent transfer of title to some 600,000 acres of established "Executive Order" reservations from the Federal government to the California Indians collectively, or at least to individual reservation groups. No deeds have been issued to Indian people as a result of this case, but it would seem clear that in making the Indians pay $1.25 for each acre of existing reservation land the Federal government made Indian ownership effective. But which Indians? Since the California Indians collectively paid for each and every reservation acre it could be argued that each Indian possesses an interest in each reservation. But the legal confusion created thereby is great indeed, especially since the 600,000 acres paid for included lands already patented to individuals and, often, resold to whites. One could go on . . . but it should be clear that the procedure followed in the 1928-1944 case can be criticized from many viewpoints, and it may well be that future lawsuits will be required to settle the confusion.

The total land claims of California Indians were not settled by the 1928-1944 case since part of the State was not covered by the eighteen treaties and since the payments made under the latter did not really constitute "just compensation" (the total gross award being $17,000,000 in exchange for the cession of some 67,000,000 acres of land).

In 1946, Congress authorized the creation of an Indian Claims Commission with broad powers to deal with any and all of the remaining claims of Indian groups. The Commission procedure was to facilitate claims cases which might never have received separate congressional approval, but cases taken to the Commission could not be appealed and normal constitutional provisions relating to just compensation were bypassed. Many California Indians pressed for a new case which would settle all of the remaining claims, and such a case was initiated in 1947 with private attorneys.

The details of this case are in many respects similar to that of 1928-1944 except that about 60 million acres were involved. After sixteen years of litigation the various attorneys agreed to a value of 47¢ per acre ($29,100,000) and, in a series of meetings held in 1963 and 1964, people of California Indian descent voted 11,427 to 3,310 to accept the settlement. In May 1965 the Commission made the settlement final, although the per capita distribution of the award still had to await congressional legislation and a new census to determine all who were eligible.

The Indian Claims Commission case suffers from many of the same legal and procedural liabilities as did the 1928-1944 case and, in addition, raises questions about the constitutionality of this entire approach to the settlement of native land claims. Suffice to state that the Indians were never afforded Fifth Amendment protections nor, specifically, did they possess the option of securing title to any of the claimed land. The Federal government, in effect, acquired a clear title to millions of acres of so-called public land for 47¢ per acre in what amounted to a "forced sale." As to the "generosity" of the government, one should note that California's national forests grossed $36,336,621 in timber sales for the Federal government during fiscal 1968 alone.

The procedure followed in the California claims case has also served to deepen factions among Indians in that state, since many natives have been very unhappy with either the amount of compensation or the failure to allow them to have the option of obtaining land instead of dollars. Those Indians desiring to retain a portion of their ancient territory will receive about $800 as payment for about 1600 acres, but with that $800 they cannot purchase even one acre of good land. In addition, many Indians believe that they were not dealt with fairly by their attorneys, that the voting at meetings was irregular, and that persons with small amounts of Indian ancestry and of non-Indian self-identity should not have been allowed to influence the outcome of the case. It should also be noted that individual groups which might have voted against the settlement had no separate voice but were simply part of a collective "California Indian" vote.

On the other hand, many Indians are pleased that at least some additional compensation will be available and look forward to future litigation to settle for the value of losses in mineral rights, timber, and other kinds of property.

Other native groups in the Far West have become involved in their own cases before the Indian Claims Commission, including groups which extend partially into California. The Washo, Northern Paiute, Western Shoshone, Southern Paiute, and Colorado River cases are all in various stages of development and all closely resemble the unified California case in general character. Resistance to the entire concept of seeking compensation for land before the Commission is greater than in California, however, especially among the Western Shoshone people. Many, perhaps a majority, of the Shoshone are opposed to the "sale" of land which they regard as being rightfully theirs, or as belonging to the Creator. But "their case" still grinds on towards a cash settlement because the government needs only to obtain authorization from one reservation council to engage attorneys for the entire "people" (however defined), and because no other option is available in practical terms (primarily due to the extra-constitutional position of Indians).

Very little compensation has been thus far received by western Indians and when it does come it will often come in a manner unacceptable to many Indians, the authorizing legislation being ordinarily drawn up by non-Indian Federal officials, attorneys, and congressmen. (Incredibly, the BIA drew up a proposed bill in the Northern Paiute case and had it submitted in Congress prior to any discussion with Indians. A comparable development occurred in 1967 and 1968 in relation to the California case.) On the other hand, many Indians will feel proud that at least' some token payment has been forced from a reluctant government and that the cases, although imperfect, can represent something of a moral victory for the natives.

Interestingly, the years of litigation and expected awards have led to many changes in native life, including: attendance at numerous meetings, the development of many new organizations, the acquisition of some degree of knowledge about legal procedures, the appearance of "Claims Case Indians" (people who never had identified themselves as being of Indian descent until the prospect of money arose), and the reinforcement of extreme suspicion of the government on the part of those opposed to the cases. Finally, many Indians have been forced by the cumbersome nature of the litigation to devote time to the claims controversies which might better have been spent on other matters.

Indian people have also continued to be involved in defensive struggles to protect their land and wealth throughout the last forty years. For instance, the Owens Valley [Indian] Board of Trustees in 1958 adopted the following resolution:

> We should also like to have the 66,620 acres of land known as the Paiute Indian Reservation... be opened to use by the Paiute Indians as grazing land and that they be reimbursed for all grazing fees, mining royalties and the like received by the federal government since 1910 plus interest on this property. This land was paid for at $1.25 per acre out of the money received by the Indians of California [in the 1928-1944 claims case]. The land obviously is the property of the Mono and Inyo County Paiute Indians... although they have been denied the right to use it.

An incredible series of correspondence followed, between Leonard Hill, BIA director for California, and State Senator Charles Brown, in which Hill made it very clear that his office intended to make no effort to restore the 66,000 acres to the Paiutes and that he was inclined to be opposed to seeking more land for Indians. In a letter of November 24, 1958, Hill stated,

> It is the policy of the bureau in California to conform to the mandate of Congress as expressed in House Concurrent Resolution No. 108 passed July 27, 1953. This resolution states: "That it is declared to be the sense of Congress that at the earliest possible time, all of the Indian tribes and individual members thereof located within the States of... California... should be freed from federal

supervision and control from all disabilities and limitations especially applicable to Indians...." Aside from keeping the Indians informed of the availability of public domain land which may be allotted under existing authority [none was available], we see no particular remedy for the plight of the Mono Basin Indians.[11]

Clearly then, the California BIA intended to use the 1953 "termination" resolution (to be discussed below) as an excuse for continuing what had long been Bureau practice, that is, to refuse to protect or to work for the interests of California Indians when those interests clashed with white interests (as in this case, with the City of Los Angeles). It should be noted that the 1953 joint congressional resolution was without the force of law, being merely the expression of the desires of a particular Congress and not being binding upon any subsequent Congress. As shall be noted below, however, such resolutions have been transformed into "administrative law" by the California BIA.

Another example of the continuing struggle for land relates to the repeated efforts of the Pyramid Lake Paiute Tribe to obtain the removal of illegal white squatters from their reservation, to obtain their share of Truckee River water, and to preserve the existence of Pyramid Lake itself. In 1938, the Indians commenced legal proceedings to recover their lands from the squatters in the face of repeated efforts by anti-Indian U. S. Senator Pat McCarran of Nevada to persuade Congress to give the whites title to the disputed land. In 1944, the Supreme Court finally ruled in favor of the Northern Paiutes, but it was still necessary to evict the squatters and that required another seven years. The whites, with the aid of Senator McCarran, resisted every step of the way, finally blocking the use of irrigation ditches needed to make the recovered lands usable. The Bureau had aided the Indians through 1949, but, by 1951, the reactionary policies of Commissioner Dillon Myer and Interior Secretary Oscar Chapman put them on Senator McCarran's side. The government attempted to prevent the tribe from retaining its private attorneys while McCarran did everything possible to prevent the Indians from developing their lands.

Many Indian organizations came to the aid of the Pyramid Lake Paiute Tribe and the battle over their right to hire their own attorneys was largely won. The water problem has not, however, been resolved to this day since white farmers continue to drain water away from the Truckee River which should be going into the reservation. A new water scheme, the Washoe Project, currently threatens the very existence of Pyramid Lake, the major future economic resource of the tribe. Court decisions have been won by the Paiutes but the continuing urban growth of the Lake Tahoe and Reno-Sparks areas is certain to drastically interfere with Truckee River flows.

Indians have also had to struggle to protect their lands from termination and from such Federal and state projects as flood-control dams. Current plans of the Army Corps of Engineers envision the flooding of the Round Valley Reservation in California, while numerous reserves have been flooded in other parts of the country. Unfortunately, the Indian people have not been in a position to resist the power of Federal agencies in most such instances. The allotment system, although in moth balls from the early 1930s to 1950, has also continued to erode the native land base since lands patented to individual Indians have usually passed to white ownership. Today, the best areas of many reservations are in the hands of non-Indians.

The Struggle Against Discrimination and Poverty

In 1920 the census counted 17,360 Indians in California and 4907 in Nevada, while the Bureau of Indian Affairs reported 16,241 in California and 5900 in Nevada. A special 1928 count of California Indians eligible for possible claims awards enumerated 23,542 persons of full or partial California native descent, although the 1930 census identified only 19,212. It would appear, therefore, that at least 4000 persons of California Indian descent were "passing" as Caucasians or as Mexican-Americans by the latter year. By 1950 at least 17,000 persons of California Indian ancestry were not counted by the census as Indians, and 36,094 persons were enrolled with the Bureau as being of California Indian descent.

A 1926 Bureau report identified 18,913 California Indians of whom only 8197 were "full-bloods," while 4149 were one-half or more of native descent, 3844 were of less than half native descent, and 2723 were unclassified "Mission Indians." Nevada possessed

5692 Indians including 3434 "full-bloods," 702 one-half or more Indian, and 286 less than half Indian. By 1931 less than one-half of California Indians were enrolled with the Bureau (10,490 of some 24,000) and 1841 of these were not residing on trust land. During the 1950s and 1960s estimates indicate that only 8000 to 9000 persons, or less, have resided on trust land, with perhaps 32,000 other California Indian individuals living elsewhere. It is clear that in California Native Americans receiving Federal assistance have declined in number while the overall population has increased, and it is also clear that intermixture with non-Indians has proceeded fairly rapidly. In Nevada, on the other hand, intermixture has proceeded more slowly and a larger proportion of Indians has remained on trust land—4362 of 5700 in 1927 and 4200 of 6700 in 1960, although the latter relationship may be invalid since 1964-1965 estimates placed the actual Nevada Indian population at 8525 to 9385. By 1960 only about 2500 Nevada Indians, out of more than 7000 individuals, were residing on those reservations with meaningful agricultural potential.

California and Nevada Indians have ordinarily been the victims of poverty and discrimination, both induced, tragically, largely through the actions of the Federal government and other white agencies. The period since the 1920s has unfortunately witnessed only a very gradual and, in some cases, negligible change in Indian material conditions of life. California and Nevada Indians have been continuously victimized by a Federal policy which has not only been hostile in the sense of seeking to acquire native land, suppress native culture and rigidly control native affairs, but also in the sense of positively discriminating against California-Nevada groups within the context of Federal Indian programs. The Federal government has tended to "short-change" the small tribes and groups of the Far West in relation to the range of services made available to the larger tribes found elsewhere. In great measure this continuing pattern of discrimination stems from the earlier failure to establish large, viable reserves for most Indians of the Far West.

During the 1950s and 1960s, discrimination against California Indians in particular was greatly accelerated by the so-called termination policy referred to earlier. For many years a group of basically anti-Indian congressmen had sought to abolish the reforms of the 1930s, and to carry the Dawes Allotment concept to its logical conclusion. They sought, in other words, to abolish tribes as corporate entities, to divide up all tribal assets among individuals, to sell those assets not so divisible, and to expose the land transferred to individuals to local taxation. The results of such a program had long been made clear by the operation of the Dawes system. Indian property would rapidly be dissipated by sale to whites, and no tribal organizations would exist to either protect native interests or to engage in corporate-level economic development projects. Without a doubt many of the groups pushing for a renewal of the Dawes program desired the above results, since congressmen from states with powerful [white] timber, mining, and stock-raising interests have been rather prominent in the movement.

During the 1950s a reactionary trend both within the Bureau of Indian Affairs and in Congress made it possible for the Dawes program, now called simply "termination," to be successfully pushed. In 1953, P.L. 280 and House Concurrent Resolution 108 initiated the process. P.L. 280 transferred many powers (over law and order, for example) to state jurisdiction without, however, sufficient clarity of language to ensure a smooth transition. H.C.R. 108, already quoted above, called for the termination of California Indians and required the Secretary of the Interior to produce a bill by January 1, 1954, designed to accomplish that purpose.

The BIA produced a series of bills which were totally unsatisfactory, not merely from the native viewpoint but from the perspective of the State of California. Basically, California Indian communities were to be cut off abruptly from Federal services with their state of poverty and under-development left "as is." The California Legislature had endorsed the idea of termination in 1953, but during 1954 made an abrupt change, largely as a result of the hearings conducted by the State Senate Interim Committee on Indian Affairs. The Committee found that most reservations were simply unprepared for termination, with a multitude of problems often including undefined boundaries, no roads, no water, no sanitation, substandard housing, and 2600 complicated heirship cases. The State was unwilling to accept the financial responsibility for correcting the failures of Bureau management and opposed the BIA's termination legislation.

Many California Indians fought against termination also,

including groups such as the Council of California Indians, the California Indians' Congress, and the Federated Indians of California, Inc. Only one group, James Martinez's Mission Indian Federation of California, completely favored the 1954 termination bills. The combined opposition of Indians, of such groups as the American Friends Service Committee, and the State of California, led to the defeat of the 1954 legislation.

In 1957 and 1958 the State Senate Interim Committee conducted another investigation and found that "with minor exceptions ... very little has been done to carry out the recommendations set forth in the [1954-1955] report" to prepare Indian reserves for termination. In spite of that fact, in 1957 the Committee recommended termination legislation which, by its nature, reveals that their opposition to the 1954 bills was not based upon any pro-Indian bias.

Briefly, the Committee's proposed bill would: 1) close tribal membership rolls so as to even exclude future-born children; 2) allow an Indian individual to initiate court proceedings to divide up tribal property; 3) require each tribe or the Secretary of the Interior to draw up a plan for the "distribution and disposal" of much reservation property; 4) require the Secretary of the Interior to draw up a plan for the "distribution and disposal" of the balance of reservation property, with the lands being divided or sold; 5) allow for a referendum on the plans but give the Secretary of the Interior authority to override any adverse vote *unless Congress takes specific action to halt him*; 6) authorize the Secretary (at his discretion presumably) to help provide training for Indians; and 7) revoke all tribal constitutions and corporate charters after the above process has occurred.

This plan was incorporated in several bills, one of which, H.R. #2824, was passed into law as P.L. 85-671 on August 18, 1958, and was made applicable to 44 rancherias in California, exempting (temporarily, at least) the larger reservations.

The California termination plan was neither necessary, just, nor wise. If the legislators were sincerely concerned about freeing Indians from the control of the Indian Bureau, that could have easily been accomplished by sponsoring an Indian-controlled non-profit corporation, or corporations, which could have contracted with the Federal government for carrying out the service functions of the Bureau. Numerous examples of Federal contracting with white non-profit (and profit-seeking) corporations existed as readily applicable precedents.

The termination legislation as proposed and adopted was quite obviously designed to destroy Indian communities, render economic development impossible, and place Indian individuals at a competitive disadvantage with whites. Let us examine this thesis further.

First, the only feasible units available for Indian economic development, the tribal corporations, were to be abolished by fiat, without a vote of the members. This would be comparable to the forced dissolution of a white corporation or, more accurately, of a white non-profit municipal corporation. Second, the internal affairs of tribal corporations were to be transferred, in fact, to the Secretary of the Interior and Congress for the transitional period and those organizations were to be prevented from controlling their own membership rolls. Third, Indians were to be completely individualized. All reservation property was to be either sold or divided into individual parcels, with none being held in corporate ownership. This is especially ironic in a state such as California where agriculture and the timber industry are overwhelmingly corporate in character. How were Indian individual owners of a few acres of timber, farmland or grazing land to compete with white corporations? Fourth, Indians with virtually no cash income (many were unemployed and on local welfare) could not be expected to do anything but sell or lease their individual parcels.

It should also be pointed out that the California termination plan was developed in a completely elitist manner by whites who did not involve Indians in any of the major decision-making steps, whether at the Bureau, Congressional, or State level. In this respect, as in others, the enactment of the 1958 legislation revealed the same tendency towards a decidedly anti-democratic procedure in so far as Indians are concerned as had the Dawes Act of 1887, the Cherokee Removal of 1838, and many other nineteenth-century actions.

The termination philosophy of the 1950s embodied the incredible stance of putting people "on their own" who had been robbed of their wealth, denigrated for years, neglected in terms of essential economic and educational development, and subjected to the stultifying experience of decades of bureaucratic manipulation without returning any appreciable quantity of their former wealth and without taking a single meaningful step to ensure their ability to compete in a complex society dominated by their former oppressors. Finally, the termination philosophy, in its high-handed and presumptuous assumption of the right to destroy Indian tribal organizations and native community life, could be said to have posed a potential threat to all forms of local group self-direction in the United States. Perhaps it is indeed far-fetched, but it is nonetheless conceivable that one day coercive programs directed against whites might be justified by the precedent established by the treatment of Indians.

In any event, the Bureau of Indian Affairs' Sacramento office moved forward vigorously to high-pressure as many rancherias as possible into being terminated, without, however, fully informing the natives of other alternatives and without providing essential services needed for an orderly transition. More significantly still, on the basis of a mere concurrent resolution of a single Congress, the BIA commenced the termination of services to virtually *all* California Indians, whether included in the 1958 legislation or not. By administrative fiat only, the Bureau withdrew college scholarships, vocational education, economic development programs, water and sanitation development projects, etc., from California Indians while still offering these services to Indians elsewhere. The Public Health Service likewise eliminated medical services for most Indians in California, while the BIA persuaded the State of California into acquiescing in the cutting off of Johnson-O'Malley funds (designated to subsidize public schools serving Indian pupils living on tax-exempt land).

This extremely discriminatory and short-sighted policy was resisted by a few Indians but they lacked any influential allies until the Indian Services Division of California Rural Legal Assistance, Inc. (an OEO-funded agency) began to call attention to what was taking place. In August, 1967, the CRLA pointed out,

> the government seems to have pursued this policy [of termination] almost fanatically, in a blind rush to cut the Indians loose from its protection and benefits, no matter how harsh the effects on them. ... Still the federal government continues to pursue the termination policy

indiscriminately and relentlessly, inducing the Indians to terminate by unfulfilled promises and in proceedings shot through with legal irregularity.[12]

CRLA staff repeatedly badgered the Sacramento BIA office with evidence of irregularities and made it clear that HCR 108 lacked any validity. The Ad Hoc Committee on California Indian Education, a new all-Indian group, also called for the restoration of Johnson-O'Malley funds and, together, CRLA and the Ad Hoc Committee succeeded in getting congressional pressure placed upon the Bureau.

Finally, in June 1968 Commissioner Robert L. Bennett announced that he had ordered the restoration of certain services to California Indians, including the right to attend BIA vocational-special schools and to receive college scholarships. A few months earlier Leonard Hill was replaced as Director of the Sacramento BIA office, thus presumably preparing the way for a policy reversal. The "latest word" is that termination is "dead" as a policy (not merely because of what happened in California, but due to the sad experiences of the Menominee, Klamath, and other terminated groups), but it is highly unlikely that such a continually popular approach to liquidating Indians can be buried as long as whites control Indian affairs.

Nevada Indians were also specifically threatened with termination when a bill was introduced in Congress in 1954 which would have cut-off services from eight groups in the State. On April 16, 1954, hearings were held in Reno, Nevada, where many Indian representatives testified that they were not ready for termination without the solution of many specific problems. The Nevada bill was not as bad as those of California since it at least provided for the option of corporate ownership of property, but it otherwise was similar to the previously discussed legislation. The bill was defeated.

California Indian Legal Services, which grew out of California Rural Legal Assistance in 1968, led the legal battle to halt termination and to make the BIA responsive in terms of such things as the management of reservation financial reserves, leasing of lands, and granting of right-of-ways. By the late 1970s CILS had repeatedly defeated the Bureau in court and had not only halted termination but had begun to make progress towards restoring some lands to trust status. On the other hand, CILS was placed under the national Legal Services Corporation in the mid-1970s and, due to new restrictions and a less imaginative staff, it began to be less effective. The Bureau, in turn, has dug in its heels to resist change as much as possible.

Little in the way or economic development occurred until about 1972 on California or Nevada reservations, although in the latter case OEO money had recently facilitated some advancement. It is most depressing indeed to read the 1966 report of the California Advisory Commission on Indian Affairs or the various reports of California Rural Legal Assistance and to realize that very little was done to improve conditions on most California reservations since the 1958-1959, 1954-1955, and 1919 reports referred to earlier. The quality of life of Indian people has improved since the early 'seventies, but such changes have come about more because of individual, off-reservation employment than because of on-reservation development, except at a few places.

Sadly, gross mismanagement and corruption have typified certain reservations and, under the "watchful" eye of the BIA, millions of dollars have been squandered. One would wish it were not so, but tribal politics can be as venal (and as vicious) as those of Chicago or Manhattan. The Indian Bureau usually does very little to halt reservation corruption.

California and Nevada Indians have also continued to suffer from many of the same kinds of discrimination experienced by other poor, non-white groups. The most blatant forms of racism would appear to have largely disappeared, but many Indians have experienced police brutality, hostile justice courts, discriminatory landlords, and prejudiced employers. Additionally, of course, Indian people suffer daily from the anti-Indian or stereotypical nature of television "westerns," and from the general pro-white bias of the communication media and advertising.

In 1960, California Indians constituted that portion of the California population with the lowest income and highest unemployment rates. Indian males, on a statewide basis, possessed a median income of $2694 (as compared with $3553 for blacks and over $5000 for whites), while 13.4% of males over the age of 25 earned less than $1000, 31.6% earned less than $2000, 45.2% earned less than $3000, and 74.8% earned less than $5000. Thus at least one-half of California Indians were below the "poverty-level" statistically, although this is an underestimate because Indian families were much larger than the average (25.4% were composed of seven or more persons as compared with 12.9% for all non-whites and 4.9% for whites). "Rural Farm" (i.e., reservation) Indian males had a median income of $1769 (as compared with $3298 for whites). Statewide Indian unemployment in 1960 was 15.1% for males (as compared with 12.7% for blacks and less than 5% for whites), while unemployment was even higher in rural areas as in the Trinity-Klamath region (21.7% for males).[13]

Nevada Indians also suffered from high unemployment and low income rates in 1960. Unemployment for non-white males in Nevada was reported at 10.1% (as compared with 5.9% for whites), while Indian rates stood at 8.2% in Elko County, 12.1% in Ormsby County, and (with blacks) at 13.2% in Washoe County. The median income for non-white males was $3184 ($4903 for all males), while 19% of non-white families or single individuals received less than $1000, 32% received less than $2000, and 45% received less than $3000 (as opposed to 24.5% for whites).[14]

In recent years new problems have arisen due to the fact that sizeable numbers of California and Nevada Indians have migrated to urban areas. More significant still has been the almost-forced migration of tens of thousands of out-of-state Indians into the San Francisco–San Jose and Los Angeles areas, thanks to a modern "trail of tears" known as the Relocation Program. Relocation was commenced during the reactionary period of the 1950s as a device for reducing population on overcrowded reservations, as a partial substitute for an unwillingness to spend money for on-reservation development, as a means to encourage "assimilation," and as a means for improving the income of individual Indians. The program was highly praised and severely criticized but, in any event, it had the effect of contributing heavily to the growth of urban Indian populations and made many natives into commuters between reservations and cities. Since the formal relocation program was halted, Indian migration has continued, largely due to poverty and unemployment, in Arizona, New Mexico, and other states. Many of the newer migrants, like the relocatees of old, give up and return home, while still others move back and forth. Nonetheless, conditions are now much improved in the cities, especially when compared with the 1950s.

There is no question that it was a traumatic experience for rural, tribally-oriented people to be moved to the heart of modern metropolises, especially when the counseling afforded the relocatees was marginal at best. In the 1950s and 1960s the relocatee was placed in a job (any job, literally) after, perhaps, some brief training (which may or may not have been related to his first job) and for a few weeks he received minimal financial assistance. Thereafter, he or she was on their own in a strange city and, not surprisingly, a high proportion ended up on "skid row" or as local welfare recipients. (In many respects it can be said that the BIA is contributing directly to the increased welfare expenses of our urban complexes.) Innumerable personal tragedies occurred, hidden beneath a mountain of statistics relating the number of initial jobs which had been secured, etc.

On the other hand, many relocatees were able to gradually adjust to the city, thanks in great measure to another new phenomenon, the appearance of urban "Indian centers" and "friendship houses." Whatever fellowship was to be found (aside from the many bars catering principally to Indians), whatever counseling was to be secured, whatever social life was available, was usually in association with one of these Indian centers or with the clubs which grew out of them. These valuable organizations, so essential to whatever success the relocation program had, received no support from the BIA and little from any Federal agencies until the Nixon Administration of 1968-1972 began seriously to provide aid for urban Indians. Nonetheless, it has been beneficial that most Indian centers started with purely local support because it has allowed most such groups to remain relatively independent and under local Indian control.

Joining the relocatees during and after World War II were thousands of self-relocated Indians, individuals driven from places like Oklahoma by racism or from other areas by lack of economic or educational opportunity. In general, the self-relocated Native Americans appear to have made a better adjustment to urban life in spite of having to obtain their own first jobs, pay their own travel expenses and obtain their own housing.

Together these various groups have created a new kind of Indian life, not completely pan-Indian (because tribal clubs and frequent trips "home" maintain a certain degree of tribal exclusiveness) but nonetheless something of an amalgamation. More significantly, the BIA may well have miscalculated if "assimilation" and "getting rid of the Indian problem" were its goals in fostering urbanization. Not only do the various clubs and centers preserve and even expand upon the Indian heritage, but the urban Indian has become politically militant and sophisticated. It is certainly true that urban-trained Indians have helped to awaken their rural relatives and have succeeded in greatly changing the nature of native politics. Since the 1970s, however, many reservation Indians have become fully as militant as urban ones.

Significantly, as of the 1960s, only (at most) 9000 Indians resided on reservations in California, less than 40,000 resided in smaller cities and rural areas, while at least 50,000 lived in metropolitan zones. A sizeable proportion of Nevada Indians now reside in the Reno-Sparks and Carson City area. The Indian population of California as of the early 1980s is estimated at as high as 250,000, with the great majority living in urbanized regions.

Mention should also be made of the urban Indian health centers and Indian education projects (and their rural counterparts) which, together, have helped greatly to improve the quality of life in California and, to a lesser degree, in parts of Nevada. These programs received initial funding during the Nixon years, although some started during the Johnson Administration as "War on Poverty" projects.

The Struggle for a Better Education

Between the 1920s and early 1940s the Bureau of Indian Affairs ceased to have any appreciable role in California-Nevada Indian education, thanks in great measure to Indian efforts to establish local public schools or to gain admittance to existing schools. This latter was facilitated by the case of Piper v. Big Pine School District (1924) in which Indians won the right to attend public schools.

Unfortunately, the public school movement failed to yield the results anticipated by the more optimistic, especially where the schools were controlled by white individuals basically hostile towards the Indian heritage and prejudiced against native pupils.

Prior to World War II it was rare indeed for an Indian to graduate from high school in California and a high school education was simply not available to many Nevada Indians living in highly anti-Indian areas such as Douglas County. It was not until the 1920s that Nevada Indians were able to receive a high school education and then, in a real sense, only at Carson City High School. In 1926 there were no Nevada Indians enrolled above grade nine at any Federal school.

A college education was simply beyond the realm of possibility for California and Nevada Indians before World War II and the number of college graduates from that period can be literally counted on one hand.

The post-war period witnessed some improvement, but not due to change in the schools. Anti-Indian personal prejudice did decline, but basically the public schools, now increasingly under white control, retained the same mono-cultural Anglo-American curricula as in earlier years. History was white history, literature was Anglo or European literature, music was in the European tradition, art was Anglo-European, cooking was white cooking, sewing was white sewing, crafts were white crafts, and so on. Needless to state, no effort was made (and little is being done now) to teach any California or Nevada Indian language in any school below the college level. English language instruction was almost always designed for the pupil from a middle-class English-speaking home.

In spite of these handicaps, far western Indian pupils, stimulated by the pressure of exceptional parents or teachers, began to graduate from high school in larger numbers after World War II and this, in turn, made it possible for college graduates to number about two score and college students to number in the dozens by 1968.

The majority of Indians have not, however, been able to advance beyond the upper years of high school on the average, and in some areas few still advance beyond the junior high school level. In 1957, a field worker for the American Friends Service Committee in northern California reported:

The drop-outs of Indian students appear to be generally high in those counties in which Indians form a sizeable proportion of the county population.... Drop-outs do not seem to occur on an unusual level in the elementary schools but begin to develop as students go on up through the high school. Very few Indian students go on to commercial, vocational, or college training.... As examples, of approximately 100 Indian students who entered Ukiah Union High School in the five years ending in 1952 only two were graduated.... In Round Valley one elementary school is entirely Indian, the white parents of that district do not allow their children to attend this school and recent attempts to unify with the adjacent white school have met with defeat on the basis of the racial issue.[15]

The 1960 census revealed that 43.3% of the Indians in California aged 14 years and older had not gone beyond the eighth grade (as compared with 25% for whites and 36% for blacks), that only 56.7% had completed one or more years of high school, that only 7.6% of males had completed one or more years of college (as compared with 12.7% for blacks, and over 25% for whites), and that only 1.8% of males had completed four or more years of college (as compared with 5.5% for all non-whites and 10.7% for whites). The median school years completed for all Indian males in California was 9.7 (as compared with 10.6 for non-whites and 11.7 for the total population). The rural median was, however, much lower (probably 8.9 or less) while the urban median was about 10.6 (as compared with 10.7 for non-whites and 12.0 for the total population).[16]

Indians would appear to have been receiving two years less schooling than the California population as a whole in 1960, and probably two and one-half years less than the white population. Still further, Indians and Mexican-Americans were at the bottom of the educational ladder among minorities, with the Mexican-Americans pulling ahead of Indians at the college level. The 1966 report of the State Advisory Commission on Indian Affairs summarized conditions by stating that

> few Indian students finish high school, few attend college, and many who have graduated from high school receive an inferior education because of a lack of teacher concern or the failure of the school system to devise compensatory teaching techniques to cope with students of differing cultural backgrounds.[17]

Educational conditions in Nevada were, if anything, more severe than those of California. The median school years completed for Indians twenty-five and older in Elko County stood in 1966 at 7.9 years and for all non-whites in Nevada at 8.8 years (as compared with 12.2 for whites). Almost 17% of the adult Indians had never been to school (compared with 0.7% of whites). Approximately 1.7% of Indian adults possessed four years of post-high-school educational experience (as compared with 8.7% of Nevada whites).[18]

This disappointing state of affairs convinced many Indians and non-Indians that the educational programs of the schools serving Indian pupils had to be radically altered and that Indian people themselves had to become meaningfully involved in educational issues. Both white-controlled segregated schools (the BIA schools) and white-controlled integrated schools (the public schools) had apparently failed. Thus many Indians began to look back towards the successful Indian-controlled schools of the past, especially those operated by the Cherokees and Choctaws.

In 1964, the American Indian Historical Society, founded in San Francisco by Mr. and Mrs. Rupert Costo, began publishing *The Indian Historian* along with special research reports. The Costos for a number of years also published *Wassaja* as a regular national newspaper. The AIHS was especially concerned with bringing an Indian viewpoint to bear upon historical writing, but it also became concerned with many related issues including the white biases of school textbooks and the non-Indian orientation of school curricula. During the fall of 1966 the Historical Society, with a grant from the Rosenberg Foundation, conducted workshops for teachers at Beaumont, Hoopa, Fresno, Berkeley, and San Francisco. The Society also launched an Indian historical, artistic, and cultural center in San Francisco, called Chautauqua House, and successfully fought for the removal of an anti-Indian text used in the Oakland schools. More recently, *The Indian Historian* has been transformed into a valuable professional-quality journal contributing to the enrichment of contemporary knowledge about Indian history and culture, while society members have continued to work for the improvement of school programs.

Another development contributing directly to increased Indian involvement in education grew out of a Conference for Teachers of California Indian Pupils held at Stanislaus State College in March

1967. The conference, funded by a grant from the legislature, brought together several dozen teachers, administrators and Indian adults. The latter, not being willing to see the conference become merely another discussion session, organized themselves into the Ad Hoc Committee on California Indian Education with the purposes of seeing that the recommendations of the conference conformed to Indian viewpoints and that a major statewide all-Indian meeting on education would be held.

The report issued as a result of the Stanislaus Conference contained many useful recommendations, including ones favoring increased Indian involvement in education, the convening of an Indian education conference, and calling for the development of California Indian-oriented courses for teachers and Indians in the universities and colleges of the State. But the Stanislaus report was not comprehensive, nor did it have the backing of a large enough group of Indians to make it a truly powerful tool for bringing about change.

During 1967, the Ad Hoc Committee, under the chairmanship of David Risling, Jr. (Hoopa), proceeded to hold numerous regional meetings designed to involve large numbers of Indians in an educational movement and to prepare for a statewide conference. The latter, with the help of the Rosenberg Foundation, was held in October 1967 at North Fork, California.

The North Fork Conference brought together about 200 Indians who thoroughly analyzed the problems involved in Indian education. The conference proceedings, including numerous specific recommendations, were then edited and published as *California Indian Education: the Report of the All-Indian Statewide Conference*. This represented an extremely significant step forward since the North Fork Conference was the first all-Indian, Indian-controlled conference on education ever held anywhere in the United States and *California Indian Education* is the first comprehensive statement dealing with education ever prepared by a large and representative group of Indian people.

Basically, the North Fork Conference called for increased Indian involvement at all levels of the educational process. It especially emphasized the role of the Indian family and community in the education of children, and it advocated the development of Indian-directed out-of-school educational projects. Stress was placed upon the value of the native heritage and the schools were called upon to transform their curricula so as to ensure than an Indian element existed in all aspects of the school's program.

The North Fork Conference also called for the restoration of Johnson-O'Malley funds (with the proviso that they be used to advance the quality of Indian education under the direction of a panel of Indians), for Indian participation in the control of BIA schools, for the development of Indian-oriented higher education programs, and for Indian membership on the State Advisory Commission on Indian Affairs. During 1968, the Ad Hoc Committee continued its activities, sponsoring successful conferences in Hoopa, Oakland and elsewhere, and making strong efforts to implement the recommendations of the North Fork Conference.

Under the leadership of David Risling, Jr., the Ad Hoc Committee became the California Indian Education Association, a national leader in grassroots organizing. During 1969, powerful right-wing State Senator John Harmer took over the chairmanship of the State Advisory Commission on Indian Affairs. Harmer attempted to strong-arm the changes that Senator Coombs had failed to get in 1968, but the CIEA, California Indian Legal Services, and UNA combined to defeat the plan. More significantly still, the CIEA and various student groups succeeded in the establishment of beginning programs in Native American Studies on several university and state college campuses. Some have since fallen victim to the "backlash," but those at Davis, UCLA, Berkeley, and several other places remain active.

In 1970 and 1971, the dream of an Indian university was finally brought closer to reality when CIEA leaders, Indian and Chicano students, and community people established D-Q University at a surplus Army communications center site near Davis, California. The Federal government had planned to illegally award the land to the University of California, but the DQU board went to court and the younger people went "over the fence" (to occupy the site). The Nixon Administration eventually awarded the land to the Indians.

The acquisition of the 650-acre DQU site was a great victory for Indian people in California. On the other hand, the new college has always had a difficult time obtaining enough financial support. But thanks to the leadership of California's David Risling, Jr., the school has weathered all crises and has notably enriched the Indian community in the region.

California Indian people can also be proud of the fact that the CIEA and Risling have led the Native world nationally since 1969 and have been key elements in virtually every new development, including the establishment of the National Indian Education Association, the passage of the Indian Education Act and the establishment of the National Advisory Council on Indian Education (with Risling appointed a member first by Nixon and later reappointed by President Gerald Ford), the establishment of the American Indian Higher Education Consortium, the development of the Coalition of Indian Controlled Schools, the implementation of Federal funding for tribally-controlled colleges in 1980, and the founding of the Native American Rights Fund (patterned after the CILS which Risling chaired for several years).

It is worthy of note that California Indians have led the way in almost every major innovation since the 1960s, with only Minnesota as a possible "rival" for progressive developments. (Washington State native peoples would probably place third, although the Pueblos of New Mexico and the Navahos have become very active since the early 1970s.)   .

Nevada, with its smaller population and more conservative political environment, has not witnessed as many changes. Nonetheless, the Inter-Tribal Council, the Walker River Paiute Tribe (under Chairman Ed Johnson), and many organizations have published books, sponsored conferences, developed community centers, established programs for elders, and made some inroads in terms of changing the public schools. Especially noteworthy is the continuing struggle of the Western Shoshone traditionalists to regain their land. Now, with the threat of the "M-X missile" system, the Shoshone land claim is assuming even greater significance.

Successes and Failures

The general conditions of California and Nevada Indian people have greatly improved since the "awakening" of the Sixties. One has only to contrast the "California Indian Days" celebration held annually at Cal Expo in Sacramento with conditions in 1967 to realize the degree to which opportunities have mushroomed. Nonetheless, many severe problems persist, especially in relation to these key issues: 1) almost no land has been restored, and the future of the tribes as social and economic entities is still in jeopardy; 2) racial prejudice still persists, especially in rural areas, along with job discrimination; 3) many schools are still indifferent to multicultural programming; 4) a relatively small middle class has benefited primarily from the changes made; 5) still very few Indians are graduating from high school and college (although more than before 1967); 6) many Indian cemeteries and sacred places are still being destroyed or desecrated; and 7) Indians still cannot obtain election to public office or major state-level appointments.

Conditions are, in general, typified by the status of the Native American Heritage Commission (recently created in California). The Commission's establishment represented a victory for Indian people in that it obtained the power to protect sacred places on State lands. Unfortunately, however, most cemeteries and old village sites are on private and Federal land and are still unprotected.

It seems that Indian people can only go so far. Whenever Indian interests clash with those of powerful non-Indian corporations or agencies, the reforms are brought to a halt. The great question of the 1980s is whether further gains can be made, gains that will have to be won from legislators whose elections depend upon financial contributions from powerful corporate interests or whose districts are influenced by Department of Defense spending.

The true testing period of "the Indian awakening" is still to come!

V. BASIC CONCEPTS FOR UNDERSTAND-ING NATIVE HISTORY AND CULTURE

Who Is An Indian?

The term "Indian" or "Indio" is, of course, an unfortunate result of the early Spaniards confusing the Americas with India. The Native American people, the persons residing in the Americas when Columbus arrived, possessed no universal or even widespread name for themselves as a group since they knew of no other kind of people to contrast themselves with. The name "Indian" has come to be used by natives themselves, although quite often Native Americans have been also called simply Americans (during the colonial era), *indigenas* (indigenes or aboriginies), *naturales* (natives), etc.

But regardless of the name, who is an Indian or Native American today? There is no clear answer to this question, since different people apply different definitions. Generally, however, most definitions rest either upon a "cultural" or a "racial" basis, with the former being used most widely in Latin America and the latter in Anglo-America. For example, in Mexico most people are very proud of being of indigenous (Indian) ancestry but do not consider themselves to be Indians unless they speak an Indian language and live in an Indian community. A Mexican of pure Indian descent participating fully in the Mexican national culture does not ordinarily think of himself as an Indian (although he may be aware of his Indian background and even occasionally refer to himself as "Indio" in certain contexts). Likewise, the person of mixed racial descent is never considered to be an Indian in Latin America unless he resides in an Indian community and speaks an Indian language.

In brief, from the Latin American perspective, to be Indian is to live an Indian way of life. This means that Indianized Europeans and mixed-bloods have on occasion been thought of as Indians.

In the United States, independent Indian communities were often able to absorb Europeans and mixed-bloods into their ranks and to define such persons as being Indian, that is, as Delaware, Comanche, etc. The Anglo-American population tended, however, to define such persons in a racial sense, as white men who had "gone Indian" rather than as Indians. Similarly, Anglo-American government officials have tended to keep rather close record of whether a person in an Indian community is "full-blood," "half-blood," "quarter-blood," etc., not being willing to fully accept a cultural definition of Indianness.

The tendency to define a person by his racial background rather than by his way of life (as is also very true in the case of United States citizens of African descent) is one facet of Anglo-American racism. (It is significant that Latin Americans, with less of a tendency towards racism, have tended to utilize cultural definitions rather than racial ones.)

The conquest of American Indian tribes by the United States tended to deprive these tribes of the ability to absorb aliens, as they had done when they were still free. Because the resources left to the tribes have not been enough to support their own people, tribal groups have generally attempted to restrict "membership" rather than to welcome those outsiders who might wish to assimilate in an Indian direction. But perhaps more significantly, the.Federal government and certain state governments have assumed the authority of defining what an Indian is. In Virginia and adjoining states many Indian tribes which had assimilated persons of African descent during the colonial period found themselves being defined by racist white governments as mulattos or Negroes, or of having some arbitrary definition of Indianness forced upon them.

In Virginia an Indian was legally defined in 1924 as a person of more than one-eighth native descent who possessed no trace of African ancestry. (In 1930 persons with less than one-quarter "Indian blood" were allowed to become whites provided they had no other non-white ancestry. Indians as such still could not possess any African descent, except that those "domiciled" on a state reservation could possess up to one-thirty-second part-Negro background.) Generally speaking, the Federal government defines an Indian as a person of one-quarter or more United States Indian descent who resides upon Federal "trust land" (reservations, colonies, or rancherias) or who has preserved membership in a tribe occupying "trust land." A person of European descent or even of

Mexican Indian descent who was allowed by a tribe to reside on tribal land, who married a person of one-quarter native descent, and who became assimilated into the local Indian culture would not be accepted as an Indian by the Federal government nor would his children be so accepted, although (as in the case of a Mexican Indian–United States Indian marriage) they might well be of five-eighths biological native descent. The Federal government takes the position that one-eighth "bloods" are non-Indian while one-quarter "bloods" are Indian, when both reside on "trust land."

To fully understand the peculiarity of this modified racial definition, one must be aware of certain facts. First, it is well to keep in mind that ordinarily assimilation and place of birth are the basic elements in defining identity. One does not, for example, ask a Scotsman how much Gaelic (Scottish) biological ancestry he possesses, nor does one refer to Scotsmen as being one-quarter Scots, one-sixteenth Scots, etc., on the basis of how much "original" Scottish ancestry they may possess. The same thing is true for most populations around the world, even including those such as the English, Irish, French, Greek, Chinese, etc., who have absorbed large numbers of aliens. Generally each nationality defines its own membership and this is ordinarily on the basis of how the individual involved defines himself. It is true that extreme racial (or religious) differences may occasionally slow this process down, but in this connection it is well to keep in mind examples such as that of the Magyars and Turks, who have probably changed their predominant physical character (from "Mongoloid" to "Caucasoid") through absorbing European aliens, and that of southern Arabs who have become largely "Negroid" through a similar process, in all three cases preserving their Magyar, Turkish or Arab peoplehood while changing, in considerable measure, their biological character.

It is probably impossible to clearly assert who is an Indian in the United States today, although certain statements can be made. First, it is clear that the Federal government's definition of Indianness is not a true definition of the latter, but is, instead, merely a description of the people "served" by the Bureau of Indian Affairs. Second, a purely "racial" definition of Indianhood cannot be applied, operationally, in the United States so long as the Mexican-American population is regarded as being legally "White with Spanish Surname," since this population is *at least* as biologically

Indian as that population being served by the BIA. Third, a "cultural" definition of Indianhood is rather difficult to apply so long as persons of full-blood United States tribal descent living an Anglo-American style of life in a non-Indian urban setting are regarded in practice as still being "Indian" (because of their physical characteristics, former tribal affiliation, or, possibly, self-definition as an "Indian").

What one must do, perhaps, is to simply describe the different "kinds" of "Indians" who reside in the United States without attempting to resolve the contradictions apparent between the various groups. Let us consider, for example, the following types of people:

(1) Several million Americans are of "pure" biological Native American descent and can be categorized as "racial Indians." Within this group, however, only about 200,000 to 300,000 are members of United States tribal organizations or communities, while an undetermined number of others have some knowledge of being related to a specific Mexican or other non-United States indigenous population.

(2) Several million Americans possess a significant degree of Indian descent, but less than "full-blood." Only about 200,000 to 300,000 of these persons are members of United States tribal organizations or communities, while an undetermined number of others have some knowledge of being related to a specific Mexican, or other, non-United States indigenous population. Quite obviously, these hybrids are not "racial Indians" but constitute, in reality, a new mixed "race" of their own. They have been called *metis* (in Canada), *mestizos, ladinos* and *cholos* (in Latin America), half-breeds, half-bloods, and Eurindians. Unfortunately, many of these terms have also been used to refer to other kinds of hybrids or to persons of mixed-cultural, as opposed to mixed-biological, characteristics.

(3) Approximately one-half million Americans belong to tribal organizations or reside in Indian communities within the United States. These persons are commonly thought of as "Indians" in their local area, or think of themselves as "Indians." But in other respects, they are an extremely varied group. The tribal groups vary, for example, from ones whose members are exclusively of part-Indian ancestry, with little or no pre-European cultural heritage, to ones whose members are virtually all "full-blood" and whose culture is

significantly non-European. Additionally, many such "Indians" do not, in fact, belong to a specific tribe or Indian community, but belong only to urban inter-tribal groups, Indian-interest clubs, or to general categories of detribalized hybrid populations such as "Mission Indians" in California or "Lumbees" in North Carolina.

A very critical problem relating to defining a person as an "Indian" simply because he belongs to a tribal or inter-tribal organization arises from the fact that although a part-Indian may be accepted as "Indian" in his own local community or in a certain region, he may often be regarded as a "mixed-blood" or even as a non-Indian by people in other communities or regions. Still further, a "mixed-blood Sioux" may be regarded as an "Indian" by whites or by non-Sioux, while at home he may be regarded very rigidly as a "mixed-blood," that is, as a kind of person who is neither "Indian" nor non-Indian (although he may be a member of the tribe and receive BIA services).

Finally, reference should be made to the fact that many persons who regard themselves as being of "pure" United States Indian descent are, in fact, partially descended from the numerous Europeans, Africans, and Mexicans commonly captured and adopted by tribes at an early date. This is especially true for tribes formerly residing in the eastern half of the United States or in areas adjacent to Mexican territory. In the Far West, Chinese and Hawaiian mixtures are not uncommon among certain Indian groups, and in Alaska, Russian, native Siberian, and Chinese ancestry is present. The memory of being descended from such early intermarriages has frequently been forgotten or is known to only a few older persons and thus has no practical impact (except where a factional feud may lead to gossip about such ancestry). Nonetheless, it is of some significance in relation to any effort to equate "racial purity" with "Indianness."

In summary, the only type of person in the United States who can be safely categorized as an "American Indian" *under any and all circumstances* is an individual who is of unmixed or virtually unmixed United States native ancestry and who 1) resides in an Indian community, 2) is a member of a tribal organization, and 3) participates in the way of life of the group to which he belongs; or, 1) resides in an urban setting (usually temporarily),

2) maintains contacts with "home," and 3) participates in the activities of inter-tribal organizations or tribal clubs.

All other classes of individuals may be categorized as "Indians," "mixed-bloods," or even "non-Indians," depending upon what definition is being applied, by whom, and where. *Perhaps the most important criteria are self-definition and how the individual is categorized in the community where he resides,* but neither of these yields a classification which will be accepted by all Indian communities.

The problem of stating who an "Indian" is, would, of course, be in great measure resolved if we ceased to refer to the peoples of the Americas as Cherokee Indians, Chickahominy Indians, Hupa Indians, etc., and instead spoke of them as Cherokee People, Chickahominy People, and Hupa People. This style would conform to usage in all other parts of the world, where, for example, we do not speak of Meo Asians, Shan Asians, Dayak Indonesians, Basque Europeans, or Swazi Africans, but rather of Meo People, Shan tribesmen, Basques, and Swazis.

The use of the term "Indian" in the way in which it is commonly used (as will be discussed subsequently) *implies that the natives of the Americas were one people, which is not true, linguistically or politically.* It might be useful to speak of individual tribes as being part of a larger unit, as when we refer to "Buriat Mongols" because the Buriats speak a Mongol language, but this practice has tended to be followed only in certain regions of the United States (as in the Southwest with Mescalero Apaches, Jicarilla Apaches, etc.).

In any event, there is no reason why we must add the word "Indian" to each group's name. Thus, we can speak of Pamunkies as easily as Pamunky Indians (and if we wish to make it clear that the Pamunkies reside in America we can refer to them as Pamunky-Americans, although the need for this is rather slight since we never find it necessary to speak of Hausa-Africans, the context usually supplying information on geographic location).

Once we think in terms of specific peoples rather than of a vague group such as "Indians," then it becomes much easier to identify individuals ethnically. If a person belongs to the Shawnee Tribe he is, in fact, a Shawnee (provided, of course, that he is accepted by other Shawnees as a Shawnee) regardless of his ancestry. *He may not be a Shawnee "Indian" but he is a Shawnee person.*

This approach to ethnic definition has the virtue of taking away from whites the power to determine the identity of a person of native descent or affiliation and giving that power to the local tribal community, where it in fact belongs.

This approach poses some problems for persons who are descended from more than one native group and who have never chosen (or perhaps been able to choose) to affiliate primarily with one tribe or community. This is especially a problem for natives who reside in areas, such as California, where many of the pre-European community-republics were destroyed by white conquest and where few viable tribal organizations have subsequently developed. Since only about 9000 California natives reside on "trust land" (out of a total 30,000 to 50,000 persons of Native Californian descent), it follows that large numbers possess no tribal organization to which they can belong since so-called "tribes," in California, are almost universally confined solely to organizations for persons who reside upon a specific piece of "trust land." Thus, for example, a person of Nisenan descent possesses no Nisenan tribe to which he can belong. He can only affiliate with some type of inter-tribal club or association or, if he resides on one of the very small reservations, with a local reservation organization. In point of fact, however, the Nisenan people (simply a language group before the conquest) possess little more than kinship relationships with each other, and consciousness of being "Indians." They possess no means whereby persons who are partially descended from another native group or from a non-Indian can be "inducted" into membership in any Nisenan organization.

In California, therefore, (as along the Atlantic Seaboard) a caste of brown-skinned people is developing which cannot effectively identify itself with any specific tribe, but which must be either "Indians" (without any other clarification) or simply "brown people." In some regions such people come to be known as "Marlboro County Indians" or "Auburn Indians," that is, they acquire rather meaningless geographical names. In still other areas, such people acquire vague nicknames like "Mission Indians," "Moors," "Issues," and "Brass Ankles."

All of these latter developments, which collectively make it difficult for persons of native descent to maintain a meaningful and specific ethnic identity, are to be regarded as disadvantageous. To become simply a "brown person" with no specific history, no heritage, and no tribal identity around which pride can be developed, is to expose oneself to the worst possible kind of existence in a society which still, for all of its ideals, ranks people on a color basis and places great emphasis upon ancestry. The actual experience of detribalized people along the Atlantic Seaboard would certainly suggest that it is advantageous to retain as much specific heritage and tribal identity as possible.

This whole question is further complicated by the fact that existing tribal organizations, as specific incorporated bodies, are almost universally the creation of the Federal government and stem from the manner in which Indians were "rounded up" or split up and forced onto particular reservations; while existing trans-reservation identifications· (such as the concepts of "Apaches," "Yokuts," or "Southern Paiutes") are the creation of white anthropologists, historians or laymen and, in many cases, possess very little operational meaning for native people.

Of course, all of these problems relating to the loss of a specific tribal or ethnic affiliation are results of conquest and white dominance and can only be resolved when Native Americans assert themselves and grasp a greater degree of mastery over their own collective fate. In so far as identity is concerned, such a development would, in some cases, result in Indian people casting off white-imposed designations in order to create or recreate groupings which are truly meaningful and practical for their own lives.

Finally, note should be taken of the fact that large numbers of colored or Afro-Americans are part-Indian, perhaps as many as one-third knowing of a specific Indian grandparent or other ancestor. Still further, hundreds of thousands of Oklahomans of African appearance (in whole or in part) are descended from citizens of the Creek, Cherokee, Seminole, and other tribes, and their Indian citizenship was guaranteed by treaties negotiated with the Federal government after the Civil War. Many of these latter people, called "Freedmen" of the Five Civilized Tribes, also have Indian blood and even speak native languages. Teachers should be aware that large numbers of "Red-Black" children, as they are called, now attend schools in such cities as Oakland, Richmond,

Los Angeles, and Sacramento, in California.

Native American peoples should no longer be the victims of externally-imposed stereotypes. Whether a native person looks like a German, an African, or a "racially-pure" Indian should make no difference to the non-Indians since we must respect both the free choice of the individual and the sweep of history, the latter being a process that tends to create myriad new types of human beings in a manner totally beyond legislative control.

What Are "Indian Cultures"?

All too frequently teachers who wish to discuss "Indian culture" in the classroom adopt the viewpoint that to do so they must deal with the "old" native way of life as it existed prior to European contact or at least prior to European conquest. "Indian culture," in brief, is perceived of as being a static thing which no longer exists (except perhaps in Arizona or New Mexico). It is generally described by laymen as an unchanging set of behavioral patterns and material objects uniformly used in the same way by all of the people in the "tribe" or group under discussion.

This viewpoint conveys a false impression of what "cuture" is and also may serve to confuse pupils of both non-Indian and Indian background. This erroneous belief serves to deprive Indians of today of a sense of identity *as Indians* since most of them obviously can not live as native people did a century ago. Unfortunately, many Native Americans also share the viewpoint of the teacher, as when they assert, nostalgically perhaps, that "Indian culture" is disappearing, that the young people are not learning "the old Indian ways."

Before discussing the above points further it is first necessary to say a few words about the concept of culture itself. This term, in its modern sense, is commonly understood as referring to the total way of life of a given people (as in the concept of "Comanche culture"), or to the somewhat related styles of behavior in a region (as with "Southwestern Culture"), or to the collective, although distinctive, ways of life followed by all human beings (as in "human culture"). Culture has also been defined by some anthropologists as referring only to those aspects of human behavior which are learned (that is, nonbiological and nonenvironmental) and to the products of such learned behavior. This writer is disposed, however, to use the term to refer to the total patterns of behavior associated with a particular people, not attempting to separate out those aspects of behavior which are environmentally or biologically determined from those which are "learned." (Principally because it is, in many instances, impossible or at least very difficult to discuss many learned patterns when they are abstracted from their biological or environmental relationships. Thus, for example, it is meaningless to discuss color prejudice as a part of Anglo-American culture if the existence of biologically-determined skin-color differences are ignored.)

In what does a "culture" (in the singular) consist? When does one pass from one culture to another? These are questions which confuse many persons who come into contact with socio-anthropological literature, and justifiably so, since few scholars are able to clearly define "a culture" or "a cultural tradition." Unfortunately for simplicity, human groups have commonly mixed together, separated, borrowed from each other, migrated, etc., to such an extent that few, if any, "boundaries" actually exist between behavioral traditions. Additionally, those "boundaries" between "cultures" which might be discerned by the scholar were, and are, largely imposed by himself upon the data and would not necessarily be meaningful to the peoples actually living in the particular area under study.

To illustrate the complexities involved, one might cite the situation in the early 1700s from Taos Pueblo (New Mexico) northeasterly into the plains. The Taos People possessed a settled horticultural tradition featuring large multi-story "apartment house" structures, an eleborate ceremonial life, etc., supplemented by some buffalo hunting and a few other traits—such as male hair style—more typical of Plains Indians. Ten leagues to the northeast lived the Apaches de la Xicarilla, a people with horticulture, irrigation ditches, pueblo-style single-story dwellings, and some emphasis upon buffalo hunting. Still further to the northeast were closely related Apache groups who practiced little or no horti-culture, lived in tipis or brush huts, and pursued the buffalo and other game for the greater part of the year.

Quite obviously, these three peoples possessed three different "systems" or "configurations" of behavior. Yet all three shared traits with each other and, in fact, were in frequent, friendly contact with one another. One could probably assert that the three systems were three separate cultures, and yet, operationally, they seem to have "blended" together in such a way as to preclude any clear-cut boundary. However, this problem only arises when we think primarily in terms of material traits abstracted from sociopolitical and linguistic characteristics.

The Taos People, a Tiwa-speaking population, clearly possessed a distinctive sense of "peoplehood" confined to themselves. Although close linguistic and cultural relatives of the Tiwa-speaking Picuries and close friends of the Tinnéh-speaking Xicarilla and Plains Apaches, the Taos clearly composed a separate, independent community-republic. This self-conscious concept of political separation must be thought of as a key element in their cultural system, having undoubtedly a great impact upon other facets of behavior.

The Plains Apache situation is less clear, for there is some evidence which would suggest that the Apaches de la Xicarilla were not a separate people from their semi-nomadic relatives to the northeast, since their dialects appear to have been very close and since the various local political organizations ("bands" or groups of related families) would appear to have acted in concert in a kind of a loose confederation during the late seventeenth and early eighteenth centuries. In this instance, it would seem that the sociopolitical "peoplehood" unit (the informal confederacy) possessed several variations in material behavior, ranging from a quasi-Pueblo style of life to a Plains style of life. Can we then speak of a "Xicarilla-Plains Apache Culture?" Probably we can, since the extremely significant linguistic and "peoplehood" elements were uniform and since, after the 1730s-1750s, the remnants of these Apache groups largely came together as the Jicarilla Apaches of modern times (sharing a more uniform cultural tradition which leaned towards the Plains style of life).

It must be borne in mind that the dispersal patterns for various specific behavioral traits will not ordinarily conform one with another, nor will they conform with ethnic (linguistic and sociopolitical) boundaries. For certain scientific purposes it may, at times, be necessary to study various behavioral characteristics abstracted from linguistic and sociopolitical data (as when a scholar discusses the "Southwestern Cultural Tradition" and thereby ignores significant language and sociopolitical divisions). *On the other hand, Native American peoples always operated within a conscious framework of social and political relations and one who wishes to understand native life as it was, and is, functioning must look at culture as an attribute of particular associations of people.*

Thus, while it might be meaningful for the student of cultural evolution to create the concept of "Colorado River Culture," the several peoples along that stream would have certainly placed more emphasis upon belonging to the Quechan, Halchidhoma, Hamakhava, or Halyikwamai republics. This emphasis upon peoplehood rather than upon overall cultural similarity, made it possible for the rather closely related Hamakhava and Halchidhoma to be almost continuously at war, while the Hamakhava were close friends and rather frequent associates of the quite culturally distinct Chemehuevi Nihwi ("Southern Paiute") people.

To summarize this discussion of culture, one might make the following points:

(1) The behavioral pattern systems of human groups are like currents in the ocean. It is possible to point out generally where a particular current exists, especially at its center or strongest point, but it is not ordinarily possible to neatly separate that current from the surrounding sea. Human cultural traditions flow together in much the same manner as currents and any attempt at charting boundaries must be regarded as only leading to rough approximations.

(2) A "culture" (in the singular) is always possessed by a particular societal unit or "people," if the term "culture" is to refer to a living, functioning, integrated whole. If we accept the above, a culture can be said to consist in the system or configuration of behavior patterns exhibited by a particular people.

(3) A culture according to this approach, may contain a number of behavioral options, but must include some sense of "peoplehood" (shared by all individuals) and a common means of oral communication (a single language or at least· one language available equally to all).

(4) In speaking of closely-related systems of behavior, we should perhaps speak of "cultures" (plural), as in "Colorado River

Cultures," although it would probably be pedantic to make too much of this point.

(5) The attempt to distinguish specific cultures one from another must always be fraught with difficulties even if socio-political units are regarded as the "container" of the culture. This is true because it is not always possible to clearly separate one "people" from another, especially in areas such as California and Nevada.

When we look at culture in connection with the lifestyle of a particular people, we find that their way of life almost always includes options or variations and, therefore, is never completely homogeneous. These options may be contradictory; they may endure for long periods of time; and they may be symptoms of the gradual shifting of a peoples' way of life from one pattern to another. For example, in the 1600s there was apparently no single, homogeneous Navaho way of life. Many Navahos were adopting Pueblo Indian traits at an increased rate, as well as Spanish-introduced items, while other, more isolated, Navahos were still oriented towards an earlier "Apache-like" way of life. But all were equally Navaho and all of the cultural traits being integrated into the lives of Navaho people were units within any generalized "Navaho culture."

We must also note that it is technically incorrect to speak of "Navaho culture," "Quechan culture," or "Sioux culture" without reference to a particular time period, unless it is fully understood that one is speaking about a fluid, changing "tradition" which has only one basic, unifying, element, that is, that it is associated with a particular people. "Navaho culture" of 1500 was different from that of 1600, which in turn was different from that of 1700, which in turn was different from 1890, which in turn was different from 1960. Although there are some traits, such as language, which probably survived with relatively little change during this one-thousand-year period, the basic unifying strand is the fact that the modern Navaho is descended sociopolitically from the Navaho of 1000 A.D. (Although he is also biologically related to Apaches, Pueblo Indians, Paiutes, Utes, Spaniards, Mexicans, and other peoples.)

If we take away such Pueblo Indian and Hispano-Mexican traits as blanketweaving, cloth garments, the clan system, sandpaintings, much of the religion, silversmithing, turquoise-working, sheep-raising, horseback-riding, agriculture, etc., we might be able to gain a better idea of how Navahos lived before 1000 A.D. But even the hunting and gathering Navahos of that early period did not possess an "original Navaho culture." Without a doubt, the Navaho way of life of 1000 was markedly different from that of their ancestors before they migrated to the Southwest. And, needless to state, one can continue this kind of analysis back to the very origins of all human behavior. In short, there is no point in time where a particular way of life can be said to be "original" or "pure" or "static." Cultural evolution constantly is in process and groups are continually borrowing from their neighbors as well as developing more or less original traits.

In short, so long as a people possess a sense of identity, of "peoplehood" (by means primarily of kinship ties and a self-consciousness of their own distinctiveness from "aliens") they can be said to possess a culture or way of life. It follows then, that the origin of the various specific traits is irrelevant as regards the question of whether or not a people possess a culture of their own.

Thus, we can correctly speak of "Powhatan Culture" as existing today even though a large number of the current behavioral characteristics of the Powhatan people of Virginia are of European or alien Indian origin. In fact, it would not make any difference if all of the traits of the Powhatan were of non-Powhatan origin, so long as the Powhatan people maintained themselves as a viable, distinct sociopolitical group with a "history" (largely internalized) of their own.

The Bulgarian people can be cited as a further illustration of this principle. The Bulgarians of today certainly possess a "Bulgarian Culture," however, their modern language is of non-Bulgarian origin, they have migrated from their ancient homeland (the Volga-Don area of Russia), their religion is non-Bulgar (Greek Christianity and Islam), and so on. But the Bulgarian people have retained their identity and history as a distinct people descended from the ancient Bulgars of the steppes of southeastern Europe. They have not lost the possession of a culture by virtue of losing (and replacing) all of their ancient behavioral patterns.

Indian cultures, then, continue to exist no matter what the origin of the particular traits found therein. (Pickup trucks are as

Navaho as Navaho blankets.) But there are two qualifying statements which must be made: first, as a people's social organization disintegrates, so too will the culture disintegrate; and, second, conquered peoples who do not control their own destiny may not possess a way of life which they feel to be an integrated way of life.

Regarding this latter point, we must understand that an independent or at least quasi-autonomous people ordinarily are free to accept or reject alien behavior patterns or products. They can, therefore, maintain a culture which is integrated and which is felt to be "their own." They are in control of the traits in question, and they are free to determine the manner in which a new trait relates to older elements of the culture. Conquered peoples, especially if experiencing a process of social disorganization, cannot ordinarily accept or reject alien behavior patterns. Thus, when their culture changes, it changes in a kind of haphazard, socially-disturbing manner (as when, for example, Anglo-Americans appropriate native economic resources, reduce the natives to a state of poverty, and force the latter to adjust as best they can).

Because of the fact of conquest, many modern Indian groups, although possessing a modern culture, do not feel that their culture is an integrated and harmonious whole. In point of fact, such post-conquest cultures are often collections of contradictory or irreconciled traits, and it can be said that the group possessing such a "culture of conquest" is the victim of its culture rather than the master of its culture. The resolution of this situation can only come about when native groups possess enough self-confidence and "power" to control the selection of their own patterns of behavior. (Such a process does not depend upon the rejection of alien traits, but, rather, upon their "rationalization" within a harmonious system.)

The possession of an integrated culture is perhaps crucial for the psychological well-being of any class of people. Only when a way of life is harmonious, integrated, and rationalized can the individual understand his relationship to other individuals; and only then can he know what kinds of behavior are acceptable or desirable according to the circumstances. It may well be that much of the alienation and anti-social behavior found in modern mass cultures stems from their being relatively nonintegrated (non-understandable). Certainly, many of the tensions of Afro-Americans derive from their not being able to deal successfully with the contradictory traits within Anglo-American culture relative to race relations. One facet of the appeal of black cultural separatism may well lie in the fact that it serves to offer an understandable, noncontradictory, set of behavioral patterns and attitudes.

Educators or community aides must be continually aware of the processes of cultural evolution and conquest. They should encourage native peoples to become explicitly conscious of the dynamics of culture change and of the problems involved in possessing a nonintegrated culture. They should do what they can to facilitate the process whereby Indian communities become masters of their own behavior. Above all, teachers must avoid the use of stereotypical materials which, in effect, allow the white man to define Indianness and Indian culture as something not possessed nor capable of being possessed by modern Indian people.

Systems of Classifying Native Groups

Teachers, Indian laymen, and others concerned with understanding the history of Native Americans are unfortunately confronted with textbooks, maps, and guides which either classify native groups in an erroneous manner or which use some system of categorization whose underlying assumptions are not fully explained.

One often, for example, sees maps of the "Indian Tribes of North America" which 1) give the impression of simultaneity for the various locations assigned to "tribes" when in fact the latter may be as much as two centuries apart [e.g., the location of the Leni-Lenápe (Delaware) may be as of the early seventeenth century, while the location of the Lakota (Sioux) is as of the mid-nineteenth century]; 2) give the impression of dealing with equivalent social units when in fact the groups shown on the map may vary from language families, to loose confederacies, to idiomalities, to actual political units; 3) assign all of the groups to a language family when, in fact, we possess only the weakest kind of evidence relating to the languages formerly spoken by many groups in northern Mexico, Texas, and the South.

Much of the published material available to teachers and laymen relating to Indians is misleading, especially when it stems from popular or general textbook sources. But scholarly sources can also be misleading in cases where the reader is not able to clearly perceive the assumptions of the author or does not understand the type of analysis being pursued.

A beginning point for misunderstanding consists in the fact that few sources are readily available which attempt to portray, via text or maps, an accurate idea of the native's own view of his socio-political life. The majority of the "tribes" or groups ordinarily mentioned in white sources are essentially the creation of non-Indians. In part this is due to the activity of white governments or missionaries, but in great measure it stems from the writings of scholars, principally anthropologists.

The names applied to native groups are very seldom the people's own names, in part because many groups depicted on maps were not self-conscious, named entities. But even when a native name has always existed, white writers have often persisted in using an alien term, as with Delaware (from Lord De la ware) instead of Leni-Lenápe, and Navaho (or Navajo) in place of Diné (Dineh). Indians themselves have gradually been forced·to "live with" or even to accept alien names because of the pressure stemming from white "custom" (and, occasionally, because of editors' demands for uniformity).

The problem of named groups becomes more serious when one finds that the units commonly dealt with in popular sources actually had no sociopolitical reality in pre-European times. For example, certain of the groups portrayed on the usual map of Indian California are *idiomalities*—groups of completely independent and perhaps even hostile people who merely spoke the same language (e.g., Wintun, Yurok, Shasta). Other groups commonly portrayed on such maps are not even idiomalities but are in fact composed of closely related, but different languages (e.g., Chumash, Pomo, Mewuk, Maidu, Costanoan, Salinan, Coast Mewuk). Still other groups are essentially fictitious creations of Spanish contact and missionization (e.g., Diegueño, Juaneño, Luiseño, Gabrieliño, Fernandeño, Serrano).

For the layman to be able to unravel the many layers of invented groups in order to understand the functional reality of native California life is a difficult task indeed. And yet it is essential because a large percentage of Indians in areas such as California are still living in a stage of sociopolitical self-consciousness rather close to that of former years and quite different from that implied by maps and textbooks.

The problem can best be understood by examining several groups, such as the Maidu, Mewuk (Miwok), and Kamia-Diegueño. Many maps simply assign the entire area of the Sierra Nevada mountains and foothills from roughly Placerville to Lake Almanor, California, to the Maidu. Other, more detailed maps divide the Maidu region into three areas, occupied by "Southern Maidu," "Northeastern Maidu," and "Northwestern Maidu." In point of fact, however, the Nisenan, Maidu, and Concow, respectively, all spoke separate languages and comprise, therefore, three separate idiomalities. To call all of them "Maidu" is very misleading, when what is really meant is "the Nisenan-Concow-Maidu group of closely related languages," or, in brief, a language family. But the process of classifying people according to a system of related languages is rather complex because, as in this example, the Nisenan-Concow-Maidu group is but a division of the California Penutian group of languages, which in turn is now thought to be part of a still larger assemblage of distantly related tongues.

The whole problem becomes still more complicated when we realize that the Maidu, Concow, and Nisenan were probably not sociopolitical units but simply idiomalities. The real sociopolitical units were local community-republics (independent communities composed of at least one village), informal confederations of communities, and ceremonial exchange-kinship territories (which will be discussed below). Ideally our maps should illustrate these latter units. When space is lacking, however, we should speak of "Nisenan-speaking communities," "Concow-speaking communities," and "Maidu-speaking communities," thus clearly specifying the kind of units being delineated.

The groups commonly designated as Mewuk (or Miwok)— Sierra Mewuk, Plains Mewuk, Bay Mewuk (Saklan), Coast Mewuk, and Lake Mewuk—pose problems very comparable to that of the so-called Maidu. Each of these groups possessed a language of its own, with the exception of the Coast Mewuk who possessed two languages. What we are dealing with is essentially a group of closely-related languages (another branch of the California Penutian family) which, in turn, divides into two further subdivisions, that of the Mewko (Plains Mewuk) and the Mewuk (Sierra Mewuk), and that of the Tuleyome (Lake Mewuk), Hukueko (Marin County), and Olamentko (Bodega Bay), with the Saklan standing alone because of an insufficiency of evidence. Each of these six language groups (idiomalities) was ordinarily composed of a number of villages or local communities and in no instances, except perhaps in the case of the Olamentko and Saklan, did the sociopolitical unit conform to the idiomality. The Mewuk-, Mewko-, and Hukueko-speaking groups appear to have been further divided by regional dialects.

The Kamia-Diegueño peoples of southern California present a little different problem from that of the above groups. The distinction between "Diegueño" and "Kamia" is purely artificial, being based upon the fact that certain Kamia-speaking people were missionized at San Diego Mission (while others were missionized in several Baja California missions and could be called Migueleños, Tomaseños, etc.). The Kamia-speaking people compose a branch of the Kamia-Cocopa-Halyikwamai-Kohuana group within the Yuman division of the Hokan language family. The Kamia are, then, an idiomality (although it may be that the Cocopa, Halyikwamai, and Kohuana people should also be included in this idiomality, depending upon whether their various tongues were mutually intelligible with Kamia). The Kamia were, however, on the margins of being a nationality, since there is considerable evidence that most, if not all, Kamia-speaking groups shared a common historical tradition of being descended from the same ancestral "first Kamia," that they shared a common sense of "being Kamia," and finally, that they possessed intravillage kinship ties by means of patrilineal lineages which were becoming nonlocalized. On the other hand, the Kamia nationality or proto-nationality had not achieved political status since the various Kamia-speaking villages, lineages and confederations were independent and occasionally mutually hostile. Thus, we must still refer to "Kamia-speaking communities" rather than to a unified Kamia people.[1]

The above analysis should serve to illustrate the complexity involved in dealing with Native American linguistic, social, and political units. The layman must understand that there are many ways of classifying native peoples and, further, that the various systems of classification may not correspond to one another. One can classify people on the basis of language, beginning with extremely minor local dialectical variations and proceeding to families of related languages and super-families composed of extremely different but probably-related language families. This type of classification does not, however, always agree with a system based upon political organization, since it is quite common for the latter to embrace people speaking different languages (as, for example, with the Comanche-Kiowa-"Kiowa Apache" confederation, the Cheyenne-Sutaio confederation, the Minsi-Unami-Unalachtigo confederation, the Iroquois confederation after the admittance of the Tuscarora, Nanticoke, Tutelo, etc., and the Western Apache-Yavapai mixed bands).

Long enduring alliance systems, although perhaps less formalized than a confederation, operated as a part of the political life of native groups, and these systems often cut across language boundaries, as with the Quechan-Kamia alliances against the Cocopa, the Quechan-Hamakhava alliance against the Maricopa, the Assiniboin Lakota-Cree alliance against the other Lakota (Sioux) groups, and so on.

Very closely related to the political life of native peoples, and integrally a part of their social-religious life, were the various ceremonial exchange systems. In the California area, for example, one finds that the people of various community-republics and villages had what appears to be a regular pattern of inviting the people of other specific localities to their ceremonies, and being invited to the other's celebrations in return. Such ceremonial exchange systems are particularly significant in California regions where distinguishable political units above the level of the village are absent, because the people who shared a common ceremonial life doubtless also shared kinship (it would be logical for mates to be acquired in conjunction with such a system) and, more significantly, probably operated as an informal political group (exchanging information, settling disputes, planning mutual activities, etc.).

It seems clear that in many areas these ceremonial exchange systems, and likewise kinship ties, cut across language boundaries. This writer's study of the Tongva of Tujunga village in southern California indicates, for example, that the Tujunga villagers and the not-too-distant Chumash-speaking villagers were intermarrying.[2] The Stonyford Pomo (Shoteah) and Wintun-speaking peoples were ceremony-sharers although these Pomo were somewhat hostile towards other Pomo-speaking peoples.

It must also be pointed out that many Indian peoples were bilingual or even multilingual. It is to be suspected that villagers in sedentary border areas, especially where intermarriage and ceremonial-sharing was frequent, were commonly bilingual from childhood (from infancy perhaps) and that the placing of such people in one or another language family is somewhat arbitrary. For example, it seems highly likely that the natives of the Chumash-Tongva border area (roughly the Los Angeles to Ventura county boundary zone) must be regarded as belonging to villages sharing something of a bilinguistic and cultural unity. This seems likely to have been the case in the Chumash-Yokuts border area, the Hupa-Yurok-Karok area, and so on. (In general, it seems likely that wherever independent or autonomous sedentary community-republics bordered upon each other, where intervillage marriage was common, and where the people were friendly, any effort to utilize language groups as a basis for identifying sociopolitical relationships is rather risky.)

Another danger involved in a purely linguistic approach to the classification of native groups consists in the fact that a given people may physically resemble people of an alien tongue more than they resemble people speaking a related language. Thus, for example, the Hupas of northwestern California, although speaking a Tinneh (Athapaskan) language, share the same physical characteristics as the surrounding Yuroks and Wiyots (Ritwan languages) and Karoks (a Hokan language). Quite clearly, the Hupa are "one people" in terms of actual biological ancestry with their near neighbors and their only apparent connection with distant Tinneh-speaking peoples (such as the Navaho), is that somehow they possess a related language. In brief, if one were to be able to construct a geneological chart for the Hupa people it would be most probably that their ancestry shared with the Yurok, Wiyot, and Karok peoples would be very much greater than that shared with Navahos, Apaches, Sarsis, and other Tinneh language groups. Which relationship is functionally more meaningful, that of actual kinship ("blood") ties or that of a remote linguistic relationship?

In a very comparable manner, the Hupas shared quite similar behavioral patterns with their near neighbors, patterns very different from that of distant Tinneh-speaking peoples. Still further, the culture of the Hupas (and certain other nearby Tinneh groups such as the Tolowa) was different from that of other Tinneh peoples located in northwestern California (such as the Kato). Areas of similar cultural configurations tend, therefore, not to be the same as areas marked out by pure linguistic criteria.

Quite obviously, then, there are many ways for classifying native groups, each with a different purpose or rationale. One can utilize language, total culture, physical characteristics, kinship, political organization, or socio-religious exchange areas, among other characteristics, as bases for significant classification. No one system can provide a complete picture of the interrelationships existing between native groups, although certain characteristics are more likely to have been meaningful to the people themselves including especially sociopolitical relationships.

It is quite clear also that analyses of Native American groups must consider the element of time, since much change has taken place both before and after intensive European contact. In the pre-European period, for example, one can note such phenomena as the gradual appearance of multivillage republics along the Colorado River (composed, as it would appear, of numerous small communities or bands gradually coming together and developing a common sense of identity), the establishment by Deganawidah of the Iroquois Confederacy ("The Great Peace") in New York, and the creation by Wahunsonacock and his kinsmen of the Powhatan Confederation in Virginia. In the post-European period one can note numerous changes, usually taking the form of the amalgamation of various previously independent republics into new unions as a response to foreign pressure, as in the Cheyenne-Sutaio merger and the unification of the Leni-Lenápe.

The evolution of Native American sociopolitical organizations did not, of course, cease with the European conquest. Some of the greatest changes have occurred under the pressure of action by non-Indian governmental agencies and through the influence of white systems of denominating Indian groups. Thus, for example, while we would be wrong to speak of "a Pomo people" before 1800 (instead we would have to refer to "Pomo-speaking peoples"), we would not be too greatly in error if we were to do so today. The various Pomo-speaking community-republics have been deprived, through the process of conquest, of their own political independence and, in many cases, of their territorial character (by relocation). In addition, the several Pomo languages are rapidly disappearing and, therefore, the surviving people possess very little reason for maintaining identity as, for example, members of the Yokayo, Kashia, or Hamfo communities. White writers constantly refer to them as "Pomo" and, in the absence of strong organizations, many Indian people have gradually come to accept the white designation. (This may not necessarily be an undesirable development since a unified Pomo people, several thousand strong, possesses more political power than a number of small groups of a few hundred individuals each.) It would also appear that a number of Miyakama (Yukan-speaking—also known as Wappo, a corruption of the word "Guapo") individuals are being absorbed into the emerging Pomo ethnic group.

In summary, the individual who desires accurate information relative to the sociopolitical organization of native America must continually be alert to the complexities involved in cataloging human groups and to the appropriate time-period. One must also be alert to the fact that many errors exist in popular writings because the authors were not familiar with the basic firsthand accounts of native culture and history, but rather depended upon secondary sources whose systems of analysis were not fully understood.

The teacher or other individual who wishes to relate some aspect of his work to a particular native people must, in most cases, check with the native people themselves in order to ascertain what they wish to be called and how they define their present stage of social organization. Particularly useful in understanding some aspects of native sociopolitical organization in the Far West are A. L. Kroeber, "The Nature of Land-Holding Groups in Aboriginal California" in *Aboriginal California*, ed. by R. F. Heizer; and R. F. Heizer, *Languages, Territories and Names of California Indian Tribes*.

Modern California Indians developing old basketry skills. Left to right: Carol Vedola, Christine Campbell, Molly Jackson, Elsie Allen (Pomos). *(Photograph courtesy of Mrs. Elsie Allen.)*

VI. A COMMUNITY-RESPONSIVE, MULTICULTURAL APPROACH TO INDIAN EDUCATION

General Theoretical Principles

Jack D. Forbes in *The Education of the Culturally Different* (1968) as well as in several other monographs and articles, *Mexican-Americans* (1967), *Afro-Americans in the Far West* (1967), and "Our Plural Heritage," *Frontier* (July 1964), has set forth much of the background for advocating community-relevant and community-responsive schools, and where culturally different communities are involved, multicultural and bilingual schools. The advocacy of this approach to education has now been taken up at the highest levels, as in the following statement made by U. S. Commissioner of Education Harold Howe, II, in May, 1968, before an audience concerned with Mexican-American education:

> You are more familiar than I with the Mexican-American cultural factors that impede a youngster's transition from home to school. But I would say that the notion of Anglo-cultural superiority—over which youngsters and their parents have no control—is a much larger factor. Until the schools realize how our society projects this conviction of superiority, this cowboy-and-Indians mentality, and takes positive steps to correct it, they will not truly succeed with Mexican-American children. Some schools are taking positive steps that have shown promise of redeeming Mexican-American children from the near-certainty of educational failure. They emphasize a bicultural, bilingual approach which says, in essence, that Mexican-American children must learn the English language and Anglo ways—but that they can do so without having to reject their knowledge of the Spanish language and of Mexican-American ways.
>
> Some of these projects go farther. They suggest that

maybe it is not a bad idea for Anglo children to learn Spanish, and to gain a familiarity with another culture. This idea has all sorts of good sense to recommend it. First of all, the evidence is clear that people learn languages best if they learn them [while] young. It is rather paradoxical that in the Southwest, some elementary schools have forbidden children to speak Spanish, while at the same time many of our secondary schools require students to learn another language—and Spanish is one of the most popular electives. Mexican-American children offer their Anglo classmates a great natural teaching resource. It is time we stopped wasting that resource and instead enable youngsters to move back and forth from one language to another without any sense of difficulty or strangeness.[1]

Numerous efforts have, in the past, been made to improve the quality of formal education available to minority pupils. Innovative efforts range from the "Indian industrial boarding school" and "intensive acculturation" approach of Colonel Richard Pratt after the Civil War, to contemporary "saturated service" compensatory efforts such as More Effective Schools. None of these compensatory efforts, when instituted by outsiders (i.e., by nonminority persons), have been unequivocally successful.[2]

There are undoubtedly many reasons for the failure of intensive compensatory education efforts but doubtless *the most fundamental is that they are confined to the school as an institutional setting when there is good evidence that the school is perhaps less significant as an instrument for enculturation or acculturation than is the home and community.* Paul F. Brandwein has asserted,

> for the first five years of life ... parents *must be considered,* in the most precise use of the term, as *teachers of children.* . . . Evidence points to these five years at home as most significant, if not *the* most significant years, in the child's life.[3]

The Coleman Report, *Equality of Educational Opportunity,* would seem to clearly indicate that the background and nonschool environment of the child is a powerful element in determining educational success or failure, while other research shows that some pupils possess "disadvantages" upon entering school which the school is never able to overcome.[4]

Educational researchers have long been aware that in most cases there is a positive correlation between socioeconomic status (SES) and measured intellectual ability.[5] Cushna points out,

> the educational process itself as well as the entire socio-economic spectrum depends upon the effectiveness of social interaction. The higher a family is upon the SES scale, the more child rearing efforts are invested in teaching the child the social graces, the ability to know how to meet the right people, and to say the right thing at the right time.[6]

Another study indicates that:

> Age does not appear to be a significant factor in the Stanford-Binet performance of Negro American children from ages 7 through 10; however, marital status of the mother and her educational level exhibit important relationship to the children's performance.
>
> These environmental factors appear to be more crucial at ages 9 and 10 than at the younger age levels of 7 and 8.
>
> Finally, the above conclusions suggest that · the intellectual develoment of minority and disadvantaged children would benefit from action directed toward stabilizing their total family situation at an early age.[7]

The significance of family and community background can be vividly observed in the academic success of Chinese-American pupils attending the same or similar schools attended by unsuccessful Indian, Mexican-American, or Afro-American pupils. The difference in achievement *cannot* be explained by the school but must rest in the strength and orientation of the Chinese-American family and in the Chinese language and cultural schooling received by the young people at home or in Chinese-operated private schools attended after public school hours. The same phenomenon is observed when middle-class Afro-American children are contrasted with poor Afro-American children, and when wealthy Latin American children are contrasted with the children of migrant farm laborers, etc.

It is clear that compensatory programs will fail when they are confined to the school since the school, as now organized, can have little impact upon the home and minority community. On the other hand, the Chinese-American experience would seem to indicate that a proud, viable ethnic minority community, with its own supplementary educational organs, can protect its youth from the negative influence of mediocre or poor schools.

James Coleman, in his *Equality of Educational Opportunity, Reconsidered,* states

> it seems clear that the appropriate measure for studying equality of educational opportunity lies in both dimensions: in the distribution of school resources, and the intensity of their effect. Only if their distribution was fully equal, and the intensity of their effect was infinitely great relative to the divergent out-of-school factors, would there be complete equality of opportunity. Since the latter cannot be the case, then it can hardly be even appropriate to speak of "equality of educational opportunity," rather to speak instead of the amount of inequality. In a system with equal resource distribution, but with less than infinite intensity of effects, there remains a degree of inequality—an inequality of opportunity not arising *from* the school system, but arising outside and not *overcome* by the school system.[8]

The above overlooks the problem that "equal resource distribution" within the schools may exist quantitatively although qualitatively the school's programs may be highly biased in favor of one segment of the population. Nonetheless, it does point out the fact that factors beyond the control of the formal educational system are operative and must be dealt with.

It should be stressed, however, that an attempt to change the Indian home and community by paternalistic-elitist reformers (whether Indian or non-Indian) is not to be advocated. The Bureau of Indian Affairs has often attempted to change Indian people during the past century, with largely disastrous results. On the other hand, a "community development" approach which emphasizes Indian participation in educational and noneducational programs will, it is believed, contribute gradually to the diminishing of negative nonschool factors.

It should be borne in mind that the negative aspects of Indian community life, as regards education, stem largely from being a conquered, powerless people long denied the right to influence school policy. This problem cannot be resolved by procedures which would further strengthen feelings of powerlessness. Community-involvement in decision-making and implementation is to be suggested as the key resource available to school personnel.

The many arguments of James B. Conant, Frank E. Karlsen, McGeorge Bundy, Murray Wax, Robert Roessel and others for a close interaction of school and community-parents will not be reviewed in detail here. Nonetheless, some of the evidence supporting emphasis upon community-involvement in education will be cited.[9]

Regarding Indian education specifically, it is necessary to stress that only two formal educational systems have ever been clearly successful. Both of these were operated by Indians and arose out of Indian needs. The Choctaw Republic operated its own school systems in Mississippi and Oklahoma until the late 1890s, developing about 200 schools and academies and sending numerous graduates to eastern colleges. It has been observed that,

> As a result of its excellent public-school system the Choctaw Nation had a much higher proportion of educated people than any of the neighboring states; the number of college graduates one encounters in any contemporary record is surprising, and the quality of written English used by the Choctaw both in their official and private correspondence is distinctly superior to that of the white people surrounding them.[10]

The Cherokee Republic developed a similar school system which was also quite successful.

> It has been estimated that Cherokees were 90% literate in their native language in the 1830s. By the 1880s the Western Cherokee (Oklahoma) had a higher English literacy level than the white population of either Texas or Arkansas.... Since the federal government took over the Cherokee school system (with coercion) in 1898, Cherokees have viewed the school as a white man's institution...over which...parents have no control.... It seems clear that the starting decline during the past sixty years of both English and Cherokee literacy in the

Cherokee tribe is chiefly the result of recent scarcity of reading materials in Cherokee and of the fact that learning to read has become associated with coercive instruction, particularly in the context of an alien and threatening school presided over by (non-Cherokees). . . . As far as Cherokee society is concerned, we have historical evidence that Cherokees can learn to read both English and Cherokee and that most of them have ceased to do so.[11]

These programs were both brought to an end by the United States Government. The schools subsequently operated *for* Cherokees and Choctaws by Federal and Oklahoma State agencies have been typical "Indian schools," with little or no parent-community involvement. They have had, as Walker attests for the Cherokees, a *negative* impact.

Contemporary research findings relative to Indian education point out the necessity for a close relationship between school and home, in view especially of the psychological problems which accompany culture change. As John F. Bryde has stated: "It seems unanimous in the literature of the social scientists that mental health problems usually accompany most culture changes." Bryde's studies of white and Indian pupils in the same school showed that

the Indian group revealed greater personality disruption and poorer adjustment. Notable among the more meaningful variables were: feeling of rejection, depression, anxiety, and tendencies to withdraw plus social, self, and emotional alienation.

Eighth grade Indians

revealed themselves as feeling caught and carried along by circumstances beyond their control, hence they were more rejected, depressed, paranoid, withdrawn, and alienated from themselves and the others. . . . The centrality of the concept of alienation is suggested as the integrating pattern explaining the behavior of the Indian students studied.[12]

Recent unpublished findings of Bernard Spilka have confirmed Bryde's analysis and have shown a close correlation between degree of "alienation" and lack of achievement. Similarly, the Coleman Report identifies the feeling of "powerlessness" as being closely correlated with negative achievement among Afro-American pupils.

William H. Kelly, a very experienced researcher in Indian education, recently stated:

> The recognition of the place of the parent and of the community in the toal process of socializing and educating Indian children is implicit in almost all [current] research [in Indian education] and is explicit [in some].
>
> In every descriptive statement of the behavior of Indian children, attention is drawn to the psychological consequences inherent in the discontinuities that exist between the home environment and the school environment. The situation can be corrected to some extent through teacher training, changes in the attitudes of educators, and curriculum changes....
>
> The solution of fundamental problems of value orientations and biculturalism, however, will require more than research. It will require the kind of participation in, and understanding of, the educational process on the part of Indian parents and leaders that will permit intelligent control of the destiny of their children after they enter school.[13]

The recommendations contained in the "Bundy Report" to the New York City schools reflect the same philosophy, in that

> the central purpose of [its recommendations] is to reconnect all the parties with an interest in the public schools of New York so that each will have more constructive power... parents and neighbors shape the child's attitude. If peers and family regard the school as an alien, unresponsive, or ineffective institution in their midst, the child will enter school in a mood of distrust, apprehension, or hostility.... If, on the other hand, the community regards the school as an agency in which they can identify, which acknowledges a responsibility for pupils achievement—in short as their own—children will enter the school with positive expectations.[14]

The ultimate test of a successful school system or educational institution is perhaps not so much the measurement of the progress of individual students along some arbitrarily-conceived curricular path, but rather how the communities served by that system or institution have enhanced their own lives, individually and collectively, because of the presence of that educational system. The Cherokee and Choctaw schools before 1890 were successful in that they arose from the felt needs of the Indian people themselves, attempted to meet those needs, and served as *integral* parts of the Indian society and culture. Most schools serving minorities today, are in fact alien extracultural institutions controlled by powerful outsiders. These schools cannot meet the needs of ongoing community self-development because they exist outside of the community, in a sociocultural sense, and cannot effectively communicate with the people being served.

Finally, it is interesting that the National Advisory Commission on Civil Disorders recommended that an important objective of programs affecting urban ghettos should be

removing the frustration of powerlessness among the disadvantaged by providing the means for them to deal with the problems that affect their own lives, and by increasing the capacity of our public and private institutions to respond to these problems.[15]

These words sum up, in one important sense, the objectives of a community-responsive approach to education.

The Indian Education Act now rewards school districts which establish Indian advisory committees and special native cultural enrichment programs. Unfortunately, some of the value of these programs has been dissipated by school administrators' desires to have a compliant, easy-to-control committee comprised largely of white persons with fractional (if any) native ancestry. Similarly, teachers are sometimes hired to head such programs who have never identified with the Indian community and who have been reclassified as Indians in order to undercut Affirmative Action. Needless to state, districts which allow such subterfuges are hostile to meaningful multicultural education.

It is also important that Indian programs in the schools purchase materials produced by Indian authors and presses whenever possible.

Suggestions for Personnel Training Programs

Much of the above discussion serves to illustrate the importance of having school personnel in minority schools who are trained especially for interacting with culturally different adults and pupils. It is now widely recognized that teachers need special training for working with minority pupils. One research study revealed that

> middle-class youngsters who have apathetic teachers are less affected than are poor children of lower-class neighborhoods who have such teachers.... Revolutionary revisions in techniques of instruction and teacher recruitment, selection, and preparatory programs appear to be necessary....[16]

The Peace Corps, faced with the problem of training personnel for working with culturally different groups has made many changes as a result of criticisms made by early volunteers. "We have moved away from the traditional college classroom approach and into field programs which attempt (over a fourteen-week period) to recreate the conditions volunteers will be confronted with overseas."[17]

A good, professional, training program should seek to develop an intensive training process which will involve the cooperation of Indian adults, institutions of higher education and other agencies. This training program should be designed to 1) acquaint the teacher with the theoretical background of working with culturally different and low-income pupils, 2) acquaint the teacher with the dynamics of social process, acculturation, and cross-cultural contacts, 3) make the teacher aware of the cultural and class assumptions and prejudices which he or she may possess, 4) thoroughly acquaint the teacher with the general history and culture of American Indians, 5) specifically acquaint the teacher with the particular local population's history, culture, and present situation, and 6) provide direct practical experience at working with minority adults and youth derived from that particular population.

It is especially important to stress that any such training program should be under the overall direction of the local Indian community wherever feasible, and should, at a minimum, involve at least co-direction by the local community. With such an approach, the training program should not only serve to bring about close parent-teacher relationships and realistic knowledge on the part of new staff, but it also should serve to provide the local community with a concrete role in the exercise of power relative to the educational system.

Suggestions for Teachers and Administrators in Public Schools

A. A school serving American Indian pupils should serve as a bridge between these students and the adult world which they will subsequently enter. This adult world will sometimes be Anglo in character, but more often it will be of a mixed Anglo-Indian culture. In any case, the school, if it is to be a bridge, must serve as a transitional experience and not as a sudden leap into a foreign set of values and practices.

Additionally, American Indians live within the margins of a society which has treated them in a rather discriminatory manner for one hundred years, and more terribly still, has attempted (consciously or otherwise) to instill in the Indian a sense of inferiority. The school must address itself to the task of bolstering the self-image of native pupils and adults in order to overcome the psychological effects of a century of conquest. This is a doubly difficult task in view of the continuing reality of life in the United States, but it must be undertaken as a central function of any school serving native groups.

For all of the above reasons, such a school needs to develop a set of strategies, in close collaboration with the local Indian community, which will make the school truly belong to the people being served, rather than to the people who operate the school system.

The following are suggestions which hopefully will help to bring about such a change.

1. The school environment should have some element of American Indian character, subject, of course, to the desires of the local native community. Such character can be created by means of murals depicting aspects of the Indian

heritage, the erection of statues depicting outstanding leaders of Indian ancestry, displays of native arts and crafts, bulletin boards depicting brown people and their accomplishments, and by the adoption of a name for the school which is relevant to our indigenous past. The expense involved in the above will not necessarily be great, as adults in the local Indian community might well become involved in projects which would have the effect of making the school "their" school.

2. Teachers and administrators in such a school should be familiar with the dialect spoken in the pupil's home and should be encouraged to utilize this language wherever appropriate in order to enhance communication both with pupils and with parents, and, especially, to help develop a positive self-image on the part of the Indian people.

3. Imaginative administrators and teachers may with to further linguistic development in schools by using the local language as an early means for introducing language concepts and for developing bi-dialectical skills.

4. If a native language or dialect of English is widely spoken in the area, an "English as a second language" technique may well prove advantageous in English instruction.

5. Where the local community is interested, an American Indian language might be offered at the secondary level along with, or in place of, European languages. The United States needs persons able to speak such important tongues as Quechua, Guarani, and Maya, and even less significant languages are useful in disciplines such as anthropology and linguistics.

6. Supplementary materials utilized in the classroom, as well as library resources, should include numerous Indian-oriented items (magazines, newspapers, books, phonograph records, films, etc.), in order to provide cross-cultural experiences for all pupils and to provide an atmosphere relevant to the native pupil's heritage.

7. Every effort should be made to acquaint pupils and visiting parents with the rich literature now available pertaining to native America. Many techniques are useful, including a

permanent display case near the main entrance to the school, a paperback library operated by students or parents, a paperback bookstore, and an extensive use of supplementary soft-cover books as a part of regular classwork. Books by Indian authors should be given special prominence, as in a display case where photographs of the author can be placed next to the book being exhibited.

8. Curricula in the school should possess a native dimension wherever appropriate. In social science courses where the development of the western United States is being discussed, attention should be given to the Indian side of our history, and to more recent American Indian developments. Courses in American Indian history might well be offered in some schools and these courses should not limit their attention to United States Indian groups alone.

9. Courses in literature should include readings in American Indian literature (in translation, if necessary) and works by and about tribal peoples.

10. Curricula in music and "music appreciation" should give attention to all classes of Native American music, including pre-European styles and music of recent origin whether from the United States, Peru, or elsewhere in the Americas. In many schools instruction in American Indian musical forms might well replace or supplement the standard band and orchestra classes, in order to provide a mechanism for enriching contemporary music.

11. The dance would appear to be an area where many young Indians can readily contribute to the enrichment of a school's program. American Indian dance styles should be included in any dance curriculum, along with other forms of the art.

12. Arts and crafts courses should acquaint all pupils with Indian arts of the Americas and should provide a close tie-in with the various folk movements still in existence.

13. American Indian cooking should be available as a part of the school's programs in home economics wherever sufficient interest exists. Indian foods should be served in the cafeteria also.

14. Since one of the primary objectives of educators should be the linking of the school with the local adult community, it follows that American Indian adults and youths should be involved in the life of the school as resource people, supplementary teachers, teacher's aides, and special-occasion speakers.

    Additionally, local advisory committees should be asked to help develop policy either for a neighborhood school or for an Indian-oriented cultural enrichment program in a districtwide or regional school. *No elements of American Indian culture should be introduced into any school without the active participation of local native people in the development of the program.*

15. Our American Indian cultural heritage, whenever brought into the school, should be treated as an integral and valuable part of our common legacy, and not as a bit of "exotica" to be used solely for the benefit of brown pupils. It should be stressed that the local historical heritages of the West are almost wholly Indian prior to the last century.

16. In a school composed of students from diverse cultural backgrounds every effort should be made to bring a little of each culture into the school. A part of this effort might involve incorporating each major ethnic celebration into the school routine (focusing on Chinese-Americans at Chinese New Year, Mexican-Americans during Cinco de Mayo, Afro-Americans during Black History Week, American Indians during a period of local celebration as at harvest time, etc.).

17. School personnel should receive special training in Native American culture and history and should have some background in anthropology or sociology. It may well be that school personnel hired for employment in schools serving Indians should have several weeks of intensive pre-service training in cross-cultural dynamics not unlike that received by Peace Corps and VISTA trainees. Such training should actively involve persons from the local community.

18. A school serving an Indian community should become closely identified with the aspirations of the local community and should function, in so far as is possible, within

the framework of the local culture. This may call for much reorientation on the part of middle-class school personnel, whether of Indian or non-Indian ancestry. It will also call for a revamping of the curricula so that course content deals with the real world perceived daily by native children. For example, courses in United States Government should describe the manner in which political action actually takes place and not an idealized version of what might be the case in some non-existent utopia. Perhaps one appropriate manner in which to teach governmental concepts might involve training secondary-level students as community organizers or community service workers.

19. School personnel who believe that it is important to examine pupils periodically in order to provide data on "ability" for future counseling or "tracking" should wish to obtain accurate information by the use of tests which are relatively unbiased. It is difficult to ascertain the potential of dialect-speaking youths by means of standard English language tests, nor can that of low-income students be predicted on the basis of tests oriented toward middle-class paraphenalia or concepts. On the other hand, biased tests will substantially predict the formal achievement level of culturally different or low-income pupils attending biased schools. Therefore, a change in tests will accomplish little unless accompanied by changes in the school, which serve to realize and enhance the potential revealed by the new test.

20. Maximum use should be made of techniques which are designed to enhance self-concept and involve the community in the life of the school, including the use of parent teaching aides, older pupils as tutors for younger pupils, and college students of minority backgrounds as paraprofessionals.

21. Most American Indians are brown skinned and, therefore, suffer psychologically to some degree from the common tendency to exalt light skin and blondeness in the United States. The use of periodicals, films, books, etc., which are of non-white origin should be useful in combating the above whether the materials are produced by Indian people or not. East Indian, Latin American, and Japanese items might be especially useful in this connection.

B. The above suggestions are basically designed to change the atmosphere of the school in order to provide greater motivation for all concerned, as well as to impart useful knowledge. In addition, many curricular and methodological innovations are available which are expected to improve learning for *all* students, and these new programs should certainly be made available to American Indian youngsters. It is to be suspected, however, that a school which is basically indifferent or hostile toward the local native culture will not succeed in stimulating greater learning merely by the use of methodological innovations unaccompanied by a change in the general orientation of the school.

C. Attention should be given to Native American history and culture in all schools, regardless of ethnic composition. Anglo-American young people grow up in a "never-never" land of mythology regarding non-whites, and it is crucial for our society's future that damaging myths be exposed and eliminated. We must bear in mind that the "white problem in America," the tendency of Anglo-Americans for three centuries to exploit and denigrate non-whites, is probably still the major hurdle blocking the advancement of brown Americans. White young people, growing up in a mythic world of prejudice against non-whites and knowing little of brown contributions, may well, as adults, frustrate many of the goals of educational programs directly involving American Indians.

The multicultural reality of American life and history should be a part of every school's curriculum.

D. In many urban and rural settings it may be that the creation of "Community Education Centers" in place of age-segregating secondary, continuation, and adult schools will contribute to the solution of a number of problems. Many communities lack sufficient facilities for "adult education," have essentially unsatisfactory "continuation schools" for their difficult students, and experience serious discipline and motivation problems in their secondary schools.

For the above reasons, it is suggested that appropriate secondary schools be transformed into multipurpose "educational centers" for the total community which they serve, after the pattern of junior colleges. To eliminate the segregated "teenage" and "adult" schools, to add to the total educational resources of a community, and to improve school-community relations, the following specific changes in secondary schools are suggested:

1. Open up all classes in the regular program to any student, regardless of age, who might benefit from the class.

2. Open up all evening "adult" classes to any student, regardless of age, and develop evening programs where none exist.

3. Combine the regular day and evening programs, along with new late afternoon and Saturday classes, into a continuous day program.

4. Provide a nursery and a preschool so that mothers of small children may enroll for classes.

5. Provide a social lounge and center, perhaps in a partially used basement area, to be decorated by the students and kept open until 10:00 p.m.

6. Provide areas, if space is available, for sewing centers, etc., for adults as well as youth.

7. Utilize teenage students as much as possible in working with the nursery, preschool, and other projects, so as to provide opportunities for the development of self-confidence and other desirable qualities.

8. Abolish all age-grading systems, so that each class consists of students capable of doing the work regardless of age.

9. Allow older teenagers to carry a partial load and still remain involved in the school's program.

10. Encourage work-experience programs.

11. Encourage the teachers, parents, adult and "regular" students to elect an advisory board to develop school policy, innovations, and enrichment experiences.

12. Alter the curriculum and orientation of the school in order to make it fully relevant to the language, culture, and desires of the community served.

13. Conduct a series of intensive community-teacher workshops to develop a full awareness of the contributions which both groups can make, and of the character and social dynamics of the local community.

Accompanying the opening up of classes to all and their extension into the evening hours and to weekends, should also be the following:

1. The development of an adequate bookstore in each school, making available a significant proportion of current educational paperbound books and periodicals;

2. Allowing instructors to offer at least one seminar-type course each semester, perhaps on a topic of their choice, but with the approval of their faculty colleagues and based upon community relevance;

3. Allowing instructors to establish their own class schedules, using the extended day period and Saturday if so desired, subject primarily to the approval of their faculty colleagues;

4. Encouraging faculty to keep abreast of new knowledge in their fields by providing scholarships which would enable teachers to take additional subject-matter coursework, or to pursue research-literature review interests during the non-teaching months.

In summary, it seems a shame indeed that in many urban and isolated rural areas where nonscholastics are in obvious need of the opportunity for additional secondary-level schooling, the only schools in their areas or neighborhoods capable of meeting these needs arbitrarily restrict themselves to certain kinds of potential students or segregate by age-groups and thereby diminish the educational opportunities of all concerned.

The physical facilities and most of the personnel needed for community education centers are already available. All that is needed now is a willingness to experiment and to innovate.

A Note on Federal and Parochial Schools

The above principles should be equally applicable to schools under Federal and denominational jurisdiction. In addition, the community-responsive approach would require the establishment of local boards which provide parents with control over the basic programs of the school.

VII. GUIDE TO RESOURCES AND FURTHER READING

Published Sources (An asterisk indicates availability in paperback and suitability for classroom use, usually at the secondary level.)

This guide is not intended to be an exhaustive bibliography of materials dealing with American Indians. It is, rather a selective guide to those items which the author considers to be especially valuable for school personnel and for classroom use.

No attempt has been made to list or analyze materials designed primarily for elementary school classroom use. Instead the reader is referred to Diane Olsen, *Indians in Literature, A Selected Annotated Bibliography For Children*, University of Minnesota, Minneapolis, Minn. (EDRS, NCR, Company, 4936 Fairmont Avenue, Bethesda, Maryland, 20014. Report Number: ED 014 353. Price for hard copy: $.72)

It should be stressed that the large number of elementary-level books about Indians are of uneven quality and should be examined by Indian parents and community leaders prior to use in any given school. The Council of Interracial Books for Children, 1841 Broadway, New York, New York 10023, publishes reviews of books for young children each month. *Every school should subscribe to this publication.*

SELECTED WORKS ON AMERICAN INDIANS (other than California and Nevada)

Source material on Indians is now available in considerable quantity. Cited below are introductory or basic works, some of which are intended for use by secondary-level students while others are intended for teachers. Most of the works cited contain bibliographies which will guide the reader to more technical or regionally focused sources. The periodicals mentioned will also provide guidance to more specialized resources.

Two bibliographies have been published by the American Indian Historical Society, 1451 Masonic Avenue, San Francisco, California.

Many periodicals contain articles about Indian history and culture. The reader should begin by examining G. P. Murdock's *Ethnographic Bibliography of North America* (latest edition available) and then proceeding to journals such as *The Indian Historian, Ethnohistory, American*

Anthropologist, Ethnology, Journal of American Folklore, American Antiquity, The Masterkey, and others. Unfortunately, most of these journals are usually technical and the nonspecialist will have to be prepared to do a great deal of digging.

Native American Poetry and Traditional Literature

*Astrov, Margot, Ed., *American Indian Prose and Poetry* (New York: Capricorn, 1962).

*Hobson, Geary, Ed., *The Remembered Earth: An Anthology of Native American Literature* (Albuquerque, New Mexico, P. O. Box 26041, 87125: Red Earth Press).

*Lowenfels, Walter, *From the Belly of the Shark* (New York: Vintage, 1973).

*Rothenberg, Jerome, Ed., *Shaking the Pumpkin: Traditional Poetry of the Indian North Americans* (New York: Doubleday, 1972).

*Sanders, Thomas E. and Walter W. Peek, Eds., *Literature of the American Indian* (Beverly Hills: Glencoe Press, 1973).

*Thompson, Stith, Ed., *Tales of the North American Indians* (Bloomington: Indiana University Press, 1966).

*Underhill, Ruth, *Singing For Power* (New York: Ballantine, 1973).

*Welch, James, *Riding the Earth Boy Forty* (New York: Harper and Row, 1971).

*Witt, Shirley Hill and Stan Steiner, Eds., *The Way: An Anthology of Indian Literature* (New York: Vintage Books, 1972).

The following quarterlies or presses also regularly publish Native poetry and have back issues available:

A (Box 206, Laguna, New Mexico 87026).

The Blue Cloud Quarterly (Marvin, South Dakota 57251).

Spawning the Medicine River (Institute of American Indian Arts, Santa Fe, New Mexico 87501).

Strawberry Press (P. O. Box 451, Bowling Green Station, New York, New York 10004).

Suntracks (Indian Studies, University of Arizona, Tucson, Arizona).

UCLA American Indian Studies Center (Los Angeles, California 90024).

Native American Fiction

*Hale, Janet Campbell, *The Owl's Song* (New York: Doubleday, 1974).

*Highwater, Jamake, *Anpao* (New York: Lippincott, 1979).

*McNickle, Darcy, *Wind From an Enemy Sky* (New York: Harper and Row, 1979).

*———, *Runner in the Sun* (New York: Holt, 1954).

*Momaday, N. Scott, *House Made of Dawn* (New York: Harper and Row, 1968).

*Russell, Roger, *The Indians' Summer* (New York: Harper and Row, 1975).

*Silko, Leslie Marmon, *Ceremony* (New York: New American Library, 1977).
*Storm, Hyemeyohsts, *Seven Arrows* (New York: Harper and Row, 1973).
*Welch, James, *Winter in the Blood* (New York: Harper and Row, 1974).

Native American Non-Fiction

*Black Elk with Joseph Epes Brown, *The Sacred Pipe* (Baltimore: Penguin Books, 1971).
*Blanco, Hugo, *Land or Death: The Peasant Struggle in Peru* (New York: Pathfinder Press, 1972).
*Burnett, Robert, *Tortured Americans* (Englewood Cliffs: Prentice-Hall, 1971).
*Burnett, Robert with John Koster, *The Road to Wounded Knee* (New York: Bantam, 1973).
*Debo, Angie, *A History of the Indians of the United States* (Norman: University of Oklahoma Press, 1970).
*Deloria, Jr., Vine, *Custer Died for Your Sins* (New York: Macmillan, 1969).
Dozier, Edward P., *Hano: A Tewa Indian Community in Arizona* (New York: Holt, Rinehart & Winston, 1966).
*Fire, John and Richard Erdoes, *Lame Deer: Seeker of Visions* (New York: Simon and Schuster, 1972).
*Forbes, Jack D., *American Words: An Introduction to Those Native Words Used in English* (Davis: Tecumseh Center, 1979).
*————, *A World Rules by Cannibals* (Davis: D-Q University, 1979).
*————, *Aztecas del Norte: The Chicanos of Aztlan* (New York: Fawcett, 1973).
————, *Native American Languages: Preservation and Self-Determination* (Davis: Tecumseh Center, 1979).
————, *The Indian in America's Past* (currently out of print).
————, *Tribes and Masses* (Davis: D-Q University, 1978).
Hungry Wolf, Adolf, *The Good Medicine Book* (New York: Warner, 1973). See also separate *Good Medicine* booklets (Box 844, Invermere, B.C., Canada).
McNickle, D'Arcy, *Indian Tribes of the United States* (London: Oxford University Press, 1962).
————, *They Came Here First: The Epic of the American Indian* (New York: J. B. Lippincott Company, 1949).
Mathews, John Joseph, *The Osages* (Norman: University of Oklahoma Press, 1961).
*Neihardt, John G., Ed., *Black Elk Speaks* (Lincoln: University of Nebraska Press, 1961).
Ortiz, Roxanne Dunbar, *The Great Sioux Nation* (San Francisco: Moon Books, 1977).
Vizenor, Gerald, *The Everlasting Sky* (New York: Crowell-Collier, 1972).

Native Autobiographies (Selected)

*Barrett, S. M., *Geronimo: His Own Story* (New York: Ballantine, 1970).

*Dyk, Walter, Ed., *Son of Old Man Hat: A Navajo Autobiography* (Lincoln: Nebraska, 1966).

*Lamb, F. Bruce, *Wizard of the Upper Amazon* (Boston: Houghton Mifflin, 1975).

*Linderman, Frank B., *Plenty-Coups: Chief of the Crows* (Lincoln: Nebraska, 1962).

*————, *Pretty Shield* (Lincoln: Nebraska, 1974).

*Lurie, Nancy O., *Mountain Wolf Woman, Sister of Crashing Thunder* (Ann Arbor: University of Michigan Press, 1966).

*Marquis, Thomas B., *A Warrior Who Fought Custer,* also known as *Wooden-Legs;* several editions.

Simmons, Leo W., Ed., *Sun Chief: Autobiography of a Hopi Indian* (New Haven: Yale University Press, 1942).

Selected Works by Non-Native Americans

*Bodard, Lucien, *Green Hell: Massacre of the Brazilian Indians* (New York: Ballantine, 1971).

*Borland, Hal, *When the Legends Die* (New York: Bantam, 1964).

Burland, Cattie et al., *Mythology of the Americas* (London: Hamlyn, 1970).

Cahn, Edgar, *Our Brother's Keeper: The Indian in White America* (New York: World, 1969).

Collier, Donald, *Indian Art of the Americas* (Chicago: National History Museum, 1959).

*Collier, John, *The Indians of the Americas* (New York: New American Library, 1947).

Colson, Elizabeth, *The Makah Indians* (Minneapolis: University of Minnesota Press, 1953).

Chronicles of American Indian Protest (New York: Council on Interracial Books for Children, 1841 Broadway, New York, 10023, 1979).

*Faron, Louis C., *The Mapuche Indians of Chile* (New York: Holt, Rinehart & Winston, 1968).

*Filler, Louis and Allen Guttmann, Eds., *The Removal of the Cherokee Nation, Manifest Destiny or National Dishonor? Problems in American Civilization* (Boston: D. C. Heath and Company, 1962).

*Hoebel, E. Adamson, *The Cheyennes* (New York: Holt, Rinehart & Winston, 1960).

*Jackson, Helen Hunt, *A Century of Dishonor* (New York: Harper and Row, 1963).

*Jacobs, Wilbur R., *Dispossessing the American Indian* (New York: Scribner's, 1972).

Jenness, Diamond, *The People of the Twilight* (Chicago: University of Chicago Press, 1959).

*Katz, Jane B., Ed., *I Am the Fire of Time: Voices of Native American Women* (New York: Dutton, 1977).

Kimball, Yefee and Jean Anderson, *The Art of American Indian Cooking* (New York: Doubleday, 1965).

Lutz, Hartmut, *D-Q University: Native American Self-Determination in Higher Education* (Davis: Tecumseh Center, 1980).

MacLeod, William C., *The American Indian Frontier* (New York: Alfred A. Kuopf, 1928).

Marquis, Arnold, *A Guide to America's Indians* (Norman: University of Oklahoma Press, 1974).

*Nabokov, Peter, Ed., *Native American Testimony* (New York: Harper and Row, 1978).

Opler, Morris E., *An Apache Life-Way* (New York: Cooper Square Publishers, 1966).

*Sandoz, Mari, *Cheyenne Autumn* (New York: Avon, 1953).

————, *Crazy Horse* (Lincoln: University of Nebraska Press, 1961).

Spencer, Robert F. et al., *The Native Americans* (New York: Harper and Row, 1965).

Squires, John L. and Robert E. McLean, *American Indian Dances: Steps, Rhythms, Costumes, and Interpretation* (New York: Ronald Press, 1965).

*Traven, B., *The Kidnapped Saint and Other Stories* (New York: Lawrence Hill, 1975). (Also other Traven books, including *The Night Visitor, The Bridge in the Jungle, The Carretta, The Cotton-Pickers,* etc.—all excellent for high school students.)

*Vogel, Virgil J., *American Indian Medicine* (New York: Ballantine, 1973).

*Wilson, Carter, *Crazy February* (Berkeley: University of California Press, 1974).

*Wilson, Edmund, *Apologies to the Iroquios* (New York: Vintage, 1966).

*Wrone, David R. and Russell S. Nelson, Jr., *Who's The Savage?* (New York: Fawcett, 1973).

Surveys of bias against Indians in American history textbooks are provided in Jack D. Forbes, "The Historian and the Indian: Racial Bias in American History," *The Americas*, April 1963 and Virgil J. Vogel, "The Indian in American History Textbooks," *Integrated Education*, May-June 1968.

SOURCES ON CALIFORNIA-NEVADA HISTORY AND CULTURE

For additional resources relating to the Native American in any particular state or sub-region, the reader will wish to consult with commissions and agencies concerned with Indian affairs, human relations, and equal employment opportunities, with local organizations, with reference librarians in the larger libraries, and with white organizations concerned with civil liberties. The larger university libraries will usually contain some unpublished material, such as master's theses or doctoral dissertations, and may well have modest collections of documentary data in their archival or "special collections" departments. State and local historical societies and museums also usually possess material of value.

Especially important collections of archival data are located at the Federal Records Center, San Francisco; Federal Records Center, Los Angeles; Bancroft Library, University of California, Berkeley; Huntington Library, San Marino; and the National Archives, Washington, D.C.

Books and Monographs

Allen, Elsie, *Pomo Basketmaking* (Happy Camp: Naturegraph Publishers, 1972).

*Angulo, Jaime de, *Indian Tales* (New York: Hill and Wang, 1953).

Bailey, Paul, Wovoka, *The Indian Messiah* (Los Angeles: Westernlore Press, 1957).

Bean, Lowell J. and Thomas C. Blackburn, *Native Californians: A Theoretical Retrospective* (Ramona, California: Ballena Press, 1976).

*Brown, Vinson, *The Pomo Indians of California and Their Neighbors* (Happy Camp: Naturegraph Publishers, 1969).

Browne, J. Ross, *The California Indians* (New York: Harper Brothers, 1864).

*Brusa, Betty War, *The Salinan Indians of California and Their Neighbors* (Happy Camp: Naturegraph Publishers, 1975).

Caughey, John, *Indians of Southern California in 1852* (San Marino: Huntington Library, 1952).

Cook, Sherburne F., *The Conflict Between the California Indians and White Civilization* (Berkeley: University of California Press, 1943; published as a part of the Ibero-Americana series).

*Downs, James F., *The Two Worlds of the Washo: Indian Tribe of California and Nevada* (New York: Holt, Rinehart & Winston).

Forbes, Jack D., *Nevada Indians Speak* (Reno: University of Nevada Press, 1967).

————, *Warriors of the Colorado: The Quechans and Their Neighbors* (Norman: University of Oklahoma Press, 1965).

Grant, Campbell, *The Rock Paintings of the Chumash* (Berkeley: University of California Press, 1965).

Harner, Nellie Shaw, "History of the Pyramid Lake Indians, 1842-1959" (Unpublished master's dissertation, Department of Arts and Science, University of Nevada, 1965).

Heizer, Robert F., Ed., *Aboriginal California: Three Studies in Culture History* (Berkeley: University of California Archaeological Research Facility, 1963).

————, "Civil Rights in California in the 1850's—A Case History" (The Kroeber Anthropological Society Paper, Fall 1964, No. 31).

————, *Languages, Territories and Names of California Indian Tribes* (Berkeley: University of California Press, 1966).

Heizer, Robert F., *Notes on Some Paviotso Personalities and Material Culture* (Carson City, Nevada: Nevada State Museum, 1960).

———— and John E. Mills, *Four Ages of Tsurai: A Documentary History of the Indian Village of Trinidad Bay* (Berkeley: University of California Press, 1952).

———— and M. A. Whipple, *The California Indians: A Source Book* (Berkeley: and Los Angeles: University of California Press, 1951).

———— and Alan F. Almquist, *The Other Californians* (Berkeley: University of California Press, 1971).

Hopkins, Sarah Winnemucca, *Life Among the Piutes: Their Wrongs and Claims* (New York: G. P. Putman's Sons, 1883).

"Indian Land Cessions in the United States," from the *18th Annual Report of the Bureau of American Ethnology, 1896-1897* (Washington, D.C.: Government Printing Office, 1899).

"The Indians of California: Bibliography" (San Francisco: American Indian Historical Society) emphasis on the northwestern area.

James, Harry C., *The Cahuilla Indians* (Los Angeles: Westernlore Press, 1960).

Johnson, B. E., *California's Gabrielino Indians* (Los Angeles: Southwest Museum, 1962).

Kelly, Isabel T., *Southern Paiute Ethnology* (Provo: University of Utah Press, 1932).

*Knudtson, Peter M., *The Wintun Indians of California and Their Neighbors* (Happy Camp: Naturegraph Publishers, 1977).

Kroeber, A. L., *Handbook of the Indians of California* (Washington, D.C.: GPO, 1925. Smithsonian Institute, Bureau of American Ethnography, Bulletin 78).

*Kroeber, Theodora, *Ishi in Two Worlds* (Berkeley: University of California Press, 1961).

————, *Ishi: Last of His Tribe* (Berkeley: Parnassus Press, 1964). For junior high school level although of interest to adults also.

*————, *The Inland Whale: Nine Stories From California Indian Legends* (Berkeley: University of California Press, 1963).

Landberg, Leif C. W., *The Chumash Indians of Southern California* (Los Angeles: Southwest Museum, 1965).

Latta, F. F., *Handbook of Yokut Indians* (Bakersfield: Kern County Museum, 1949).

Masson, Marcelle, *A Bag of Bones* (Happy Camp: Naturegraph Publishers, 1966).

Merriam, C. Hart, *Studies of California Indians* (Berkeley: University of California Press, 1962).

Murray, Keith A., *The Modocs and Their War* (Norman: University of Oklahoma Press, 1965).

*Potts, Marie, *The Northern Maidu* (Happy Camp: Naturegraph Publishers, 1977).

Price, John Andrew, "Washo Economy" (master's thesis, University of Utah, April 1962).

Reid, Hugo, *Indians of California* (Berkeley: University of California Press, 1939).

Robinson, W. W., *The Indians of Los Angeles, Story of the Liquidation of a People* (Los Angeles, 1952).

Scott, Lalla, Ed., *Karnee: A Paiute Narrative* (Reno: University of Nevada Press, 1966).

*Simpson, Richard, *Ooti: A Maidu Legacy* (Millbrae, California: Celestial Arts, 1976).

Underhill, Ruth M., *Indians of Southern California* (Ph.D., Associate Supervisor of Indian Education, Sherman Pamphlets #2. A publication of the Education Division, United States Office of Indian Affairs, Haskell Institute Printing Department, Lawrence, Kansas.) A very general and somewhat erroneous introduction.

————, *The Northern Paiute Indians of California and Nevada* (United States Department of the Interior, Bureau of Indian Affairs, 1941). Very general and containing errors.

Walker, Edwin F., *Indians of Southern California* (Southwest Museum Leaflets No. 10, Southwest Museum, Highland Park, Los Angeles, Calif. 90042).

Wheat, Margaret, *Primitive Survival Arts of the Northern Paiute* (Reno: University of Nevada Press, 1968).

The following presses should be contacted for up-to-date lists of all their available publications on California or Nevada Indians:

Ballena Press, Ramona, CA 92065

The Indian Historian Press, 1451 Masonic, San Francisco, CA 94117

..lki Museum Press, Morongo Indian Reservation, Banning, CA 92220

...er-Tribal Council of Nevada, Inc., 1995 E. 2nd St., Reno, Nevada 89503

Walker River Paiute Tribe, Schurz, Nevada 89427

UCLA American Indian Studies Center, Los Angeles, CA 90024

Periodicals and Serial Publications

The bulk of material useful for in-depth studies relating to any particular group of California-Nevada Indians are to be found in such publications as the University of California's *Publications in American Archaeology and Ethnology, Anthropological Records, Publications in Linguistics, Archaeological Survey Report,* and *Ibero-Americana,* the series of the Nevada State Museum, the reports of the *Great Basin Anthropological Conference,* the Smithsonian Institute—Bureau of American Ethnology *Bulletin* and *Annual Report,* the University of Utah Anthropological Papers, and various historical and anthropological quarterlies.

The following list of reports and articles is meant to be illustrative only, that is, to show the reader the range covered by articles and types of journals.

Beals, Ralph L., "Ethnology of the Nisenan," *University of California Publications in American Archaeology and Ethnology*, v. 31, no. 6, 1933.

Brimlow, George F., "The Life of Sarah Winnemucca: The Formative Years." *Oregon Historical Quarterly*, v. 53, no. 2, June 1952.

Cook, S. F., "Migration and Urbanization of the Indians of California," *Human Biology*, February, 1943, v. 15, no. 1.

————"Aboriginal Population of the San Joaquin Valley," *Anthropological Records* 16:2 (Berkeley: University of California Press, 1955).

————"Population Trends Among the California Mission Indians," *Ibero-Americana*: 17 (Berkeley: University of California Press, 1940).

Drucker, Philip, "The Tolowa and Their Southwest Oregon Kin," *University of California Publications in American Archaeology and Ethnology*, v. 36, no. 4, 1937.

Ellison, William H., "The Federal Indian Policy in California, 1846-1860," *Mississippi Valley Historical Review*, v. 9, 1922.

Evans, William Edward, "The Garra Uprising: Conflict Between San Diego Indians and Settlers in 1851," *California Historical Society Quarterly*, v. XLV, no. 4, December 1966.

Forde, C. Daryll, "Ethnography of the Yuma Indians," *University of California Publications in American Archaeology and Ethnology*, v. 28, no. 4.

Gifford, E. W., "The Northfork Mono," *University of California Publications in American Archaeology and Ethnology*, v. 31, no. 2, 1932.

Grosscup, Gorden L., "Lovelock Northern Paiute and Culture Change," *Nevada State Museum Papers*, no. 9 (Thelma D. Calhound, editor, published in Carson City, Nevada, January 1963).

Riddell, Francis A., "Honey Lake Paiute Ethnography," *Anthropological Papers*, no. 4 (Nevada State Museum, Carson City, Nevada, December 1960).

Kasch, Charles, "The Yokayo Rancheria," *California Historical Society Quarterly*, v. XXVI, no. 3, September 1947.

Kelly, Isabel T., "Ethnography of the Surprise Valley Paiute," *University of California Publications in American Archaeology and Ethnology*, v. 31, no. 3, 1932.

Kroeber, A. L., "Types of Indian Cultures in California," *University of California Publications in American Archaeology and Ethnology*, v. 19, no. 5.

Merriam, C. Hart, "Ethnographic Notes on California Indian Tribes." Compiled and edited by R. F. Heizer, *Reports of the University of California Archaeological Survey*, no. 68, Part I, University of California Archaeological Facility, Department of Anthropology, Berkeley, 1966.

Merriam, C. Hart, "Ethnological Notes on California Indian Tribes. II. Ethnological Notes on Northern and Southern California Tribes." Compiled and edited by R. F. Heizer. *Reports of the University of California Archaeological Survey,* no. 68, Part II, February 1967, University of California Archaeological Research Facility, Department of Anthropology.

Miller, William C., ed., "The Pyramid Lake Indian War, 1860," *Nevada Historical Society Quarterly,* v. 1, no.1-2 (Nevada 1957).

Steward, J. H., "Ethnography of the Owens Valley Paiute," *University of California Publications in American Archaeology and Ethnology,* v. 33, no. 3, 1933.

"The Stone and Kelsey 'Massacre' on the Shores of Clear Lake in 1849, the Indian Viewpoint," *California Historical Society Quarterly,* v. XI, no. 3, September 1932.

Strong, William Duncan, "Aboriginal Society in Southern California," *University of California Publications in American Archaeology and Ethnology,* v. 27 (Berkeley: University of California Press, 1929).

Watkins, Frances E., "Charles F. Lummis and the Sequoya League," *Southern California Quarterly,* June-September 1944, v. 26, nos. 2 & 3.

Young, Lucy, "Out of the Past: A True Indian Story," told by Lucy Young of Round Valley Indian Reservation to Edith V. A. Murray, *California Historical Society Quarterly,* v. XX, no. 4, December 1941.

Articles and Reports

Scholarly articles on contemporary Indian affairs usually appear in journals such as *Human Organization, Phylon, Journal of American Indian Education, Current Anthropology, América Indigena, Boletin Indigenista,* and journals concerned with economic development and cultural change.

The best source of information on current affairs stems, of course, from Indian publications. Many tribal councils mimeograph their minutes and these can sometimes be obtained by subscription. Some tribes, and many inter-tribal groups, have formal publications. Some Indian publications are listed below (the best sources are asterisked).

The American Indian, American Indian Council, Inc., 3053 16th Street, San Francisco, CA 94103. Published monthly; sent on request.

Akwesasne Notes, Mohawk Nation via Rooseveltown, NY 13683.

American Indian Bulletin, Inter-Tribal Friendship House, 523 E. 14th Street, Oakland, CA 94606.

Apache Drumbeat, P. O. Box 356, San Carlos, AZ 85550.

Association of Indian Manpower Programs *News,* 7100 Bowling Drive, Suite 180, Sacramento, CA 95823.

Association of American Indian Physicians *Newsletter,* 6801 So. Western, Suite 206, Oklahoma City, OK 73139.

California Indian Days *Newsletter,* P. O. Box 15649, Sacramento, CA 95813.

Cherokee Newsletter, Finis Smith, Box 473, Tahlequah, OK 74464.

The Drum, P. O. Box 1069, Inuvik, N.W.T., Canada.

Drumbeat. Inter-Tribal Friendship House, 523 East 14th Street, Oakland, CA 94606.

Early American, Ad Hoc Committee on California Indian Education, 1349 Crawford Road, Modesto, CA 95352.

The Indian Historian – Official Publication of the American Indian Historical Society, Inc., The Chautauqua House, 1451 Masonic Avenue, San Francisco, CA 94117.

Jicarilla Chieftain, Dulce, NM 87528.

The NCAI Sentinel, National Congress of American Indians, 1346 Connecticut Avenue, N.W., Room 1019, Washington, D.C. 20036.

The Native Nevadan (Official Newspaper of the Inter-Tribal Council of Nevada, Inc.), 1995 E. 2nd Street, Reno, Nevada 89503. Published monthly.

Native Press, Box 1919, Yellowknife, N.W.T., Canada.

The Navajo Times, Window Rock, AZ 86515.

Rosebud Sioux Herald, Tribal Office, Rosebud, SD 57570.

Sacramento Indian Center News, 1912 F Street, Sacramento, CA 95814.

Treaty Council News, 777 United Nations Plaza, New York, NY 10017.

The Tribal Spokesman, 2220 Watt Avenue, Suite C-13, Sacramento, CA 95825.

Tundra Times, Box 1287, Fairbanks, AK 99701.

War Cry, Box 379, Pine Ridge, SD 57770.

Wassaja (Same address as *The Indian Historian*).

Yakima Nation Review, P. O. Box 386, Toppenish, WA 98948.

SOURCES ON NATIVE INDIAN EDUCATION

A number of bibliographies are available including one in Jack D. Forbes, *Education of the Culturally Different: A Multi-Cultural Approach* (Berkeley: Far West Laboratory, 1968). This latter includes references to materials relating to culture change, conquest and colonialism and their relationship to education, as well as a list of other bibliographies. The ERIC Clearinghouse at New Mexico State University, Las Cruces, New Mexico, provides the most comprehensive source of recent studies on Indian education. Contact them for lists of titles available on microfiche or as reprints.

Additional items, worthy of special note or difficult to find in most bibliographies, include:

Anderson, James G. and Dwight Safar, *The Influence of Differential Community Perceptions on the Provision of Equal Educational Opportunities* (New Mexico State University Research Center, 1967).

Brown, Anthony D., *A Johnson-O'Malley Educational Program for California Indians* (Sacramento: State Advisory Commission on Indian Affairs, June 1967).

Bryde, John F., "Indian Educational Needs" (Denver, Colorado: Upper Midwest Regional Educational Laboratory Conference on Indian Education, February 8-9, 1967).

Dumont, Robert V., Jr. and Murray L. Wax, ms., "The Cherokee School Society and the Intercultural Classroom."

The Education of Indian Children in Canada (Toronto: Ryerson Press, 1965).

An Experiment in Programmed Cross-Cultural Education: The Import of the Cherokee Primer for the Cherokee Community and for the Behavioral Sciences. (Carnegie Corporation Cross-Cultural Education Project of the University of Chicago).

Fennessey, James, *An Exploratory Study of Non-English Speaking Homes and Academic Performance* (Baltimore: John Hopkins University Center for the Study of Social Organization of Schools, 1967).

Forbes, Jack D., "An American Indian University: A Proposal for Survival," *Journal of American Indian Education*, January 1966.

————, *Racism, Scholarship and Cultural Pluralism in Higher Education* (Davis: Tecumseh Center, 1977).

———— and Howard Adams, *A Model of Grass-Roots Community Development: The D-Q University Native American Language Education Project* (Davis: Tecumseh Center, 1976).

Fuchs, Estelle, "Innovation at Rough Rock," *Saturday Review* (September 16, 1967).

Fuchs, Estelle and Robert Havighurst, *To Live On This Earth: American Indian Education* (New York: Doubleday, 1973).

Gast, David K., *Minority Americans in Children's Literature* (reprinted from *Elementary English*, January 1967).

Gudschinsky, Sarah C., *How To Learn an Unwritten Language*, Summer Institute of Linguistics (Studies in Anthropological Method, eds: George and Louise Spindler, Stanford University, 1967).

Hickman, John M. and Jack Brown, *Aymara Biculturalism and Sociopsychological Adjustment in Bolivia* (Cornell University, Andean Indian Community Research and Development Project, ms.).

Indian Integration in Nevada Public Schools (Nevada State Department of Education, 1966).

Kelley, William H., *Current Research on American Indian Education: A Critical Review of Selected Ongoing Studies* (Bureau of Ethnic Research, University of Arizona, Tucson).

King, Richard A., *The School at Mopass* (New York: Holt, Rinehart & Winston, 1967).

King, Richard A., "A Study of Values in a Canadian School" (Microfilm, Stanford International Development Education Center, Stanford University).

Leighton, Dorothea C., and Clyde Kluckholm, *Children of the People: The Navaho Individual and His Development* (Cambridge: Harvard University Press, 1947).

Lund, Betty Faye, "A Survey of Comparative Achievement and Scholarship Records of California Indian Children in the Auburn Public Schools" (unpublished master's thesis, Sacramento State College, 1963).

Lutz, Hartmut, *D-Q University* (Davis: Tecumseh Center, 1980).

Modiano, Nancy, "Reading Comprehension in the National Language: A Comparative Study of Bilingual and All-Spanish," doctor's thesis, New York University, 1966.

Musser, Donald K., "An Investigation of Indian Student Drop-outs at Ukiah Union High School" (ms. 1952).

Rancharan-Crowley, Pearl, "Creole Culture: Outcast in West Indian Schools," *The School Review*, v. 69, 1962.

Reichert, Joshua and Miguel Trujillo, eds., *Perspectives on Contemporary Native American and Chicano Educational Thought* (Davis: D-Q University, 1973-1974).

Roessel, Robert A., Jr., *Handbook for Indian Education* (Los Angeles: Amerindian Publishing Company, 1967).

The Treatment of Minorities in Secondary School Textbooks (Anti-Defamation League of B'nai B'rith, 515 Madison Avenue, New York, 1963).

Wall, Leon C., "Indian Education in Nevada, 1861-1951" (unpublished master's thesis, Department of Education, University of Nevada, 1952).

Wax, Rosalie H., "The Warrior Dropouts," *Trans-action*, May 1967.

Whitman, Carl, Jr., "Comprehensive Renovation of the Education Program" (mimeographed).

Wilson, Herbert, *Evaluation of Social Action Education Programs: Case Study of UNESCO Center at Patzcuaro, Mexico* (Stanford University Inter-library Loan Service, Stanford International Development Education Center).

Wolcott, Harvey F., *A Kwakiutl Village and School* (New York: Holt, Rinehart & Winston, 1967).

Audio-Visual Sources

The acquisition of audio-visual materials of appropriate quality and relevance is always a difficult and never-ending task. Perhaps the following suggestions will open up new avenues for the gathering together of such aids, but it must be borne in mind that no guidebook can take the place of imagination and perseverance on the part of school personnel.

The local Native American community will ultimately comprise the best source for the greater part of audio-visual materials used in any school. No matter where such materials are acquired, they should be reviewed by representatives of the local community. Illustrations from national magazines may seem quite appropriate to middle-class teachers, but may be unacceptable to local Native American people; or it may well be that the total context in which illustrations or other media are used may be acceptable while the individual units are not, or vice versa.

RECORDINGS

The Archive of Folk Song of the Library of Congress publishes a catalog of available recordings, entitled *Folk Music*. This catalog is available from the U. S. Government Printing Office, Washington, D.C. 20402. Available in the Archive of Folk Song are songs from the Iroquois, Seneca, Mexican Indians, Chippewa, Sioux, Quechan (Yuma), Cocopa, Yaqui, Pawnee, Northern Ute, Papago, Nootka, Quileute, Menominee, Mandan, Hidatsa, Kiowa, Delaware, Cherokee, Choctaw, Creek, Paiute, Washo, Ute, Bannock, Shoshone, Comanche, Cheyenne, Caddo, Wichita, Navaho, Taos, San Ildefono, Zuni, and Hopi peoples. These records may be ordered from the Library of Congress, Music Division, Recording Laboratory, Washington, D.C. 20540.

Columbia Records, Education Department, 799 Seventh Avenue, New York 10019, also has previously issued a brochure which lists the folk records available on the "Columbia" and "Epic" labels. Interested persons should write to the above address for current information on this series.

Canyon Records, 834 North Seventh Avenue, Phoenix, Arizona 85006, offers a selection of predominantly Navaho and Southwest Indian music. Write to the above address for the latest price lists and other information.

Folkways Records, 121 West 47th Street, New York 10019, has an excellent selection of Native American recordings such as "Healing Songs of the American Indians," "Anthology of Brazilian Indian Music," "Indian Music of the Pacific Northwest Coast," and "Mushroom Ceremony of the Mazatec Indians of Mexico." Write to the above address for price lists and information. Similarly, write to Ethnic Folkways Records, 165 West 46th Street, New York 10019, for information on their Native American recordings. Folkways/Scholastic Records, 50 West 44th Street, New York 10019, also has issued several recordings of Indian music.

A visit to a good record store specializing in folk music will reveal numerous other recordings of American Indian music or, if such a store is not readily available, lists of such recordings may be acquired from individual record companies, or through the current *Schwann Record and Tape Guide* on hand at most record stores.

The *Educator's Guide to Free Social Studies Materials* lists recordings available at no charge from various kinds of agencies; however, these must be examined carefully for evidence of propaganda. Such recordings need to be reviewed carefully by appropriate persons in order to validate accuracy and perspective.

The *National Audio Tape Catalog* (National Education Association, 1201 16th Street, N.W., Washington, D.C. 20036) presents narratives on a wide variety of subjects concerning the Native American (e.g., American Primitive Painting, Legends of the Aztecs, the Seneca Language, and "America's First Citizens—The American Indian Before the White Man").

PICTURES, POSTERS, ARTS AND CRAFTS

Magazines can be excellent sources of pictures for bulletin boards, along with local newspapers. Posters and illustrative material depicting current aspects of Native American life may be obtained from the consulates of American governments as well as from airlines serving Central and South America. Another source of illustrative material might be the chambers of commerce in states where Native Americans live. Inquiries should also be made to the New Mexico State Tourist Bureau, Capitol Building, Santa Fe, New Mexico 87501, and to the Santa Fe Film Bureau, the Acheson, Topeka & Santa Fe Railroad, 80 East Jackson Blvd., Chicago, Illinois 60604, for additional free material.

State and local museums and historical societies will provide upon request copies of photographs in their collection on Native Americans. There is usually a small charge for this service. It is always advisable to write first for information. Other institutions which also offer this service are given below.

Heye Foundation, Museum of the American Indian, 3751 Broadway, New York, NY 10032.

Still Pictures Section, National Archives, Washington, D.C. 20408.

Gallup Intertribal Indian Ceremonial Association, Second and Hill Streets, Gallup, NM 87301.

Southwest Museum, Highland Park, Los Angeles, CA 90042.

Useful sources for Native American arts and crafts are given below.

Alaska Indian Arts, Inc. Box 271, Haines, AK 99827.

Alaska Native Arts & Crafts, Inc., Box 889, Juneau, AK 99801.

American Indian Foundation, 26265 West River Road, Grosse Ile, MI 48138.

Fort McDermitt Arts & Crafts, Box 88, McDermitt, NV 89421.

Hopi Arts & Crafts Guild, Oraibi, AZ 86039.

Ka-Eyta, Inc., Harlem, MT 59526.

Mescalero Apache Tribe, Box 176, Mescalero, NM 88340.

Navajo Arts & Crafts Guild, Window Rock, AZ 86515.

Oklahoma Cherokee Indian Arts & Crafts Center, P. O. Box 533, Tahlequah, OK 74464.

Oklahoma Indian Arts & Crafts Cooperative, Box 749, Anadarko, OK 73005.

University and public libraries have many books containing pictures and information regarding Native Americans or can obtain them through inter-library loans. Many libraries are equipped to make photocopies of illustrations from their collections.

Naturegraph Publishers, Inc., P. O. Box 1075, Happy Camp, CA 96039, has published Indian maps in color of the Pomo, Salinan, and Wintun regions of California. These maps are included in Naturegraph's American Indian Map Book Series, which should be especially useful to many California schools.

The gathering together of an adequate supply of posters and pictures can be an excellent parent-teacher cooperative project. Involving the parents in such an endeavor will serve to activate local sources of material and will also help to ensure the acceptability of the items placed on display.

FILMS AND FILMSTRIPS

Commercial concerns are producing films and filmstrips for the school market dealing with Native American history, culture and contemporary issues. The accuracy and acceptability of these commercial products is not uniformly high, however, and they should be previewed before purchased by persons familiar with current conditions and recent research, including individuals from the local Native American community.

The Oakland, California, schools have produced a "Resource Guide for Teaching About Contributions of Minorities to American Culture" (1966) which lists and describes some of the commercial educational films dealing with the above subjects. Readers will also wish to check with their local educational television station for information on the availability of some of the excellent television productions dealing with Native Americans.

Listed below are those organizations which offer a wide selection of films for *lease or purchase* on Native Americans. Catalogs of these collections may be available at local public libraries and universities or obtained by writing to these organizations directly.

Educational Motion Pictures, Audio-Visual Center, Division of University Extension, Indiana University, Bloomington, IN 47401.

University of California Extension Media Center, 2223 Fulton Street, Berkeley, CA 94720.

Encyclopedia Britannica Films, Inc., 7250 MacArthur Blvd., Oakland, CA 94605.

There are also those organizations which will loan their films *without charge*. However, the propagandistic element in these "free" films is apt to be extremely high. Write to them for catalogs or for additional information.

The Educator's Guide to Free Social Studies Materials, Educator's Progress Service, Randolph, WI 53956.

Modern Talking Pictures, 927 19th Street, N.W., Washington, D.C. 20006.

The Atchison, Topeka and Santa Fe Railway Company, Public Relations Department, 314 Railway Exchange, 80 East Jackson Blvd., Chicago, IL 60600.

New Mexico Department of Development, 302 Galisteo Street, Santa Fe, NM 87501.

The Bureau of Indian Affairs has several films which, however, must be purchased. A film on the Washo is available from Western Artists Corp., 512 Calle Alamo, Santa Barbara, CA 93105, while many other films are listed in an index issued by the National Information Center for Educational Media, University of Southern California, Los Angeles, California.

Motion pictures produced in non-white countries, such as India and Japan, might well be made available in assemblies so as to help reinforce efforts as cross-cultural education and to vividly convey a sense of the rich legacies of non-European peoples. This may be especially important in communities lacking in theaters showing international films.

Guides to 16 mm. commercial films should be useful in locating suitable motion pictures and making contacts with distributors. Some useful guides are listed below.

Films in Review, National Board of Reviewers of Motion Pictures, Inc., 31 Union Square, New York, NY 10003. Reviews United States 35 mm. films.

Film Reports, Film Board National Organization, 522 Fifth Avenue, New York, NY 10036. Monthly, free to libraries. Reviews United States and foreign 35 mm. films.

International Motion Picture Almanac, Quigley Publishing Co., 1270 Sixth Avenue, New York, NY 10009. A guide to 35 mm. films.

Title Guide to the Talkies, 1947-1963, by R. B. Dimmitt, 2 v. (New York: Scarecrow Press, 1965). An annotated guide to 35 mm. films.

Several commercial firms publish catalogs of commercial-type movies which are available for schools on 16 mm. film. Among these are: Brandon International Films, Western Cinema Guild Inc., 244 Kearny Street, San Francisco, CA 94108; and Teaching Film Custodians, 25 West 43rd Street, New York 10036.

There are many other guides and catalogs available dealing with "educational films" especially prepared for school audiences and these should be obtainable in any district's audio-visual office. Bernard Klein's *Guide to American Educational Directories* (New York: McGraw-Hill, 1965) should serve as an initial source in case such guides have not been collected locally.

CALIFORNIA-NEVADA NATIVE AMERICAN HISTORY CHART

HIGHLIGHTS OF HISTORY OF INDIANS IN CALIFORNIA AND NEVADA SINCE 1539

Date	Locality	Event
1539-1769	California-Arizona	Visited by Spanish expeditions. Generally these first white contacts with the natives were peaceable, and trade goods were introduced.
1744	S. E. California	Halchidhoma of Colorado River are trading for horses. Horses came slowly to be used by California-Nevada natives, but spread rapidly after 1770s.
1769-1800	California coast	Most coastal missions and forts established. Many Indians Christianized and taken into mission to work. Indians react peaceably or with fear at first, not understanding Spanish duplicity and plans of conquest.
1775	San Diego	Mission destroyed by Kamia. First serious revolt against missions.
1776	San Francisco	Attack on San Francisco by Indians revolting against cruel treatment.
1781	Colorado River	Quechan rebel and destroy Spanish garrisons because Spanish are offensive to them. Salvador Palma (Olleyquotequiebe), his brother, Ygnacio Palma, and other Quechan leaders, as well as Francisco Xavier, a Halyikwamai, lead brave fight. Spanish are completely driven out of this area.
1782-1783	Colorado River	Quechans repulse later attacks. Nationhood of Quechans preserved. Success mainly due to political unity and sophistication of these people.
1785	Los Angeles area	Tongvas attack and almost take San Gabriel Mission. The Hapchi-vitam and a woman religious leader, Toypurina, lead the revolt.
1793-1795	San Francisco area	Indians flee mission to start revolt across Bay among the Saklan and Cuchillones (Little Knives). Charquin (Charkeen) leads the struggle. Pits dug by natives to trap attacking Spaniards on horses.
1804	Salinas Valley	Chief Guchapa of Cholan refuses to aid San Miguel Mission to secure converts. He is later arrested after fight and forced, by holding his son as hostage, to help Christianize his people.

Date	Locality	Event
1809-1840	Bodega Bay area	Russians come to Bodega Bay area and then found Ft. Ross. Russians are friendly with Indians and even supply them with arms against the Spaniards. The Russians leave when slaughter of sea otters brings end to their fur trade.
1819	Calif. coast	By this date over 40,000 Indians have died from white-brought diseases.
1822	Calif. coast	Coastal California becomes part of Mexican Republic. Conditions remain same for conquered natives at first, but seeds of new revolt brewing.
1824	Marin County	Hukueko put up heroic resistance against Mexicans. Leaders, such as Pomponio, Marin and Quintin, hide in woods and attack or ambush Mexicans.
1827-1839	San Joaquin Valley	Warfare and border fights and raids rage between Mexicans and natives (mainly Yokuts). Estanislao and Cipriano (ex-mission Indians) escape and lead in clever and heroic battles, often defeating Mexicans by aid of fortifications.
1834-1847	Sonoma Co., Calif.	Mariano and Salvador Vallejo ruthlessly carve out empire. They enslave Indians and Salvador treats the natives with extreme cruelty. Sametoy (or Solano), Suisun leader, helps Mexicans, but leaders like Ampay of the Yolos and Saccara of the Sotoyomes (a Pomo group near Healdsburg) fight back valiantly, assisted by Miyakmas (Wappos) and Tuleyomes (south of Clear Lake).
1840s-1860s	Nevada	Slave-raids from New Mexico harm Southern Paiutes; Anglo travelers destroy food of Humboldt River Paiutes and Shoshones. Nevada Indians begin to feel direct effects of invasion after early friendly contacts with whites.
1848-1849	California	Gold Rush upsets Indian economy and many Indians seek gold to buy food. Stone-Kelsey outfit in Clear Lake area, like some other whites, enslave Indians for mining and ranching. Their cruelty causes Pomos Shuk and Xasis to execute them, bringing brutal massacre of Pomos by Anglos.
1851-1852	Southern California	Cahuillas, Kamias, Quechans, etc., angered by great injustices, stage final revolt against Anglos, which is crushed by U. S. forces. Antonio Guarra, a Kupanga-kitom, is chief leader in this bitter fight.
1851-1865	California & Nevada	Treaties made with many groups, later repudiated or broken by Congress.

Date	Locality	Event
1860	Nevada	Northern Paiutes win victory at Pyramid Lake against white militia. As usual Indians were attacked first and Indian girls kidnapped.
1869-1875	California & Nevada	First "Ghost Dance" spreads; a religious revival to bring back the good days.
1870-1885	California & Nevada	Sarah Winnemucca (Northern Paiute) campaigns for native rights and dignity.
1872-1873	N. E. California	Modoc War shows how small group of Indians hold off army. Captain Jack (Kentipoos) cleverly uses rugged lava caves for defense against attack.
1883-1914	Mendocino Co., Calif.	Round Valley Indians attempt to burn government boarding school five times. Natives actively resist Bureau of Indians Affairs' oppressive school programs.
1887-1890	Nevada	Wovoka (Northern Paiute prophet) revives the "Ghost Dance," in which Indians seek spiritual recovery and strength. Spreads mainly to Plains tribes.
1890-1895	Western Nevada	Senator William Stewart tries to take away reservations. Northern Paiutes successfully resist Stewart and keep lands.
1904	No. California	Yokayo Pomo go to court to successfully defend their land rights.
1910-1911	No. Nevada	"Shoshone Mike" leads last Indian fighting in country near Elko.
1917	Lake County	Ethan Anderson (Pomo) wins court case to allow nonreservation Indian voting rights.
1918	Lake & Mendocino Cos.	Society of Northern California Indians organized to seek long-denied justice.
1920	California	Northern California Indians seek legislation allowing them to be paid for lost lands. This eventually results in the California Indian Claims cases.
1920-1922	So. California	Federation of Mission Indians resists injustices; persecuted by government.
1924	Inyo County	Indians win legal right to attend California public schools (Piper vs. Big Pine, S.D.).
1944	No. Nevada	Supreme Court rules in favor of Indian land rights at Pyramid Lake Reservation.
1964-1969	California & Nevada	American Indian Historical Society (led by Costos) fights for true Indian history.
1967-1969	California	Ad Hoc Committee on Indian Education, chairmaned by David Risling (Hoopa), begins vital work to improve Indian education.

Date	Locality	Event
1968	No. Nevada	Stanley Smart kills deer out of season to test Indian hunting rights in court. Western Shoshones drive white hunters off their lands. Nevada Indians awaken.
1968	California & Nevada	United Native Americans organized in San Francisco to unite all American Indians.
1968	National focus	American Indian Movement and *Akwesasne Notes* founded.
1969	National focus	Louis R. Bruce, Mohawk-Sioux, appointed as Commissioner of Indian Affairs; soon begins effort to reform the BIA. Termination repudiated by Republican leadership.
1969-1971	National focus	Wave of "occupations" by Indians, at Alcatraz, DQU, Fort Lawton, etc.
1970	National focus	Zuni Tribe is first tribe to take over BIA operations at local level; American Indian Press Association organized; Nixon restores Blue Lake to Taos, supports "self-determination" but "old-guard" in the BIA fights reforms.
1971-1972	National focus	BIA in constant turmoil as Interior Secretary Rogers Morton and Robert Robertson of the Vice President's staff block reforms; Pyramid Lake, Black Mesa, Four Corners, and Alaska oil battles rage. ·
1972	National focus	National Tribal Chairmen's Association becomes new conservative power in Indian world, works with BIA "old-guard;" large amounts of money channeled to tribal leadership by Nixon officials; fight over Indian natural resources intensifies; BIA building occupied to force changes in government policy.
1973-1976	National focus	"Old-guard" regains control over BIA, most reforms halted completely; government moves against AIM during and after Wounded Knee occupation; "self-determination" abandoned by Nixon-Ford administrations.
1976-1980	National focus	Carter Administration ignores Indian affairs, allows it to drift while Indian resources become a major issue in the energy crisis; pollution and ecological destruction in Indian areas becomes a major concern.

APPENDIX

Linguistic Classification of California and Nevada Indians

The following represents an attempt to classify the idiomalities of California within the several divisions and branches of the seven language families represented in the two states. This system of classification is tentative and exploratory, because many of the various languages have not been analyzed thoroughly by trained linguists, many are known only by incomplete vocabularies, and a number have become extinct without leaving any record.

Several points should be noted: first, the author has tried to use a native term wherever feasible but other names are included for comparison; second, the names of idiomalities (a group speaking a single language or several mutually intelligible dialects) are printed in a bold type face; third, groups shown in italics indicates uncertainty as to whether that particular group's idiom was intelligible to the preceding group; fourth, the numbers in brackets refer to the map of "California Idiomality Areas;" and, finally, *it is very likely that few, if any, of these linguistic divisions meant anything to Indian people with the exception of the idiomalities themselves and these latter seldom possessed political significance.*

I. Hokan language family

  A. Northern California branch

    1. Palaihnihan (Pit River) division

      a. **Elemewi** (Achomawi, Achumawi) dialects [6]

      b. **Atsugewi-Apwúrokai** dialects [16]

    2. Shastan division

      a. **Shasta-Konomihu** dialects [3]

      b. **Kahutineruk** (New River, Tlohomtatoi) language [9]

      c. **Okwanuchu** (Okwanutsu) language [7]

    3. Karok division

      a. **Karok** (Karuk-v-arara) dialects [2]

    4. Chimariko division

      a. **Chimariko** language [12]

  B. Yana-Yahi branch

    1. Yana division

      a. **Yana** dialects [15]

    2. Yahi division

      a. **Yahi** language [18]

C. Pomoan branch
1. **Shotéah** (Northeastern) language [84]
2. **Kashia** (Southwestern) language [33]
3. **Hámfo** (Southeastern) language [27]
4. **Northern Pomo** dialects [24]
5. **Central Pomo** dialects [25]
6. **Eastern Pomo** language [26]
7. *Weshumtatah* (Southern Pomo) dialects [34]

D. Washiu branch
1. **Washo** (Washoe, Washoo) language [31]

E. Esselen branch
1. **Esselen** language [55]

F. Iskoman branch
1. Tepothálap division
   a. **Tepothálap** (Énnesen, Salinan) dialects [57]
2. Stishini-Chumashan division
   a. Stishini subdivision
      1. **Stishini** (Ticho, Obispeño) language [60]
   b. Chumashan subdivision
      1. *Kagimuswas* (Akkili, Purisimeño) language [66]
      2. *Tsamála* (Kasákompéa, Ynezeño) language [67]
      3. *Tsmúwich* (Barbareno, Kasswáh) language [68]
      4. **Mishkonaká** (Mishanákan, Ventureño) language [69]
      5. *Káshinasmú* (Cuyam, Cuyama) language [61]
      6. *Tokya* (Tecuya, Tashlipum) language [70]
      7. **Limú** (Minawa, Mitchúmash, Santa Cruz Island) language [74]
      8. *Naskwe* (Nicalke, Hurmal, Santa Rosa Island) language [73]
      9. *Wimat* (Wima, Tuakam, San Miguel Island) language [72]

G. Yuman branch
1. Pipai division
   a. **Quechan-Maricopa-Halchidhoma** dialects [81]
   b. **Hamakhava** (Mohave) language [80]
2. Ipai division
   a. **Cocopa-Halyikwamai-Kohuana** language
   b. **Kamia** (Ipai, Tipai, Diegueño, Migueleño, Tomaseño) dialects [82]
3. Pai division (not in California or Nevada)
   a. **Paipai** language
   b. Eastern Pai subdivision
      1. **Yavapai** dialects
      2. **Walpai-Havasupai** dialects

II. Penutian language family

A. Maidu-Concow-Nisenan branch
  1. **Maidu** dialects [17]
  2. **Concow** dialects [19]
  3. **Nisenan** dialects [30]

B. Mewan-Win branch
  1. Wintu-Nomlaki division
     a. **Wintu** (Northern Wintoon) dialects [8]
     b. **Wintun** (Nomlaki) dialects [20]
  2. Patwin-Suisun division
     a. **Patwin** (Win, Puiwin) dialects [29]
     b. *Suisun* dialect or language [38]
  3. Mewan division
     a. **Mewuk** (Miwok) dialects or languages [40-42]
     b. **Mewko** (Plains Miwok) language or dialects [39]
     c. *Saklan* (Bay Miwok) language [45]
     d. Hukeuko-Olamentko-Tuleyome subdivision
        1. **Tuleyome** (Lake Miwok) language [28]
        2. Hukueko-Olamentko (Coast Miwok) group
           a. **Hukueko** dialects [37]
           b. **Olamentko** language [36]

C. Ohlonean (Costanoan) branch
  1. Muwekma division
     a. **Ohlone** (San Francisco, Santa Cruz, Santa Clara, San Jose) dialects [43]
     b. **Huichun-Karkin** (San Pablo) dialects [44]
  2. Mutsun-Rumsen division
     a. **Mutsun** (Humontwash, San Juan Bautista) dialects [54]
     b. **Rumsen** (Monterey) dialects [53]
     c. **Chalón** (Soledad) dialects [56]

D. Yokuts branch
  1. Tchoyotche ("river") division
     a. Tchoyotche (Jatchikamne, Cholvone, Chulamni) language [46]
  2. "Valley" division
     a. **Yokots** (Valley) dialects [47]
     b. *Yukots* (North Foothill, Chukchansi group) dialects [48]
  3. "Foothill" division
     a. **Mayi** (Foothill) dialects [49]
     b. **Palewyami** (Ta-at) language [58]
     c. **Toxi** (Buena Vista Lake) dialects [62]

III. Lutuamian language family

A. **Modoc** language [4]

IV. Yukian language family

   A. **Ukoht-ontilka** (Coast Yuki) language [23]

   B. *Huchno'm* language [22]

   C. *Yuki* dialects [21]

   D. Mijakma ("Wappo") dialects [35]

V. Ritwan language family (perhaps Ritwan-Algonkian)

   A. **Sulatelak** (Wiyot) language [13]

   B. **Yurok** (Yuruk) dialects [10]

VI. Tinneh (Athapaskan) language family

   A. **Tolowa** (Huss) dialects [1]

   B. Hoopa-Whilkut branch

      1. **Hoopa-Whilkut-Chilula** dialects [11]

   C. Nung-gah-hl branch

      1. **Nung-gah-hl** (Kato, Mattole, Sinkyone, Wailaki, Nongatl, etc.) dialects [14]

VII. Uto-Aztecan language family

   A. Numic (Shoshonean) branch

      1. Nehmeh division

         a. **Nehmeh** (Nehmuh, Northern Paiute-Bannock) language [5]

         b. *Neuma* (Pitanakwat, Owens Valley Paiute) language [51]

         c. *Nim* (Mono, Monache) dialects [50]

      2. Nihmih division

         a. **Nihmih** (Shoshone-Comanche) language [52]

         b. *Panamint* (Koso, Death Valley Shoshone) language [52]

      3. Nihwi division

         a. **Nihwi** (Ute-Southern Paiute-Chemehuevi) language [65]

         b. **Nu-ú-a** (Kawaiisu, Tehachapi) language [63]

   B. Tubatulabal branch

      1. **Tubatulabal-Palagewan-Bankalachi** dialects [59]

   C. Vitamic branch (Takic, "Southern California Shoshonean")

      1. **Tongva** (Vitam, Gabrieleño, Fernandeño) language or dialects [76]

      2. Maringayam-Kitanemuk ("Serrano")

         a. **Maringayam** (Serrano, Vanyume, Möhinayam) dialects [77]

         b. *Kitanemuk* language [71]

      3. Iviatim-kitom division

         a. **Iviatim** (Cahuilla, Palm Springs, Wanakik) dialects [79]

         b. **Atáhum** (Luiseño-Juaneño-Soboba) dialects [78]

         c. *Kupanga-kitom* (Cupeño) language [83]

      4. *Ghalashat* (Nicoleño) language [75]

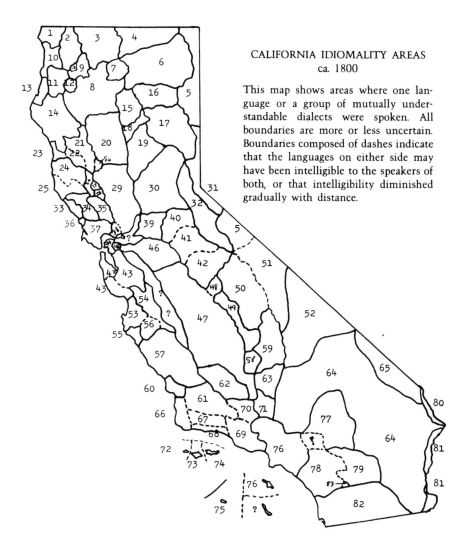

CALIFORNIA IDIOMALITY AREAS
ca. 1800

This map shows areas where one language or a group of mutually understandable dialects were spoken. All boundaries are more or less uncertain. Boundaries composed of dashes indicate that the languages on either side may have been intelligible to the speakers of both, or that intelligibility diminished gradually with distance.

Key to "California Idiomality Areas" Map

1. Tolowa (or Huss) dialects.
2. Karok (Karuk) dialects.
3. Shasta-Konomihu dialects.
4. Modoc language.
5. Nehmeh (Northern Paiute-Bannock) language.
6. Elemewi (Pit River or Achomawi) dialects.
7. Okwanuchu language.
8. Wintu ("Northern Wintoon") dialects.
9. Kahutineruk (Tlohomtahoi or New River) language.
10. Yurok (Yuruk) dialects.
11. Hoopa-Whilkut-Chilula dialects.
12. Chimariko language.
13. Sulatelak (Wiyot) language.
14. Nung-gah-hl dialects.
15. Yana dialects.
16. Atsugewi-Apwúrokai dialects.
17. Maidu dialects.
18. Yahi language.
19. Concow dialects.
20. Wintu (Nomlaki) dialects.
21. Yuki dialects.
22. Huchno'm dialects.
23. Ukoht-ontilka (Coast Yuki) language.
24. Northern Pomo dialects.
25. Central Pomo dialects.
26. Eastern Pomo language.
27. Hámfo (Southeastern Pomo) language.
28. Tuleyome ("Lake Miwok") language.
29. Patwin dialects.
30. Nisenan dialects.
31. Washo (Washoe, Washoo) language.
32. Uninhabited joint use area.
33. Kashia (Kashaya) language.
34. Weshumtatah (Southern Pomo) dialects.
35. Miyakma ("Wappo") dialects.
36. Olamentko ("Bodega Miwok") language.
37. Hukueko ("Coast Miwok") dialects.
38. Suisun language.
39. Mewko (Plains Miwok) language.
40. Northern Mewuk dialects.
41. Central Mewuk dialects.
42. Southern Mewuk dialects.
43. Ohlone (San Francisco, Santa Cruz, Santa Clara, San Jose) dialects.
44. Huichun-Karkin dialects.
45. Saklan language.
46. Tchoyotche (Cholovon, Chulamni) dialects.

47. Yokots ("Valley Yokuts") dialects.
48. Yukots ("North Foothill Yokuts," Chuckchansi) dialects.
49. Mayi ("Central Foothill Yokuts") dialects.
50. Nim (Mono) dialects.
51. Neuma (Pitanakwat, Owens Valley Paiute) language.
52. Panamint Shoshones (Koso, Death Valley Shoshone) language.
53. Rumsen dialects.
54. Mutsún (Humontwash) dialects.
55. Esselen language.
56. Chalón dialects.
57. Tepothálap (Énnesen, Salinan) dialects.
58. Palewyami (Ta-at) language.
59. Tubatulabal dialects.
60. Stishini (Ticho, San Luis Obispo) language.
61. Káshinasmú (Cuyama) language.
62. Toxi (Buena Vista Lake Yokuts) dialects.
63. Nu-ú-a (Kawaiisu, Tehachapi) language.
64. No permanent occupation or uncertain (note: post-1800 movements of Chemehuevi Nihwi are not reflected on this map).
65. Nihwi (Ute–Southern Paiute–Chemehuevi) language.
66. Kagimuswas (Akkili, Purisima) language.
67. Tsamála (Kasákompéa, Santa Ynez) language.
68. Tsmúwich (Kasswáh, Santa Barbara) language.
69. Mishkonaká (Miskanákan, Ventura) language.
70. Tokya (Tecuya, Tashlipum) language.
71. Kitanemuk language.
72. Wimat (Tuakam, San Miguel) language.
73. Naskwe (Nicalke, Hurmal, Santa Rosa) language.
74. Limú (Santa Cruz) language.
75. Ghalashat (San Nicolas) language.
76. Tongva (Gabrieleño-Fernandeño) dialects.
77. Maringayam (Serrano, Vanyume) dialects.
78. Atáhum (Luiseño-Juaneño-Soboba) dialects.
79. Iviatim (Cahuilla, Palm Springs, Wanakik) dialects.
80. Hamakhava (Mohave) language.
81. Pipai (Quechan – Halchidhoma) dialects.
82. Kamia (Ipai-Tipai) dialects.
83. Kupanga-kitom (Cupeño) language.
84. Shotéah (Northeastern Pomo) language.

[Notes: This map is based in part on the works of A. L. Kroeber, C. H. Merriam, and R. F. Heizer, as well as upon numerous individual ethnographic and documentary sources. It is, therefore, a synthesis of a great amount of data and the author must accept sole blame for errors. Many boundaries are highly tentative, especially since the information for the coast south of San Francisco is often based upon earlier information than that for the interior. The target date for the map is ca. 1800, except that some coastal groups had already been partially displaced by that date. Interior area boundaries are based upon a calculated guess that conditions were largely the same in 1800 as in ca. 1850.]

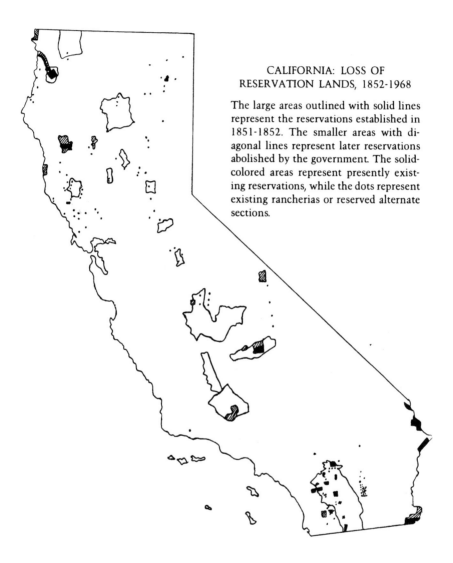

CALIFORNIA: LOSS OF
RESERVATION LANDS, 1852-1968

The large areas outlined with solid lines
represent the reservations established in
1851-1852. The smaller areas with diagonal lines represent later reservations
abolished by the government. The solid-
colored areas represent presently existing reservations, while the dots represent
existing rancherias or reserved alternate
sections.

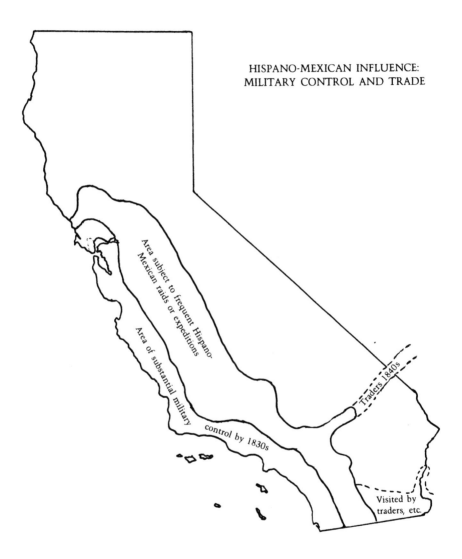

HISPANO-MEXICAN INFLUENCE:
MILITARY CONTROL AND TRADE

Area subject to frequent Hispano-Mexican raids or expeditions

Area of substantial military control by 1830s

Traders 1840s

Visited by traders, etc.

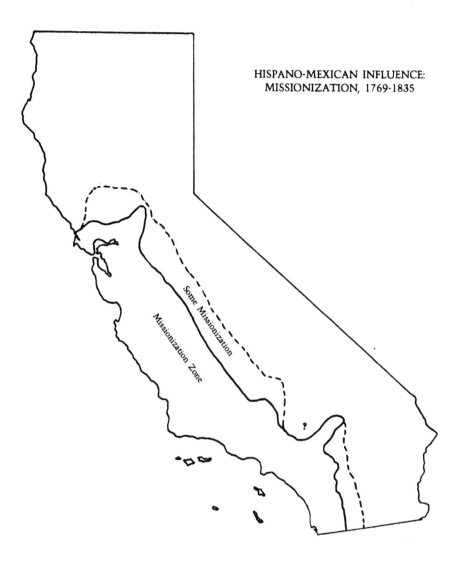

HISPANO-MEXICAN INFLUENCE:
MISSIONIZATION, 1769-1835

Some Missionization

Missionization Zone

?

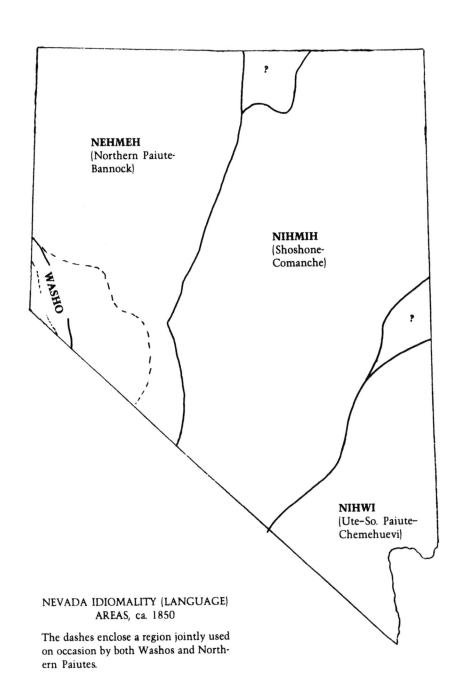

NEVADA IDIOMALITY (LANGUAGE)
AREAS, ca. 1850

The dashes enclose a region jointly used
on occasion by both Washos and Northern Paiutes.

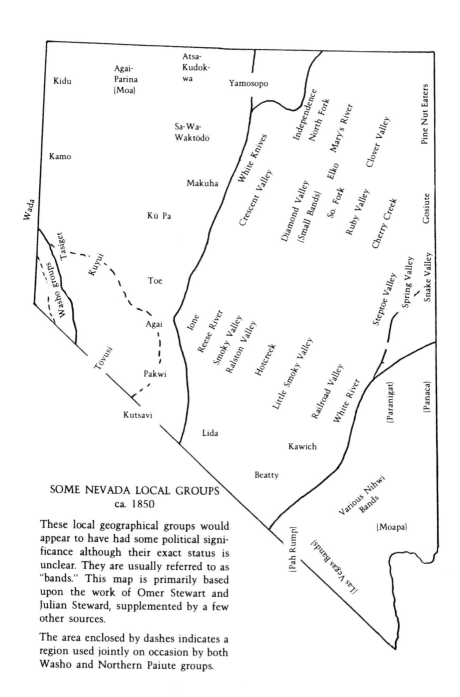

SOME NEVADA LOCAL GROUPS
ca. 1850

These local geographical groups would appear to have had some political significance although their exact status is unclear. They are usually referred to as "bands." This map is primarily based upon the work of Omer Stewart and Julian Steward, supplemented by a few other sources.

The area enclosed by dashes indicates a region used jointly on occasion by both Washo and Northern Paiute groups.

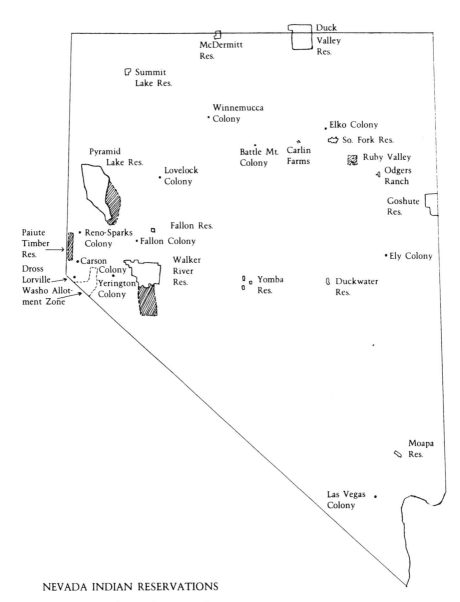

NEVADA INDIAN RESERVATIONS

Land which has been taken away from
the reservations is marked with diagonal
lines.

FOOTNOTES

Chapter I:

1. See Jack D. Forbes, *The Indian in America's Past* (1964), for further information on race mixture.
2. Forbes, "The Historian and the Indian: Racial Bias in American History," *The Americas,* April 1963, pp. 349-362.
3. Brown, "The Spiritual Legacy of the American Indian," *Tomorrow,* Autumn 1964, pp. 297-307.
4. *Ibid.*
5. Forbes, *Tribes and Masses: Explorations in Red, White, and Black,* D-Q University Press, 1979.
6. Collier, *Indians of the Americas,* 1948, pp. 7 ff.
7. Forbes, "The Indian: Looking Glass into the Souls of White Americans," *Liberator,* August 1966, pp. 6-9; September 1966, pp. 14-17; and reproduced in Forbes, *Tribes and Masses: Explorations in Red, White, and Black,* D-Q University Press, 1979.

Chapter II:

1. See Forbes, *Afro-Americans in the Far West,* 1967, for a discussion of the concept of race.
2. Jennings and Norbeck, eds., *Prehistoric Man in the New World,* 1964, p. 161.
3. See Forbes, *Warriors of the Colorado,* 1965.
4. Heizer, "The Western Coast of North America," in Jennings and Norbeck, *Prehistoric Man in the New World,* p. 128.
5. It should be noted, however, that it may be difficult to argue for a diffusion of maritime cultures from the Bering Sea area to the Northwest Coast if the currently known time difference is only 500 years (3000 b.p. in the Bering region and 2500 b.p. in the Fraser River delta of British Columbia), since the uncertainty of archaeological knowledge in this area renders such dates highly problematic. The early Columbia River riverine-maritime adaptation could indicate an independent origin in North America.
6. See, for example, Thor Heyerdahl, "Feasible Ocean Routes to and from the Americas in Pre-Columbian Times," *American Antiquity,* v. 28, no. 4, 1963.
7. The best general sources for information on this archaeological period include the chapters by R. F. Heizer, Jesse D. Jennings and Alex D. Krieger, in Jennings and Norbeck, eds., *Prehistoric Man in the New World,* 1964; and R. F. Heizer and M. A. Whipple, eds., *The California Indians: A Source Book,* 1951.
8. Interestingly, the Spaniards referred to their Filipino crewmen as "Yndios Luzones," i.e., "Luzon Indians."
9. Forbes, *Warriors of the Colorado,* 1965 [Alarcón].
10. *Ibid.*
11. See Forbes, *Warriors of the Colorado,* 1965, and *Apache, Navajo and Spaniard,* 1960, for discussion of the advance of the Spanish Empire into northern Mexico and the Southwest.

12. H. H. Bancroft, *History of California*, v. II, p. 150.

13. Indian leaders in the missions, appointed by the missionaries, were required for example, to lash their fellow Indians in minor disciplinary cases.

14. See Forbes, *Warriors of the Colorado*, for the full story of the Quechan war for independence.

15. See Forbes, "Indian Horticulture West and Northwest of the Colorado River," *Journal of the West*, January 1963.

16. See Robert F. Heizer, "Walla Walls Indian Expeditions to the Sacramento Valley," *California Historical Society Quarterly*, March 1942, pp. 1-7, and Alice B. Maloney, "Shasta Was Shatasta in 1814," *California Historical Society Quarterly*, September 1945, pp. 229-234.

17. Five thousand Valley Indians were also carried off to the coastal missions before 1833, but some of these returned. See S. F. Cook, "Aboriginal Population of the San Joaquin Valley," *Anthropological Records*, v. 16, no. 2, and "The Epidemic of 1830-1833," *Univ. of California Publications in American Archaeology and Ethnology*, v. 43, no. 3, pp. 303-326.

18. In 1834 a total of 111 Moquelumnes and 41 Cosumnes, among others, were baptized at San Jose Mission.

19. John C. Frémont.

20. *Ibid.*

21. Visit to Carcoas of 1834.

22. Michael White, *ms.*, Bancroft Library, C-D 173, University of California, Berkeley.

23. Bancroft [California Valley].

24. Charles E. Pancoast, *A Quaker 49'er*, 1930, p. 298.

25. C. Hart Merriam, *Studies of California Indians*, 1955, pp. 20-21.

26. William Ralganal Benson, "The Stone and Kelsey 'Massacre' on the shores of Clear Lake in 1849," *California Historical Society Quarterly*, September 1932, pp. 266-273.

27. Stephen Bonsal, *Edward Fitzgerald Beale*, 1912, p. 177.

28. See Theodora Kroeber, *Ishi in Two Worlds*, 1967, for further details.

Chapter III:

1. Horace Bell, *Reminiscences of a Ranger*, 1881, p. 116.

2. Bancroft [Diggers].

3. This doctrine, which is still held, in effect, by the U. S. Government, blatantly violates both the Fifth Amendment to the Constitution and the Treaty of Guadalupe Hidalgo.

4. Thirty-seventh Congress, 2nd Session, Senate Ex. Doc. No. 1, v. 1, p. 759.

5. John W. Caughey, ed., *The Indians of Southern California in 1852*, 1952, pp. 16, 21.

6. Quoted in William H. Ellison, "The Federal Indian Policy in California, 1846-1860," Ph.D. dissertation, University of California, Berkeley, 1919, pp. 206-208.

7. See Forbes, "The Public Domain and Indian Property Rights in Nevada," *Nevada State Bar Journal*, July 1965.

8. In 1855, the Tejon Reservation was greatly reduced in size. Just what Beale did for the Tejon Indians is unclear. His successor found only 700 Indians

at Tejon, living in native-style houses, and gathering wild foods for part of their subsistence. Beale later became the owner of Tejon and thereafter used the local Indians as laborers.

9. J. Ross Browne, *The California Indians*, pamphlet, no date.
10. *Fifty-first Annual Report of the Board of Indian Commissioners*, 1920, p. 40.
11. Jackson and Kinney, "Report on the Condition of the Mission Indians...," 1883, p. 12.
12. Malcolm McDowell, 1919.
13. At Hoopa Reservation.
14. See Forbes, ed., *Nevada Indians Speak*, 1967, pp. 168-176.
15. Round Valley agent.
16. *Ibid.*
17. Round Valley School superintendent.
18. Records of Col. Lafayette Dorrington, 1915-1923, Item 102, various boxes, Federal Records Center, San Francisco.
19. *Fifty-first Annual Report of the Board of Indian Commissioners*, 1920, p. 69.
20. *Ibid.*
21. *Report of the Board of Indian Commissioners*, 1923, p. 22.
22. *Ibid.*

Chapter IV:

1. Cramer v. United States with quote from U. S. v. Kagama [1886], in C. S. Goodrich, "The Legal Status of the California Indian," *California Law Review*, March 1926, pp. 161-162.
2. L. F. Schmeckebier, *The Office of Indian Affairs*, 1927, p. 90.
3. *Report of the Commissioner of Indian Affairs*, 1922, p. 20.
4. *Ibid*, pp. 20-21.
5. Oscar H. Lipps, *The Case of the California Indians*, U. S. Indian School Print Shop, Chemawa, Oregon, 1932.
6. *Ibid.*
7. *Report of the Commissioner of Indian Affairs*, 1922, p. 18.
8. Kenneth M. Johnson, *K-344 or the California Indians vs. the United States*, 1966, pp. 64-65.
9. *Ibid*, p. 67.
10. *Ibid*, p. 73.
11. *Progress Report... by the Senate Interim Committee on California Indian Affairs*, 1959, pp. 68, 73 ff.
12. "California Rural Legal Caseload," August 1967, p. 21.
13. *American Indians in California*, State Department of Industrial Relations, 1965.
14. Elmer Rusco, *Minority Groups in Nevada*, 1966, pp. 34-37.
15. Letters of Frank A. Quinn in *Progress Report... by the Senate Interior Committee on California Indian Affairs*, 1955, pp. 56, 58.
16. *American Indians in California*, State Department of Industrial Relations, 1965.
17. Report of the State Advisory Commission on Indian Affairs, 1966.
18. Elmer Rusco, *Minority Groups in Nevada*, 1966.

Chapter V:

1. See Forbes, *Warriors of the Colorado*, 1965, for a detailed discussion of the Kamia.

2. See Forbes, "The Tongva of Tujunga to 1801."

Chapter VI:

1. *Report on Education of the Disadvantaged*, v. 1, no. 4, May 15, 1968, p. 12.
2. For a discussion of MES, see *The Center Forum*, November 4, 1967, pp. 3-4, and *The New Republic*, September 23, 1967, p. 18.
3. Paul F. Brandwein, "Memorandum: Concerning a 'New' School System," ms., 1967.
4. See, for example, Y. T. Witherspoon, "The Measurement of Indian Children's Achievement in the Academic Tool Subjects," University of Utah Bureau of Indian Services.
5. See, for example, Havighurst and Breese, *Journal of Educational Psychology*, v. 38, 1947, pp. 241-247.
6. Cushna, "Some affiliative correlates of social class," 1966, ms.
7. Roberts, Dickerson, and Horton, "Performance of Negro American Children Ages 7-10 on the Stanford-Binet by Selected Background Factors," American Psychological Association, September 2, 1966, ms.
8. Coleman, *Equality of Educational Opportunity, Reconsidered.*
9. See Forbes, *The Education of the Culturally Different: A Multi-Cultural Approach*, especially pp. 15 ff.
10. Angie Debo, *The Rise and Fall of the Choctaw Republic*, p. 242.
11. Williard Walker, "An Experiment in Programmed Cross-Cultural Education," 1965.
12. John F. Bryde, "Indian Education and Mental Health," 1967, ms.
13. William H. Kelly, "Current Research on American Indian Education: A Critical Review of Ongoing Studies," 1967.
14. "Bundy Report."
15. National Advisory Commission on Civil Disorders.
16. From a study of 212 teachers and their pupils in 52 schools, carried out by Albert H. Yee under a USOE grant. *Education U.S.A.*, November 17, 1966, p. 72.
17. Jack Vaughn, "The Peace Corps: New We Are Seven," *Saturday Review*, January 6, 1968, p. 22.

INDEX

(NOTE: Please study carefully the map of the Indian linguistic groups in California, on page 223, and the accompanying key. Also study the maps on pages 229 and 230 of linguistic areas and groups found in Nevada. Many Indian groups not found in this index will be found on these maps. Obviously in a book of this size not all of the Indian groups in these two states can be discussed.)